Study Guide and Workbook
To Accompany
Economics of Development

Malcolm Gillis
Dwight H. Perkins
Michael Roemer
Donald R. Snodgrass

Second Edition

by
Bruce R. Bolnick
Northeastern University

W·W·Norton & Company
New York   London

ISBN 0-393-95550-8

W. W. Norton & Company, Inc., 500 Fith Avenue, New York, N.Y. 10110
W. W. Norton & Company Ltd., 37 Great Russell Street, London WC1B 3NU

2 3 4 5 6 7 8 9 0

Contents

Preface

To the Student

Do you find that you can absorb more from your reading if you first have had a preview of the material? After reading through a chapter of one of your school books, have you ever wondered, "What exactly am I supposed to *know* from all this?" Do you find it useful to have practice tests that provide feedback on your understanding and recall of course material, and help you to spot material in need of more careful study? Do you like to see additional applications of concepts, formulas, and tools covered in class? Is your comprehension enhanced by exercises that lead you systematically through analytical and technical material, in detail?

If your answer to any of these questions is yes, then you will find this Study Guide and Workbook to be a valuable aid to learning the economics of development. First, an introductory chapter reviews some basic principles of economics that are used repeatedly in the textbook. Then, for each chapter of the textbook, the Study Guide provides:

1. An overview of the contents.

2. A summary of the main learning objectives.

3. A list of additional key terms that you should understand and be able to explain.

4. A list of economic tools and techniques developed or applied in the chapter.

5. A self-test containing between fifteen and thirty completion, true-false, and multiple-choice questions.

6. A "Worked Example" that analyzes in detail an application of one major technical tool or economic concept from the chapter.

7. Exercises that walk you step-by-step through applications of each major analytical topic and tool in the chapter.

This Study Guide is designed to help make your study time more productive, and to *help you to learn* the technical and analytical material. The best way to master this material is by doing exercises. Think of this analogy: you don't learn to play the oboe just by reading a book and listening to lectures, no matter how clear the book and the lectures may be.

Please note that all answers for the self-tests are provided in this book. The answers for the exercises, however, are not included here, because some instructors will prefer to use the exercises as homework problem sets. If your instructor does not intend to have exercises handed in and graded, he or she will determine the best method for making the answers available to you.

I hope that you will find the material in the Study Guide to be challenging and rewarding—and even enjoyable.

To the Instructor

One of the outstanding strengths of the textbook is that it integrates solid applications of economic analysis into the discussion of the economics of development. This Study Guide and Workbook provides pedagogical support that most students need to absorb the material more easily and more thoroughly. It contains summaries that point out what they should know; question sets that provide feedback on major concepts, facts, terms, and tools; examples illustrating basic analytical material; and problem sets that provide "hands on" experience with the economics of development.

In using the Study Guide for your course, four points should be called to your attention. First, as mentioned in the note to the students above, answers to the exercises are not included here. You will find them instead in the Instructor's Manual. This procedure gives you the option of assigning some or all of the exercises as homework problems to be submitted and marked, or as take-home examination material. In return for this flexibility, you will have to make available to the students the answers for exercises that are not to be handed in. This can be done by distributing copies of the answers, by posting the answers, by placing them on reserve—or any other method that you find most convenient.

Second, you may not want to hold your students responsible for one hundred percent of the material in some chapters. The format of the Study Guide allows you to identify specific learning objectives, key terms, and economic tools and exercises, that you want them to master. Third, you might consider helping to motivate your students to use the Study Guide by adopting an explicit policy of using questions from this book—either as is, or with minor variations—on course exams. I have used both of the devices mentioned here with considerable success.

Finally, I welcome your comments on the Study Guide. You can contact me at the Department of Economics, Northeastern University, Boston, MA 02115.

Acknowledgments

I am pleased to acknowledge my debt of gratitude to those who encouraged me to proceed with this project, and those who helped me to produce the final product. The first group consists of the authors of the textbook—Malcolm Gillis, Dwight Perkins, Michael Roemer, and Donald Snodgrass—as well as Drake McFeely at W. W. Norton. Also, my wife Doreen and my son Daniel must be thanked for their tremendous support, encouragement, and patience.

My work on the Study Guide was assisted greatly by comments received from Drake McFeely, Michael Roemer, Donald Snodgrass, and R. L. Curry of California State University at Sacramento. Many of my undergraduate and graduate students at Northeastern University have provided invaluable help by test-driving earlier drafts. Finally, the project depended on the expeditious and cheerful efforts of Jennifer Dawson, who compiled the manuscript.

Boston, Mass.   BRB
February 1987

Economic Principles: A Refresher

The economics of development is an applied economics course in which basic tools such as supply-and-demand analysis and fundamental concepts such as GNP and elasticity are used repeatedly. As the authors state in their preface, "these tools contribute substantially to our understanding of development problems and their solution." Of equal importance is that by using the tools and concepts in this course, your own understanding of economics will be reinforced.

A major objective of this Study Guide is to help you to master the economic tools and concepts. This introductory chapter reviews some of the basic principles of economics that you will encounter frequently in the textbook. If you have not studied introductory economics you should read through this material carefully. If you feel rusty on the principles of economics you can use this chapter as a refresher.

Principles of Macroeconomics: A Selective Review

Gross National Product (GNP)   A nation's GNP is defined as the market value of all **final** goods and services the nation produces during a given year. Final goods and services are those which are not used up as part of the production of other goods that year. **Intermediate** goods such as steel used to make cars are not counted in measuring GNP. This does not mean steel production is neglected; rather, its value is already counted as part of the value of the final good, cars.

Final goods are often aggregated into four broad categories representing different sources of expenditure on goods and services: consumption (C), investment (I), government spending on goods and services (G), and "net exports," which refers to the difference between exports and imports (E-M). To understand the last category, keep in mind that exports are goods that have been produced domestically, whereas imports are foreign-produced goods that must be netted out from the various expenditure totals. The result is a basic national income accounting identity:

$$GNP = C + I + G + (E\text{-}M).$$

The investment term here, I, refers to **gross** investment in physical capital goods (machines, factories). Gross investment includes both replacement of the capital stock that is depreciating, and net increases in the nation's capital stock to increase future productive capacity. The latter component alone is called **net** investment.

In computing GNP, an economy's various final products are aggregated by adding up their market values, i.e., price times the quantity produced. Notice that the price of a car exceeds the value of production activity taking place within the automobile industry because it includes the value of steel, glass, energy, and many other components that were produced in other industries. **Value-added** is defined as the value of an industry's output over and above the value of the intermediate goods used in production; this is equivalent to the gross payments to the **factors of production**—labor, capital and land—employed in that industry.

The total value of the automobiles can be broken down into the value-added in the automobile industry, plus the value-added in the steel and glass industries, and so on. Thus the aggregate value of the economy's final products corresponds to the aggregate value of income payments to factors of production in the economy. For this reason, GNP, though a measure of production, is also used as a measure of incomes generated by the economy.

As a measure of total incomes generated by the economy, GNP can be broken into components representing how the incomes are used. Broadly speaking, the uses of income fall into three categories: tax payments (T), consumption spending (C), and saving (S). In symbols, we have another national accounting identity:

$$GNP = C + S + T.$$

Saving here is the residual—income not used for consumption by either government or by the private sector. Saving permits resources to flow to production of capital goods (investment) rather than to current consumption goods. Hence saving is one fundamental factor determining growth. Economic growth also depends on accumulation of **human capital** (e.g., education) and on technological advances that improve productivity.

Closely related to GNP is **gross domestic product** (GDP), which measures the value of all final goods and services produced within a geographically defined economy rather than an economy defined in terms of "nationality." The difference is that GDP, unlike GNP, includes value-added that is generated within a country but accrues to nonresident foreigners. On the other hand, GDP excludes incomes earned from foreign sources by a country's nationals or residents. For most LDCs the first of these two factors outweighs the second, so GDP is usually a larger number than GNP.

Equilibrium GNP The concept of equilibrium GNP (or GDP) is a key element in Keynesian macroeconomic theory. When aggregate planned expenditure (E_p) exceeds aggregate production (GNP), producers will tend to respond by expanding output—assuming that the economy is not operating at capacity already. Similarly, when E_p falls short of GNP, there will be a tendency for output to drop. In either case, the adjustments tend to close the gap between E_p and GNP. The economy moves toward an equilibrium level of GNP where E_p = GNP, in which case there is no further inherent tendency for GNP to change.

Note that E_p can be decomposed into planned consumption expenditures plus planned investment expenditures. Also, we have seen that GNP = $C + S + T$. Since taxes (T) are ultimately either consumed or saved by the government, GNP can also be decomposed very broadly into income used for consumption plus income used for savings. From these decompositions it is easy to show that the basic equilibrium condition, E_p = GNP, may be expressed equally well in the form:

$$\text{savings} = \text{(planned) investment.}$$

Per-Capita Income A country's per-capita income is simply the GNP per person, calculated as:

$$\text{per-capita income} = \text{GNP/population.}$$

Since each country compiles GNP statistics using its own national currency, international GNP comparisons require conversions into some common currency value, usually U.S. dollars. See Chapter 3 for a complete discussion.

Real vs. Nominal Magnitudes GNP, per-capita income, and many other economic magnitudes are measured in value terms based upon market prices. This creates problems of comparability over time when price levels are rising. For example, relative to some "base year" such as 1980, a country's GNP might double by 1987 without a "real" change in the volume of production simply because inflation doubles prices.

This problem can be cured by using base-year prices to value each of the goods and services entering GNP for 1987, rather than using the current 1987 prices. GNP measured in "current prices" is called **nominal** GNP; in contrast, **real** GNP is measured using constant prices of a specified base year. Real magnitudes are those that have been corrected for inflation.

Notice that the use of base-year prices is equivalent to dividing nominal GNP by a factor representing the extent to which the relevant prices have risen. In the above example, prices have doubled, so nominal GNP would be divided by 2 to get real GNP. In the textbook, growth rates of GNP, per-capita income, or the output of particular sectors generally refer to real magnitudes. On the other hand, ratio variables such as the share of agriculture in GNP are generally defined in current prices.

The distinction between real and nominal magnitudes arises in other contexts as well. For example, the term "real wages," used in Chapter 4, refers to the wage rate relative to the price of goods. If wages and prices both double, the real wage remains unchanged. Similarly, the "real interest rate" discussed in Chapters 6 and 13 refers to the effective interest rate earned or paid on financial transactions after controlling for the effects of inflation.

Basic Growth-Rate Math   Consider a country with per-capita income (PCI) of $200 in 1980 and $213 in 1981 (in constant 1980 prices). The country's PCI grew by a factor of $213/200 = 1.065$. This is the same thing as saying that the growth rate (g) for the year was $g = 0.065$, or 6.5%.

Similarly, if PCI for 1980 was $200 and the growth rate for the subsequent year was 6.5%, this means PCI grew by a factor of $1.065 = (1 + g)$. So PCI for 1981 equals $213 (= 1.065 \times 200). With sustained growth of 6.5% per year, the level of PCI would increase each year by a factor of $(1 + g)$. After 5 years, PCI would expand from $200 to:

$$200 \times (1.065) \times (1.065) \times (1.065) \times (1.065) \times (1.065)$$
$$= 200 \times (1.065)^5 = 274.$$

With 10 years of such growth, PCI would increase by a factor of $(1.065)^{10} = 1.877$, to $375. With 20 years the result would be $200 \times (1.065)^{20} = 705. It is hard not to be impressed with the power of compound growth.

Reformulating the example, suppose that a country's PCI has increased from $200 to $375 over a period of ten years. What was the *annual* rate of growth during that decade? The answer lies in finding g such that $(1 + g)^{10} = 375/200 = 1.875$. This gives $g = 0.065$, or 6.5% per annum. Many hand calculators can promptly solve this problem.

Suppose three variables are related such that $A \times B = C$. Let g represent the growth rate for each variable, expressed in decimal units. The formula expressing the relationship between the three growth rates is:

$$[1 + g(A)] \, [1 + g(B)] = [1 + g(C)].$$

Looking at this from a slightly different angle, we see that when $A = C/B$ then:

$$[1 + g(A)] = [1 + g(C)]/[1 + g(B)].$$

So if a country's GNP grows at 8% per year while the population grows at 3.5% per year, then the growth rate of per-capita income (= GNP/population) can be calculated as:

$$[1 + g(PCI)] = [1 + .08]/[1 + .035] = 1.043, \text{ or}$$
$$g(PCI) = 0.043 = 4.3\%.$$

When working with low growth rates, a convenient approximation is commonly used. The approximation formula is:

$$g(A) + g(B) = g(C), \text{ or } g(A) = g(C) - g(B).$$

In the above example, this approximation gives a rate of growth of per-capita income of $g(PCI) = 0.08 - 0.035 = 0.045 = 4.5\%$. With larger growth-rate figures the approximation becomes quite inaccurate and should be avoided.

Principles of Microeconomics: A Selective Review

Production Possibilities Frontier The production possibilities frontier (PPF) illustrates the fundamental problem of scarcity facing every economy. It does so using the very simple case of an economy that produces only two goods (X and Y). Figure 1 shows an economy with the capacity to produce Y_{max} of good Y if it were to devote all of its resources to Y. Or it could produce X_{max} if it were to devote all of its resources to X. Or it could allocate its resources to achieve a point such as A, involving production of both goods. The PPF shows all such feasible combinations of production of X and Y.

At any point such as A, more Y can be produced only by reallocating resources away from production of good X. The loss of X is called the **opportunity cost** of additional Y. Similarly, extra production of X entails an opportunity cost in the form of the Y which must be foregone. The slope of the PPF at each point embodies the terms of this tradeoff.

An economy that is underutilizing its resources, or one that is producing inefficiently would be operating at a point inside the PPF, such as point B. In this case the economy has the capacity to produce more of both goods. Many LDCs could increase production significantly by adopting policies that encourage available resources to be used more fully and more productively. However, a point lying outside the PPF, such as point C, cannot be produced unless the economy's productive capacity expands.

Economic efficiency for an economy involves operating on the economy's PPF—and also selecting the "best" attainable combination of X and Y. The "best" attainable point is illustrated in the text using

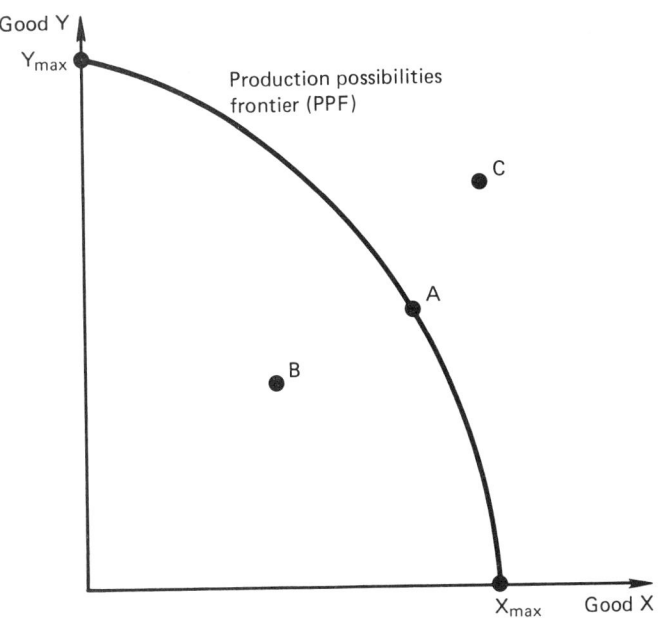

Figure 1

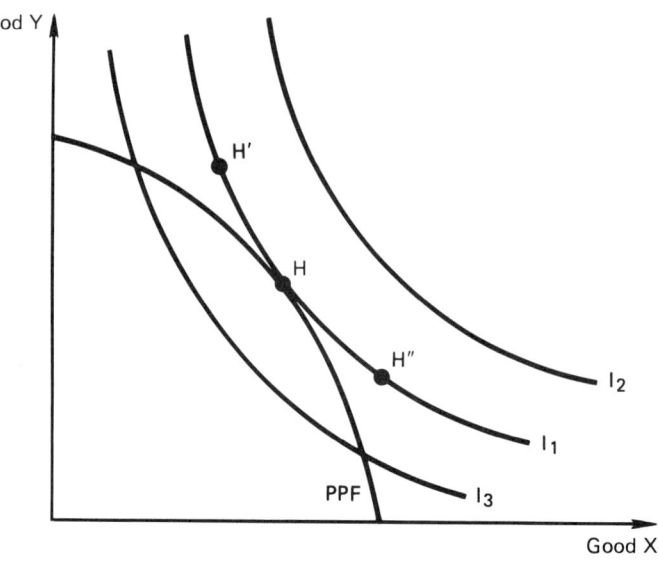

Figure 2

indifference curves to represent society's preferences. Consider point H in Figure 2. This point represents a certain amount of goods X and Y, and hence a particular level of welfare. The same level of social welfare could be achieved with less X, if enough extra Y were available, as at point H'. Or with less Y, if extra X were available, as at point H''. The curve I_1 connecting all such points of equal welfare is an indifference curve. Lying farther from the origin, another indifference curve such as I_2 connects points yielding a higher level of welfare. A curve closer to the origin, such as I_3, contains combinations of X and Y yielding a lower level of welfare.

Given the PPF in Figure 2, point H is the best outcome since it lies on the highest indifference curve the economy can attain from its limited resources. Chapter 15 will explain how trade can open up new possibilities and permit the economy to achieve a point outside the PPF, such as point C in Figure 1.

Markets Except in a highly centralized command economy, markets play a vital role in determining how resources are allocated, how much of each good or service will be produced, what prices will be paid for products or inputs, and who will receive what incomes. Quite generally, a market consists of interacting buyers and sellers engaged in transactions for a particular set of products or services. **Factor markets** are markets for factors of production such as labor, capital, and land. **Product markets** are markets for goods and services.

A **competitive market** is one in which the number of buyers and sellers is large enough that no single participant is able to manipulate the market price significantly. In a competitive market, buyers and sellers respond to market-determined prices. Where markets are reasonably competitive, they serve as an efficient social mechanism for decentralized coordination of individual production, sales, and demand decisions.

Supply and Demand   Principles of supply and demand provide the basis for understanding the market mechanism, and many development policy issues that involve market operations. The key to supply and demand is to analyze separately the behavior of the buyers and sellers: how would buyers react *if* faced with various possible market prices? How would sellers react? The **equilibrium price** is that which coordinates the supply and demand decisions.

The law of demand states that as the price of any good X rises, the quantity that buyers are willing and able to buy will fall, and vice versa. This behavior is summarized in the negatively sloped **market-demand curve**, as shown in Figure 3. Clearly the amount of X demanded at a given price depends on other factors such as consumer incomes, tastes, and prices of related goods. The demand curve shows how buyers react to various prices assuming these other factors are held constant. A change in any of these related variables will shift the position of the demand curve. For example, an increase in consumer incomes would mean that more X is demanded at any given price. The demand curve would then shift to the right.

In similar fashion the **supply curve** shows the alternative quantities that sellers would be able and willing to put up for sale at various possible market prices. In general, a higher price will induce production that had not been profitable at a lower price, as well as the entry of new suppliers into the market. Thus the market-supply curve typically has an upward slope: higher prices, higher quantity supplied.

The quantity of X that suppliers choose to supply depends on more than just the price of X. The decision depends also on factors such as the

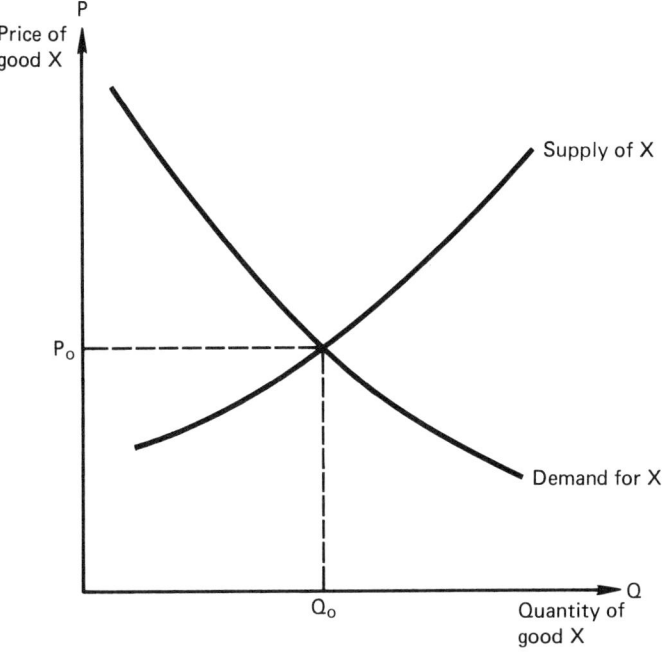

Figure 3

available capacity and production costs. The supply curve is drawn assuming these other factors are held constant, and will shift position when these variables change. For example, given a market price for X, an increase in costs would render some marginal units of production unprofitable. So supply would decline. On the graph the supply curve would shift to the left.

With the supply and demand curves shown in Figure 3, P_0 is the equilibrium price. At that price, the quantity Q_0 that suppliers decide to supply coincides with the quantity that demanders choose to demand. Furthermore, a price of P_0 is the natural outcome of **market forces** in a competitive market. At any price above P_0, the excess of supply over demand will cause the price to soften; and at any price below P_0 the inherent excess demand will create a powerful tendency for the price to rise.

The market equilibrium has very important economic properties. Suppose $P_0 = \$10$, and that buyers and sellers choose to buy and sell 500 units of X at this price. The fact that the buyers are willing and able to buy 500 X, but not more, implies that each of these units of X is worth foregoing \$10 of other things. It also implies that additional units are not worth \$10.

On the other hand, the suppliers' decision to sell 500 X, but not more, implies that the cost of producing each of these 500 units (including an adequate profit margin to compensate for the use of capital) is covered by the \$10 price. It also implies that extra units would involve a cost exceeding \$10.

Put these together. For every unit of output up to the market equilibrium of 500, the value to consumers exceeds the cost of production, whereas for every unit in excess of 500 the cost exceeds the value! In this sense, the market picks out the "best" level of production, and hence the best point on the economy's PPF. The market price serves a dual role here: it provides the incentive for production, while rationing the supply to the buyers for whom the product is worth at least the cost of production.

This conclusion applies only to competitive markets. The claim that the market output is "best" also must be questioned if there are serious inequities in the underlying distribution of income and purchasing power. These qualifications are often very pertinent to analysis of economic problems in LDCs, where monopoly power and nonmarket allocation decisions are frequently observed features of the economic landscape.

Elasticity   "Elasticity" means responsiveness. How responsive is the quantity demanded to a change in the price? The answer is the "price elasticity of demand." How does the capital to labor ratio in cement production respond to a change in the relative price of these two factors? The answer is the "elasticity of substitution." Elasticity is a convenient tool for summarizing response effects.

More specifically, elasticity is a calculation of **proportional** responsiveness. If a price increase of 15% produces a 10% decline in the quantity demanded, the elasticity is $10/15 = .667$ (in absolute value). The denominator is the percentage change in the independent variable, and the numerator is the percentage change in the dependent variable[1]. The response is **inelastic** if the value of the elasticity is less than one (in absolute value); it is **elastic** if the value is greater than one; a value just equal to one is referred to as **unitary elasticity**.

Production Functions and Isoquants   A production function identifies how much of an output can be produced from a given set of inputs. Let Q be the quantity of output, and suppose that capital (K) and labor (L) are the only factors of production. The production function for this case can be expressed generally as $Q = F(K,L)$.

The **marginal product** of a factor of production is the amount of *extra* Q that could be produced if one extra unit of the factor were added, holding other factors unchanged. As more and more of one factor is added to a fixed amount of the others, the marginal product of the variable factor typically declines. This means that increments to output grow smaller and smaller. Economists call this the **law of diminishing returns** to a factor of production.

A factor's **marginal revenue product** is the extra **value** of output that could be produced with one extra unit of the factor. In competitive markets, the marginal revenue product is simply the factor's marginal product times the price of the good being produced.

Production functions are often diagrammed as **isoquants**. An isoquant is a line showing the alternative factor combinations that could be used to produce a given level of output. In Figure 4, $Q = 100$ tons of steel can be produced using 50 units of capital along with 30 units of labor (point *A*). Or this output can be produced using a more labor intensive process involving only 20 units of K and 60 units of L (point *B*). Or it can be produced using any of the other factor combinations lying on the curve $Q = 100$. The curve labeled $Q = 200$ shows the various combinations of capital and labor sufficient to produce an output of 200 tons of steel. A similar curve can be drawn for any possible value of Q. These curves are isoquants.

Which production technique would actually be used? This depends on the relative prices of the factors of production. Producers generally try to use the production technique that minimizes costs for producing any given output. If capital were expensive relative to labor, then a point to the southeast would be used, whereas a point to the northwest would be preferred by producers facing labor costs that were high relative to capital costs.

The elasticity of substitution measures how responsive the capital to labor ratio is to a change in relative factor prices. Isoquants that are

---

[1]The percentage change in any variable X is usually calculated as:

$$[X(1) - X(0)]/X(0) = [X(1)/X(0)] - 1.$$

As an example, if $X(0) = 50$ and $X(1) = 63$, the percentage change is equal to $(63 - 50)/50 = 0.26$, or 26%. For calculating elasticity, however, a second method is often used: the average of $X(0)$ and $X(1)$ replaces $X(0)$ itself as the denominator. In the example, this would give a percentage change equal to $(63 - 50)/56.5 = 0.23$, or 23%. Except where specified otherwise, you should use the simpler approach, with X_0 as the denominator, for all exercises in this Study Guide.

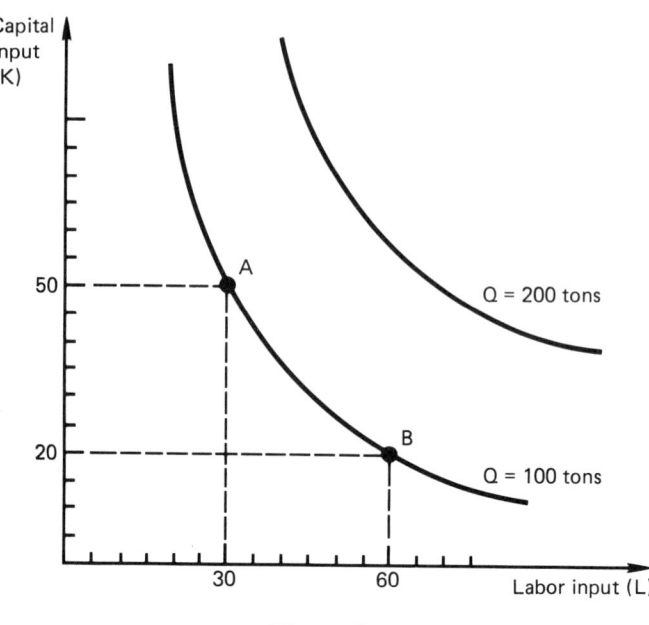

Figure 4

relatively "unbowed" reflect a high **elasticity of substitution,** or a capital to labor mix that responds strongly to changes in relative factor prices. Isoquants that are tightly bowed reflect a very low elasticity of substitution; in this case there is little room for changing the capital to labor mix. The important case of L-shaped isoquants is discussed in Chapter 3.

Monopoly Behavior A firm has **monopoly power** when it is large enough to influence significantly the price of its product in the market. In perfect competition, prices are determined by the market and each firm responds with an output decision. In contrast, a monopolist can choose what price to charge. A **pure monopoly** exists when there is a sole producer who can select the product price without fear of losing customers to competitors.

The law of demand does impose a constraint on the monopolist: the higher the price selected, the smaller the volume of output that can be sold. This constraint can be graphed as the demand curve facing the monopolist, as shown in Figure 5.

Suppose that the monopolist chooses to charge the price P and sell Q units of output. The firm's total revenue would be $P \times Q$. By how much would revenue increase if another unit of output were to be sold? The demand curve shows that $Q + 1$ units of output could be sold only if the monopolist were to charge a lower price. The gain in the sale of one more unit would be offset to some extent by lower revenues on the first Q units. Hence the **marginal revenue**—defined as the extra revenue produced by a unit increase in quantity—is less than the price shown on the demand curve. The line *MR* in Figure 5 shows the marginal revenue associated with each unit of output.

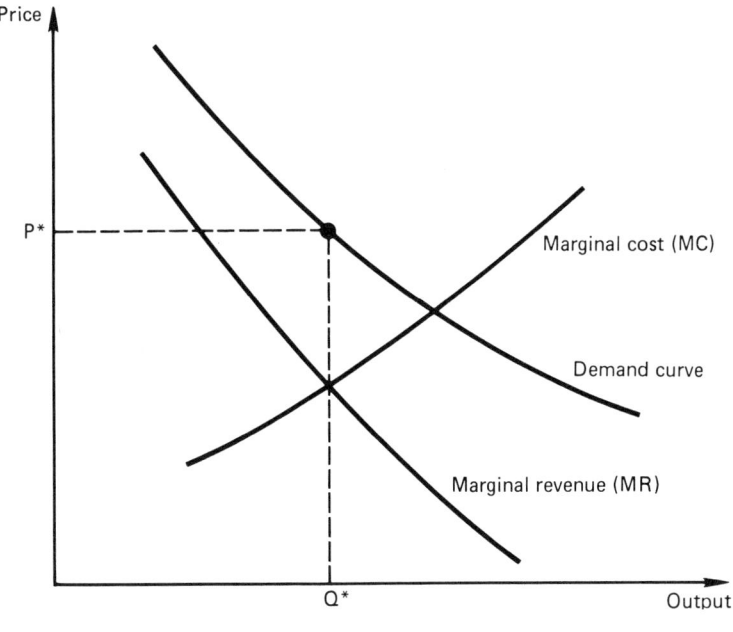

Figure 5

Given the demand curve, which price would the monopolist choose? As long as the marginal revenue produced by an additional unit of output exceeds the **marginal costs** (*MC*) of producing that unit, extra output will increase profits despite the necessity of lowering price. The monopolist will produce up to the point where *MR* equals *MC* and charge the price that the demand curve allows for that level of sales. In Figure 4, the curve *MC* shows the marginal cost of each successive unit of output. The profit maximizing output if then *Q**, and the monopoly price is *P**.

Compared to a competitive market, a monopolist will find it profitable to restrict output and charge a higher price. As a result, the market efficiency arguments presented above are violated in monopolized markets.

Exchange Rate   The exchange rate is the price of foreign currency. Consider the case of India, with the U.S. dollar as the foreign currency and the Indian rupee as the domestic currency. If it takes 12 Indian rupees to buy a U.S. dollar, then the exchange rate is 12 rupees per dollar. An increase in the price of foreign exchange means that more domestic currency is needed to buy a dollar (i.e., more rupees per dollar). In other words, the domestic currency becomes less valuable relative to the value of the dollar. Hence an increase in the price of foreign exchange is referred to as a **devaluation**.

In each country, such as India, there will be a market for foreign exchange (e.g., dollars). There will be a supply curve representing dollars supplied to India for the purchase of Indian goods or as capital flows into India, at any given exchange rate. Similarly, there will be a demand curve representing dollars required by Indians for the purchase of U.S.

goods or for investment in dollar assets. With a **floating exchange rate**, the supply and demand conditions determine the price of foreign currency. In most LDCs, the government either sets a **fixed exchange rate** or manages this important price by interventions in the market for foreign exchange. When the price of foreign exchange is held below its equilibrium value, the domestic currency is **overvalued**.

Key Terms and Concepts

Competitive market
Compound growth
Current and constant prices

Demand curve
Devaluation

Economic efficiency
Economic growth
Elasticity
Elasticity of substitution
Equilibrium price
Exchange rate

Factor markets
Factors of production
Final goods and services
Fixed exchange rate
Floating exchange rate

Gross vs. net investment
Gross National Product (GNP)
Gross Domestic Product (GDP)
Growth-rate calculations

Human capital

Indifference curves

Intermediate goods
Investment
Isoquants

Law of demand
Law of diminishing returns

Marginal cost
Marginal revenue
Marginal revenue product
Marginal product
Markets
Monopoly

Opportunity cost
Overvalued currency

Per-capita income
Production function
Production possibilities frontier (PPF)

Real vs. nominal

Savings
Supply and demand
Supply curve

Value-added

CHAPTER 1   Introduction: Worlds Apart

Overview

This chapter introduces the main character in the development story: the less-developed countries (LDCs). The chapter portrays the vast disparity in standards of living between citizens of the LDCs and citizens of the developed countries. After explaining the terminology used to distinguish these "two very different worlds," the text defines the concept of economic development, with emphasis on the diversity of conditions among countries falling within the category of LDCs. The term LDC covers a wide continuum of economic and social characteristics. Though the development process is marked by broad structural regularities, there is considerable variation among individual countries.

Since 1965 income per capita has been rising for most LDCs. Industrial development has been relatively rapid. Especially important, virtually all the LDCs have managed to achieve major improvements in health and education. But successful development is a complex process. No simple formula assures success, nor does any simple set of barriers explain disappointments. Instead of offering easy answers, the text will explore major elements of the development process through a combination of economic theory, analysis of the empirical record, and discussion of institutional conditions in the developing countries.

Main Learning Objectives

After studying this chapter you ought to understand and be able to explain:

1. The disparity between the standards of living of people living in **developed countries** and those living in **less-developed countries.**

2. The various terms used to distinguish between developed countries and developing countries, including the five-part classification used by the World Bank.

3. The distinction between **economic growth** and **economic development.**

4. Some of the basic structural regularities characterizing the **development continuum.**

5. The extent of progress achieved by developing countries since 1965.

6. The idea that no single policy or strategy provides a simple key to the complex process of economic development.

Additional Key Terms, Concepts, and Institutions

Can you identify and explain each of the following?

third-world countries
industrial countries
North versus South
epoch of modern economic growth
modernization
institutional context

Economic Tools and Techniques

From what you have learned in this chapter, can you:

1. Analyze the pattern of structural change that accompanies economic development, using cross-country data such as that shown in Tables 1–1 and 1–3 in the text? (For comprehensive, up-to-date data, check the Annex to the annual *World Development Report* of the World Bank.)

Self-Test

Completion

1. The application of science to problems of economic production is the key element in the epoch of _____.

2. In the World Bank's classification system, Saudi Arabia is categorized as a _____.

3. In the World Bank's classification system, countries such as Malaysia, the Philippines, Egypt, and Kenya fall in the group of _____-income countries.

4. U.S. restrictions on peanut imports help farmers in _____ and harm farmers in _____.

5. The acronym "LDC" stands for _____.

6. _____ that are badly distorted from their free-market values can stifle or misdirect initiative and hence reduce growth.

True-False If false, can you explain why?

_____ 1. The terms economic growth and economic development are interchangeable, each referring to a rise in national income per capita.

_____ 2. The price paid to peanut farmers in Senegal is lower than that paid to peanut farmers in the United States largely because in Senegal farmers have to sell their crops to private traders.

_____ 3. By the World Bank definition, low-income countries are those with income less than $1,000 per capita (in 1983 dollars).

_____ 4. Modernization is a term referring to social and political development, as well as economic development.

_____ 5. Due to the great progress made by 1983, the adult literacy rate in all of the low-income countries was above 50%.

_____ 6. The economics of development relies primarily on theory because data are not available to provide an empirical record of the LDCs.

Multiple Choice

1. Which of the following terms does not belong with the others?
   a. LDCs
   b. low-income countries
   c. North
   d. third world

2. Which of the following is *not* typically an element of the structural change accompanying development?
   a. An increase in agriculture as a share of GNP.
   b. An increase in manufacturing as a share of GNP.
   c. An increase in urbanization of the population.
   d. All of the above are typical elements.

3. Cherno Sar's village in Senegal lacks which of the following amenities?
   a. electricity
   b. a school
   c. a health clinic
   d. piped water
   e. all of the above

4. Which of the following is *not* classified as an industrial economy by the World Bank?
   a. Norway
   b. Australia
   c. Brazil
   d. Switzerland

5. From the data tables in the text, which of the following generalizations about low income countries is broadly valid?
   a. life expectancy remains less than 40 years
   b. around 90% of the labor force works in agriculture
   c. GNP per capita did not increase from 1965 to 1983
   d. death rates declined sharply from 1965 to 1983
   e. none of the above

6. How do economists applying economic theory to the study of
   development tend to treat the institutional context?
   a. It is ignored.
   b. It is taken as given.
   c. It is incorporated as an explicit variable in the economic analysis.
   d. It is assumed to be irrelevant.

Applications

Worked Example: Examining Cross-Country Development Patterns

Cross-country data are frequently used for inductive analysis of
development patterns, as well as for testing theoretical hypotheses about
development. What can we learn from the data about patterns of energy
consumption?

In Figure 1–1 the horizontal axis measures per capita GNP (call this
Y) in 1983 U.S. dollars. The vertical axis measures energy consumption
per capita (call this E) in kilograms of coal equivalent. The data for each
country can be considered as providing one observation about the
relationship between Y and E. Only the data for low-income and middle-
income countries reported in textbook Table 1–1 are used here. The
result is the scatter of points shown in Figure 1–1.

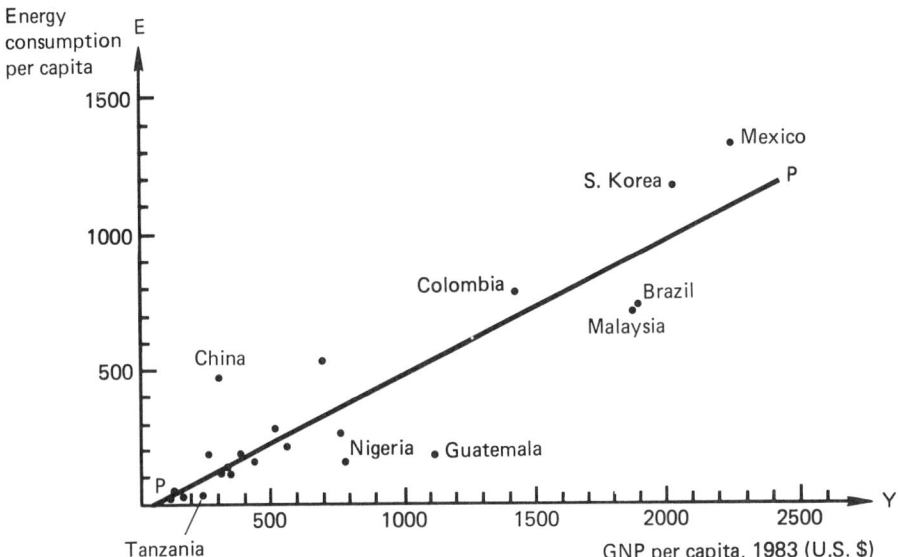

Figure 1–1

There is a visible pattern to the scatter of points. To quantify the pattern, economists use statistical techniques such as regression analysis, which can be thought of as a calculation of the "best fit" line through the data. The line PP in Figure 1–1 is the best-fit regression line for the plotted data (calculated to be $E = -27.41 + .50\ Y$).

The various observations obviously don't stick very closely to line PP. Deviations from line PP could be explained by considering additional explanatory variables. In addition to GNP per capita, one might expect an economy's **structure** to be an important determinant of E. Indeed, in countries such as Mexico, Korea, and Colombia, with E values well above the "pattern" line, agriculture's share of the labor force is below average (text Table 1–1). And in countries such as Tanzania, Nigeria, Guatemala, and Malaysia, having E values well below the line, agriculture's share of the labor force is well above average. As always, there are exceptions to such generalizations: look at the data for China and Brazil.

Exercises

1. Now it is your turn to examine a development pattern. Specifically, consider the differences in adult literacy rates (call this LIT) across the continuum of development as measured by GNP per capita (call this Y).

   a. To simplify the exercise, only three group-wise average values of LIT and Y will be used here. Look at the textbook Table 1–1 to find the values of LIT and Y for:

      low-income countries (including India and China)

      LIT = _____, Y = _____;

      middle-income countries

      LIT = _____, Y = _____;

      industrial market economies

      LIT = _____, Y = _____.

   b. (i) In Figure 1–2 plot the three points corresponding to the above data, and draw line segments connecting these data observations.
      (ii) What do you observe? [Note: the horizontal axis is drawn using a logarithmic scale, so each doubling of Y is represented by the same distance along the axis. The slope of a straight line in this diagram represents the effect of a given *percentage* change in Y on the value of LIT.]

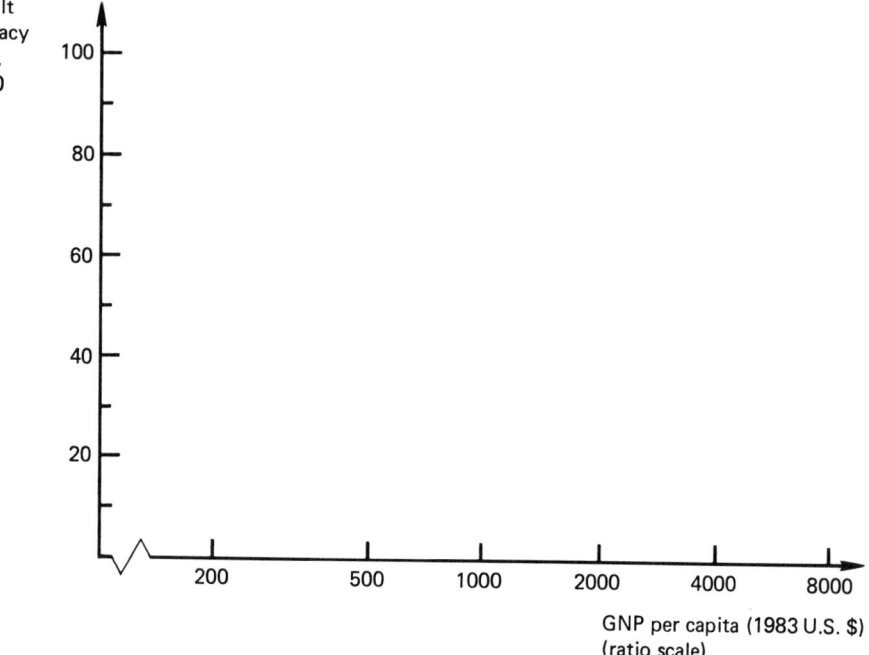

Adult literacy rate, 1980 (%)

GNP per capita (1983 U.S. $) (ratio scale)

Figure 1–2

c. Now examine some individual countries in relation to the average pattern.

    (i) After referring to textbook Table 1–1, list the LIT and Y values for each of the following countries.

	LIT	Y
Sri Lanka	_____	_____
Pakistan	_____	_____
Bolivia	_____	_____
Nigeria	_____	_____
South Korea	_____	_____

   (ii) Plot and connect these data points on Figure 1–2.

  (iii) What factors other than Y might account for the deviations in country LIT values from the average pattern you have identified in part a.

d. Do these data reveal a standard "pattern" of changes in the adult literacy rate across the continuum of developing countries?

2. Figure 1—3 shows a cross-country development pattern, but the labels need to be identified. Match the following labels with the letters shown in Figure 1—3.

Label	*Letter*
Percentage of age group enrolled in primary school	_____
GNP per capita	_____
1965	_____
1982	_____

3. The text portrays the vast disparities in work conditions and standards of living between a peanut farmer in the United States and one in Senegal. Write a similar word portrait of the differences in work conditions and standards of living for:

a. A bank clerk in Calcultta versus one in New York City.

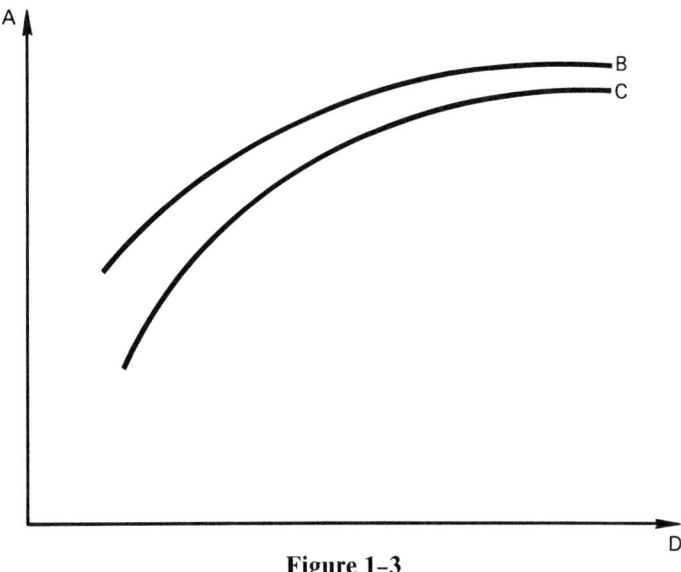

Figure 1–3

b. A traditional textile worker in Indonesia versus a textile worker in Massachusetts.

4. *Optional* The text mentions that for some low-income countries such as Sri Lanka, Kenya, and Pakistan, growth in per-capita GNP "was fast enough to double incomes in thirty years." A convenient way to grasp the significance of different growth rates is to calculate the corresponding "doubling time": how long would it take for some variable to double in value if it grows continously at the rate $R\%$ per year? The answer is found by calculating the value of T (time) from the equation: $e^{rT} = 2$, where $r = R/100$ is the growth rate expressed as a decimal. Conveniently, this equation can be expressed in the form $rT = \ln 2 = .69$. With the growth rate expressed as a percentage rather than a decimal, just remember the formula $R \times T = 69$, or $T = 69/R$. So if $R = 2.5\%$ (which was Pakistan's growth rate during 1965–1983) then $T = 69/2.5 = 28$ years.

a. Using the growth rates of GNP per capita shown in text Table 1–2, calculate the number of years it would take for per-capita GNP to double in:

	Growth Rate	Doubling Time
India	_____ %	_____ years
Sri Lanka	_____ %	_____ years
Tanzania	_____ %	_____ years
Ghana	_____ %	_____ years
South Korea	_____ %	_____ years

b. If each country were to sustain the growth rate it experienced during the period 1965–1983, how many years would it take for GNP per capita to grow eight-fold? What level of GNP per capita (in 1983 dollars) would then be attained?

India	_____ years to GNP per capita = $_____
Sri Lanka	_____ years to GNP per capita = $_____
Tanzania	_____ years to GNP per capita = $_____
Ghana	_____ years to GNP per capita = $_____
South Korea	_____ years to GNP per capita = $_____

c. Consider what can happen to the "gap" in incomes between the rich and poor nations over time.

   (i) As calculated above, at India's 1.5% per-annum rate of growth, it would take _____ years for per-capita income to double from $260 to $520 (1983 dollars).

   (ii) In 1983 West Germany's per-capita GNP was $11,430. If per-capita income in West Germany grew at India's slow rate of just 1.5% per annum, it would increase *in a single year* by

$$\$\underline{\hspace{2cm}}!$$

   (iii) To surpass Germany's 1983 level of GNP per capita, India's GNP per capita would have to double more than five times over again. What annual growth rate (R) would accomplish the task of doubling incomes five times over again in one century?

$$R = \underline{\hspace{2cm}} \%$$

[Hint: incomes would have to double every 20 years.]

Note: In Chapter 3 it will be seen that for comparing per-capita GNPs, the data actually overstate the income gap between India and Germany by a factor of three.

Answers to Self-Test

Completion

1. modern economic growth
2. capital-surplus oil exporter
3. middle
4. the United States, peanut exporting countries such as Senegal
5. less-developed countries
6. prices

True-False

1. F	4. T
2. F	5. F
3. F	6. F

Multiple Choice

1. c	4. c
2. a	5. d
3. e	6. b

CHAPTER 2
Starting Modern Economic Growth

Overview

Chapter 2 considers why the transition to modern economic growth has been retarded or aborted in some countries. There is no single key to explain why some countries stagnate while others grow. Countries have approached the task of development from very different conditions and histories, including the heritage of colonialism. Some countries started to develop with favorable educational, commercial, cultural, and political systems; others did not. No one factor can be singled out as a prerequisite for success, since it is usually possible to find substitutes.

The primary obstacles to development include political and social phenomena. Political instability and lack of political support for effective development policy have been especially serious impediments. Social conditions, such as insufficient entrepreneurship and motivation, also have been widely discussed. Finally, international conditions are widely regarded as. a major obstacle. An important school of thought stemming from Marxian analysis cites capitalist imperialism, with collaboration from local elites, as a basic cause of underdevelopment. But international influences can also be positive forces for development. The balance depends on the particular circumstances of each country.

Main Learning Objectives

After studying this chapter you ought to understand and be able to explain:

1. The important differences in historical background among LDCs, and how these differences have influenced the ease of transition to modern economic growth.

2. The concept of **substitutes** in the context of considering the **prerequisites** for development.

3. How political instability, colonial rule, and political unwillingness to implement development policies have created serious obstacles to development.

4. The debate about how a nation's social values, such as **entrepreneurship** and **achievement motivation**, relate to initiating development.

5. The theories of **imperialism** that identify international capitalism in alliance with local elites as the fundamental obstacle to development.

6. The potential for international conditions to benefit rather than to hinder development.

7. The fundamental point that there is no simple explanation for why some countries develop and others do not.

Additional Key Terms, Concepts, and Institutions

Can you identify and explain each of the following?

modern economic growth
colonialism
stable environment
innovation
blocked minorities
need achievement
advantages of backwardness

Economic Tools and Techniques

From what you have learned in this chapter, can you:

1. State the basic premises of the **theory of comparative advantage** and the theory of **vent for surplus?**

2. Explain how the Marxian concepts of **declining rate of profit** and **surplus** developed into the theory of imperialism?

Self-Test

Completion

1. The failure to achieve sustained development has been as much a

   _____ and _____ phenomenon as an economic one.

2. According to Gerschenkron, there are usually _____ for most presumed prerequisites to modern economic growth.

3. Gerschenkron also argued that there are advantages of _____, including the ability of developing countries to learn from the experience of already advanced nations.

4. Psychologist David McClelland proposed the idea that societies in

   which people possessing _____ motivation are plentiful will more easily experience economic development.

5. According to the text, the various theories of imperialism share the common view that an LDC can develop only if it severs its ties to

   the _____ _____ system.

True-False If false, you should be able to explain why.

_____ 1. Europe's development experience demonstrates that a prior accumulation of wealth is a necessary prerequisite for modern economic growth.

_____ 2. A major difference between the colonial heritage of India and that of Indonesia is that at independence India already possessed a large number of educated and experienced managers.

_____ 3. Because an effective policy for pursuing economic development will ultimately benefit all groups in an economy, such policies do not involve hard political trade-offs.

_____ 4. Blocked minorities consist of immigrant groups or minority communities whose members succeed as entrepreneurs because they are not allowed to advance through other routes.

_____ 5. In Furtado's analysis, imperialism is caused primarily by the need of capitalist firms to assure secure sources of raw materials.

Multiple Choice

1. In the context of initiating development, the term "stable environ-ment" refers to:
   a. avoiding political disruptions such as wars, coups, and frequent policy reversals.
   b. protecting a country's natural ecological heritage from damage due to development.
   c. keeping inflation low.
   d. avoiding rapid structural change due to industrialization.

2. Which of the following is *not* a frequent source of political unwillingness to adopt policies that promote growth?
   a. growth is not considered as a desirable objective
   b. in the short run such policies often hurt the interests of politically influential groups
   c. alternative political goals such as a military build-up take precedence
   d. to some degree growth and equity goals can conflict

3. Which of the following is an essential trait for an individual to become an entrepreneur, according to Schumpeter?
   a. management ability
   b. a willingness to assume risks in pursuit of profits
   c. considerable personal wealth that can be invested to start an enterprise
   d. all of the above

4. "Vent for surplus" refers to:
   a. trade that makes it possible to make productive use of an abundant resource.
   b. the Marxian concept of exploitation of labor.
   c. a country exporting more than it imports.
   d. using tax powers to raise capital as a substitute for an underdeveloped banking system.

5. In the traditional Marxian analysis, the purpose of imperialism is to transfer _____ from the colonies in order to offset the declining _____ in the capitalist center.
   a. labor; army of unemployed
   b. surplus; rate of profit
   c. raw materials; growth rate
   d. capital; wage rate

Applications

Worked Example: Political Economy of Underdevelopment

The text states that political obstacles often make it very difficult for governments to adopt effective development policies. In modern theories of imperialism, political economists contend that the economic system itself creates a class structure that becomes a breeding ground for such political obstacles.

Consider the hypothetical case of the tiny island nation of Kelapa. The population of Kelapa falls into three classes: peasants (90% of the population), urban workers (5%), and the elites (5%). The peasants are very poor. They occupy 10% of the land, on which they grow coconuts for consumption and sale. The elites own the remaining 90% of the land, on which they graze cattle to produce beef, which only they can afford. The elites run the government and they head the military. In partnership with multinational corporations, they own the nation's highly protected major industrial enterprises. As crucial supporters of the government, urban workers are well paid and enjoy a standard of living much better than that of the peasants.

The political *posture* of the government strongly favors equitable growth and development. Indeed, there are active aid-supported programs of agricultural extension, rural public works, and universal primary education.

But simultaneously, peasants are required to sell their coconuts to a government marketing board at a price well below the world market value of the product. The government then sells some of these low-priced coconuts to urban workers for food, some to large farmers for cattle feed, and some are used to feed the army. The rest are exported for foreign exchange, which in turn is used to import military hardware, industrial supplies, and consumer goods for the elites and the urban workers. The net effect is to squeeze the poor coconut producers to benefit the other groups. In addition, both marketed coconut output and overall economic growth are stagnating because the price being paid to the peasants for coconuts is so low.

According to economists, the appropriate remedy includes higher procurement prices for coconuts, more equitable distribution of land, lower protection for inefficient domestic industries, and less spending on military equipment. Kelapa's policymakers, being well-trained economists, agree that these policies would contribute greatly to growth and social equity. Can they implement the necessary reforms?

Not with the landowners refusing to assent to land reforms, nor with the urban workers refusing to accept higher coconut prices. Likewise, the generals flatly reject any cut in military imports, while the industrialists insist that protectionism continue. The class structure of the economy in Kelapa is both an incubator for bad policies and a formidable barrier to reform.

Exercises

1. This exercise explores political economy obstacles to development in Buah-Buah, an island to the east of Kelapa (see the Worked Example). Answers to the following questions may require a bit of imagination, as well as some economic logic and an understanding of the material from Chapter 2.

    a. Heavy industries in Buah-Buah are state-owned. Operating with grossly excessive staffs and very high costs, these enterprises absorb large subsidies from the government budget—funds that could be used for development projects. Policymakers agree that it would be highly desirable to eliminate these subsidies. Yet they are unwilling to do so. What kinds of social or political conditions might account for this unwillingness?

    b. Inflation is rampant in Buah-Buah, primarily due to large government budget deficits financed by printing money. The deficits result from a combination of very heavy expenditures and very low tax collections. Policymakers agree that a lower inflation rate is highly desirable, yet they are unwilling to reduce the government budget deficit. What kinds of social or political conditions might account for this unwillingness?

    c. Government spending on health care goes mainly to building and operating modern hospitals in the cities. At the same time, the vast majority of the people have little access to any kind of modern health care. Policymakers agree that it would be highly desirable to reallocate health care funds to rural health centers. Yet they are unwilling to do so. What kinds of social or political conditions might account for this unwillingness?

d. The government issues operating licenses to firms in commerce, transportation, construction, and industry. The resulting bureaucratic red tape and regulatory restrictions have stunted growth of the private sector. Buah-Buah's policymakers agree that the economy would benefit if freed of these restrictions. But they are unwilling to change existing policies. What kinds of social or political conditions might account for this unwillingness?

2. a. Identify and briefly explain three *disadvantages* faced by countries that have begun to develop in the second half of the twentieth century, as compared to countries that began to develop two hundred years ago.

b. Identify and briefly explain three *advantages* faced by countries that have begun to develop in the second half of the twentieth century, as compared to countries that began to develop two hundred years ago.

3. This exercise checks your understanding of the theories of imperialism as outlined in the text.

a. In the Marxist analysis, how did colonialism affect the expected decline in the rate of profits on capital and the overthrow of the capitalist class?

b. According to modern theories of imperialism, through what means can capitalist powers in the post-colonial era drain surplus from LDCs?

c. (i) What would motivate local elites in an LDC to ally with foreign capitalists?

(ii) How would such an alliance stifle a country's growth and development?

d. Think about the following statement. Do you agree or disagree? Briefly explain. Regardless of your position, do you recognize an element of truth in the contrary position? Briefly explain.

"Progress for a developing nation is possible if and only if its ties to the international capitalist system are severed."

4. The text points out that a nation can gain through international trade. This exercise provides a preliminary look at the gains from trade, a topic to be covered in depth in Chapter 15.

a. Suppose that steel and popcorn are produced in both Mexico and the United States. Prices in the two countries are shown below. For simplicity the Mexican prices have been converted to a dollar equivalent.

Commodity	Price in Mexico	Price in United States
Steel (per ton)	$500	$300
Popcorn (per ton)	$200	$300

In this situation, can you see the trade opportunities that exist? Specifically, it would be profitable for:

Mexico to export _____ to the United States.

Mexico to import _____ from the United States.

b. (i) Though exporters and importers might profit, not everyone in Mexico necessarily benefits from trade. With Americans now

buying _____ from Mexico, total demand for this Mexican product increases, and the price in Mexico is likely to

_____.

   (ii) What group in Mexico would be hurt as a result of the export activity?

   (iii) On the other hand, imports of _____ from the United States would expand the total supply of this product in Mexico's market. So the price in Mexico is likely to

_____.

   (iv) What group in Mexico would be hurt as a result of the import activity?

c. Although some Mexicans benefit and some are hurt by such trade, there is reason to believe that Mexico as a whole achieves a net gain. Assume that the initial prices in Mexico roughly reflect the opportunity costs of resources used in production. Consider the trade pattern as providing an indirect method of "producing" the import good via reallocating resources to the export good.
   (i) With direct domestic production, 1,000 tons of the import

good uses $_____ worth of Mexican resources.

   (ii) For exactly the same resource cost, _____ tons of the export good can be produced, then sold in the United States

for $_____.

   (iii) With these earnings, _____ tons of the import good can be obtained! Thus there is an unambiguous potential net gain from trade for Mexico. This example illustrates the theory of comparative advantage.

d. Even with unambiguous potential net gains from trade for an LDC, political and social considerations intrude on the economic analysis in a number of ways.

   (i) First, the potential net gain may be captured by only a narrow class of beneficiaries. Can you give a brief illustration of how this might occur? [Hint: maybe the export earnings will be used to import something else.]

   (ii) Second, even where net gains to the people as a whole might be realized, policymakers might act to prevent these trades from occurring. What political factors might explain such actions?

   (iii) [More difficult] Third, the domestic prices in the LDC might not be even roughly related to the opportunity cost of the resources used in production of each good. If so, the market would generate trade patterns that involve a real loss for the country. Can you give a brief illustration of how this might occur?

Answers to Self-Test

Completion

1. political, social
2. substitutes
3. backwardness
4. need achievement (or just achievement)
5. international capitalist

True-False

1. F	4. T
2. T	5. F
3. F	

Multiple Choice

1. a	4. a
2. a	5. b
3. b	

CHAPTER 3   Growth and Structural Change

Overview

This vital chapter examines the broad features of growth and structural change that characterize economic development, and presents the main theoretical and empirical approaches economists use to understand this subject. The analysis begins with an explanation of the statistical problems inherent in measurements of gross national product (GNP) that figure prominently in studies of growth and structural change. The underlying determinants of an economy's aggregate growth rate are examined—first using a traditional model based on capital accumulation (the Harrod-Domar model), and then using a neoclassical framework that permits a broader evaluation of the sources of growth. Studies based on the latter approach reveal that improvements in productivity and efficiency can be as important as capital accumulation in contributing to LDC economic growth.

Systematic structural changes accompany economic growth. Among these are an increase in the share of industry in GNP and increased urbanization. Although "normal" (i.e., average) patterns have been studied statistically, no one path of structural change is appropriate for all countries to follow. Simplified versions of standard two-sector models of development are examined to provide a deeper understanding of the links between industrial development and progress in agriculture. Case studies of China and Kenya illustrate the lessons from these models. Finally, the chapter discusses both empirical and theoretical analyses of the pattern of structural change within the industrial sector.

Main Learning Objectives

After studying this chapter you ought to understand and be able to explain:

1. The definition of **gross national product** (GNP) and the problems that arise in measuring GNP, including the **exchange-rate conversion problem** and the **index-number problem**.

2. The implications of the simple **Harrod-Domar** model and the more general **sources of growth** analysis of the determinants of economic growth in LDCs.

3. Why industrialization and urbanization systematically accompany development, and how these **patterns of development** have been estimated empirically.

4. How the pace of industrialization is related to conditions in agriculture and the rate of population growth, in the context of both the **two-sector labor-surplus model** and the **two-sector neoclassical model** of development.

5. The shifts from **early industries** to **late industries** that characterize development of the structure of the industrial sector.

6. The debate about **balanced growth** vs. **unbalanced growth** in connection with the pattern of industrial development.

7. The underlying theme of the chapter: that many regularities characterize the development process, but each country must identify the path and pattern of development most suitable to its own conditions.

Additional Key Terms, Concepts, and Institutions

Can you identify and explain each of the following?

takeoff
value-added
non-traded goods and services
real vs. nominal GNP
aggregate production function
ICOR
Engel's Law
marginal product and average product of labor
terms of trade between industry and agriculture
turning point (in the Fei-Ranis model)
big push, or critical minimum effort
backward and forward linkages

Economic Tools and Techniques

From what you have learned in this chapter, can you:

1. Apply the **exchange-rate method** and the **individual price method** to convert a country's GNP data into an international standard currency such as the dollar?

2. Show how measured GNP growth depends on which year's prices are used to compute changes in **real** GNP?

3. Apply the basic **Harrod-Domar** equation ($g = s/k$) and the sources of growth equation (Equation 3–6 in the text) to analyze economic growth?

4. Use **isoquants** to illustrate and explain **fixed-coefficient production functions** and **neoclassical production functions**?

5. Explain and interpret the patterns of development estimated by Chenery and colleagues, including the sense in which they can be considered as **normal patterns?**

6. Explain the meaning of each curve in textbook Figure 3−7, the relationship between these curves, and the theoretical lessons from the **Fei-Ranis version** of the labor-surplus model?

7. Explain the key differences between the neoclassical two-sector model and the labor-surplus model, making use of textbook Figures 3−7 and 3−8?

Self-Test

Completion

1. If the bakery industry produces $10 million worth of bread using $8 million worth of intermediate goods such as flour, the difference ($2 million) is the _____ in the bakery industry.

2. Suppose that Korea has a per-capita GNP of 3 million won and an exchange rate of 1,000 won per dollar. Using the exchange rate to convert to dollars, Korea's per-capita GNP is $_____.

3. In a country where industry is growing faster than agriculture, measured GNP growth will be _____ if real GNP is calculated using a base year with high agriculture prices.

4. ICOR stands for the _____.

5. The underlying assumption of the Harrod-Domar growth model is that growth is mainly determined by accumulation of _____.

6. Curves that show the combinations of inputs that produce equal amounts of output are called _____.

7. During the 1970s Indonesia had an ICOR of 2.6 while India had an ICOR of 6.0. This suggests that scarce capital was being used more efficiently in _____.

8. The textbook contends that it would be best to drop the term "normal" pattern of development and speak instead of an _____ pattern.

9. The Lewis and Fei-Ranis two-sector models assume the presence of _____ surplus in rural areas.

10. The Fei-Ranis model assumes that the rural wage does not fall below the _____ product of farm labor.

11. To measure _____ GNP, the impact of inflation is eliminated by consistently using a single year's prices to calculate the value of goods and services.

12. Chenery and Taylor use the term _____ industry to describe an industry that uses simple technologies to produce essential goods.

True-False If false, you should be able to explain why.

_____ 1. GNP is defined as the sum of the value of all final goods and services plus all intermediate goods produced in an economy.

_____ 2. Value-added in the textile industry is equal to the value of payments to factors of production working in the industry.

_____ 3. When the usual exchange-rate method is used to convert GNP statistics into dollars, GNP levels for low-income countries like India are substantially overstated.

_____ 4. If the aggregate production function is neoclassical, then the capital-output ratio is a variable that can be controlled to some extent by policy.

_____ 5. A major conclusion from empirical studies of the "sources of growth" is that productivity and efficiency are far less important for LDCs than capital accumulation.

_____ 6. Chenery and his colleagues found that large countries, small industry-oriented countries, and small primary-product exporters all follow a single "normal" pattern of development.

_____ 7. Empirical evidence shows that in countries with higher levels of per-capita income, a higher share of GNP is produced in agriculture.

_____ 8. In the Fei-Ranis model, the "turning point" in development is the point where labor demand has risen enough that real wages begin to rise.

_____ 9. The neoclassical two-sector model assumes that wages in agriculture are determined by the marginal product of labor, not by an institutionally fixed wage.

_____ 10. With a positive marginal product of labor in agriculture, agricultural production will decline when workers move off the farm, *ceteris paribus* (i.e., other things being equal).

_____ 11. Until the late 1970s, Kenya was not a labor-surplus economy, so population growth led to higher levels of food production.

_____ 12. Industrialization requires a "big push" because of the necessity for balanced growth on both the demand side and the supply side.

Multiple Choice

1. The textbook discusses two problems with the common interpretation of the concept of "takeoff." Specifically, takeoff does not imply that (choose two):
   a. development proceeds along a predetermined common path.
   b. per-capita incomes will be increasing.
   c. a country is experiencing modern economic growth.
   d. development progress has become automatic.

2. What is the special significance of non-traded goods in relation to GNP-measurement problems?
   a. Such goods do not enter GNP because they are intermediate goods.
   b. Such goods do not enter GNP because they are not traded in the market.
   c. There is no value-added in production of such goods.
   d. The value of such goods is not properly captured by the exchange-rate conversion method for international comparisons.

3. From 1975 to 1980 real GNP in Costa Rica grew by 2 billion colones (the national currency). Investment during this period totaled 10 billion colones. The ICOR:
   a. was 5.0.
   b. was 0.2.
   c. was 8 billion colones.
   d. cannot be determined without knowing the savings rate.

4. When isoquants are L-shaped, the production function is:
   a. aggregate.
   b. neoclassical.
   c. fixed-coefficient.
   d. Marxist.

5. Consider a country with an ICOR of 6.0 in which GNP must rise by 2% per annum to prevent a decline in per-capita income. This requires a savings rate of:
   a. 12%.
   b. 3%.
   c. 8%.
   d. 2%.

6. The central idea of Engel's Law is that as family incomes rise,
   a. the amount of money they spend on food declines.
   b. the proportion of their budget spent on food declines.
   c. they prefer to migrate to urban areas.
   d. the savings rate increases.

7. Two basic assumptions used in David Ricardo's nineteenth-century model of development have played an important role in more modern theories. One of these is the assumption of:
   a. fixed-coefficient production functions.
   b. labor surplus.
   c. zero population growth.
   d. backward linkages.

8. In the Fei-Ranis model, terms of trade between industry and agriculture turn against _____ when industry's demand for labor increases beyond the point where labor's _____ in agriculture is zero.
   a. labor, wage
   b. industry, marginal product
   c. agriculture, supply curve
   d. exports, institutionally fixed wage

9. China's efforts to cope with its labor surplus have included all of the following policies except:
   a. control of population growth.
   b. use of less mechanized farming methods.
   c. sharp reduction in food imports.
   d. encouraging growth of labor-intensive industries in the urban areas.

10. Which of the following is a backward-linkage effect from establishing a steel factory?
   a. stimulus to construction activities using steel beams.
   b. stimulus to coal mining.
   c. stimulus to employment through job creation.
   d. all of the above are backward-linkage effects.

Applications

Worked Example: The Fei-Ranis Model

How does the lack of progress in *agriculture* hinder the development of *industry*?

Consider the case of Machismo, a small country that neglected agriculture in its drive to industrialize. Initially, the entire labor force of 1,000 worked on farms producing bananas, worth 10 pesos per pound. Figure 3–1 shows the agricultural production function. You can see that the last 100 workers added nothing to farm output. Their marginal product was zero. With 1,000 workers producing 1.8 million pounds of bananas per year, each worker consumed 1,800 pounds (18,000 pesos worth) per year.

Workers were willing to migrate to urban industrial jobs as long as they were paid enough to eat as well as their farm pals. Initially, then, industry could attract labor supply with a wage of 18,000 pesos per year.

After 100 workers had moved to industry, the situation looked like this: a labor force of 900 worked in agriculture producing (still) 1.8 million pounds of bananas, enough for each rural worker and each urban worker to eat 1,800 pounds per year, as usual. But once another 100 workers had migrated to industry, conditions changed markedly. With only 800 workers left on the farms, banana production dropped to 1.62 million pounds per year. Those who left for the city no longer had a zero marginal product on the farm. Workers now demanded 1.8 million pounds but because only 1.62 million pounds were produced, banana prices rose to 12 pesos per pound. At this price rural and urban workers chose to eat only 1,620 pounds per year. Demand equaled supply (1.62 million pounds), but the terms of trade between agriculture and industry had shifted against industry.

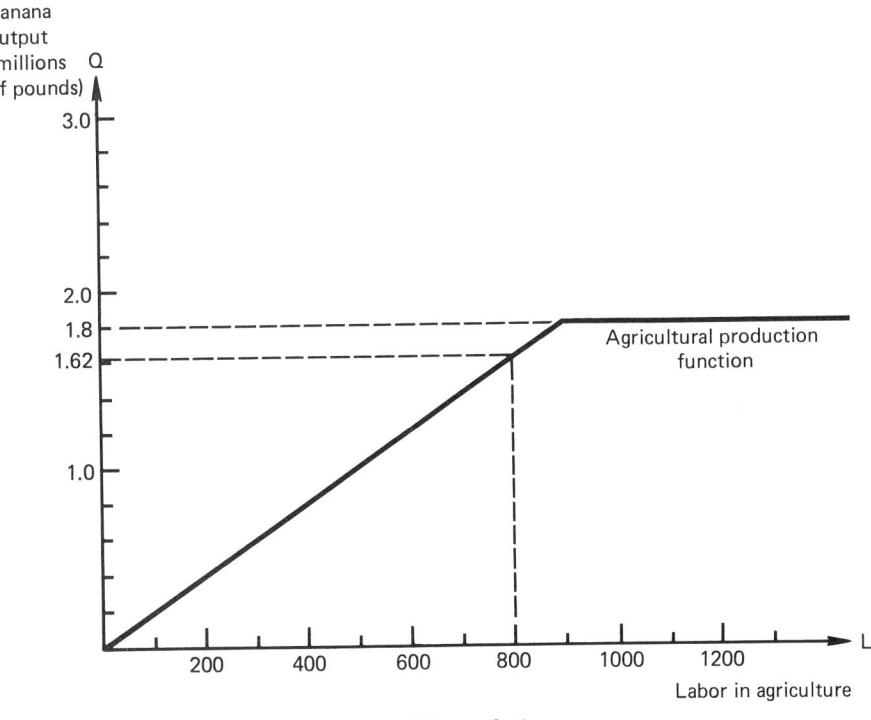

Figure 3–1

Even though each urban worker consumed fewer bananas, the higher banana price meant that each worker's food bill was now 19,440 pesos per year (= 1,620 pounds × 12 pesos/pound). Without higher wages to meet the higher food costs, workers would have chosen to move back to the farm. In Figure 3–2, the supply curve of labor to industry (S_0S_0) reflects these circumstances. Industry could hire as many as 100 workers at a wage of 18,000 pesos. But to hire 200 workers, the industrial wage had to rise to 19,440 pesos (point *B*). Note that despite the higher wage, the workers are not better off; their real wage and their consumption of bananas has declined.

Suppose instead that agricultural productivity had risen to maintain production of 1.8 million pounds of bananas despite fewer rural workers (via a shift in the production function in agriculture). Then banana prices would not have risen. Rural and urban workers alike would not have had to reduce banana consumption levels. The supply curve of labor to industry would not have turned up at point *A*. Given the demand curve (*DD*) for labor in industry, employment could have expanded out to point *C* rather than point *B*. In short, by neglecting agricultural productivity, Machismo ended up with fewer jobs, lower real income, fewer goods, and lower profits for reinvestment and growth.

Three observations: First, this example refers to an increase in the nominal price of bananas; it is more accurate to say that the shortage caused the price of bananas to rise *relative to* the price of industrial goods. Second, had it been possible to import bananas, industrial labor costs might not have increased as much. But the need for food imports would then have drained valuable foreign exchange, again cramping

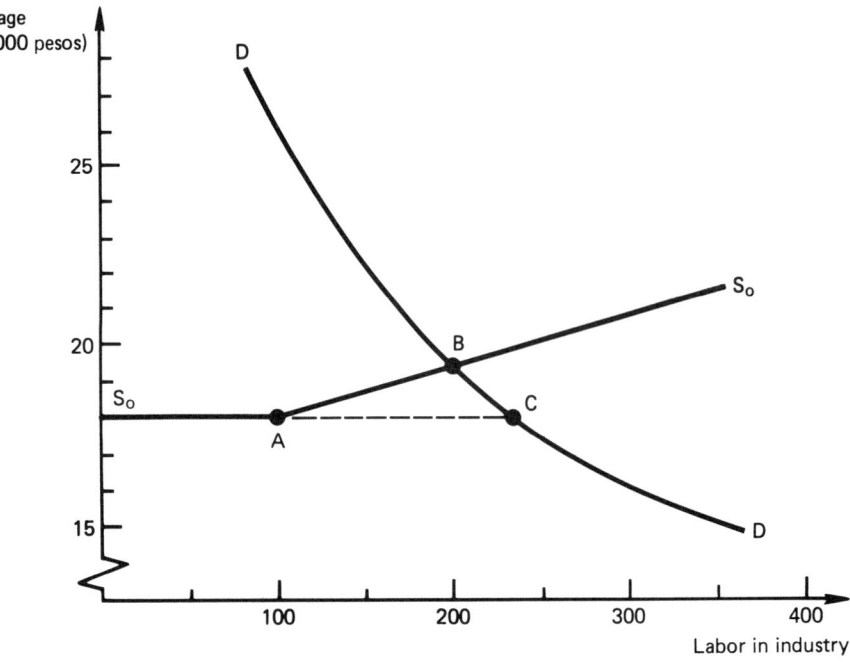

Figure 3-2

industrialization and growth. Finally, in a neoclassical version of the story there would have been no horizontal portion to curve S_0S_0 in Figure 3-2. If so, neglect of agricultural productivity would have pinched banana output even before industrial employment had expanded beyond point A.

Exercises

1. It is your turn to analyze the two-sector labor-surplus model. This exercise uses Figures 3-1 and 3-2 discussed above. Be sure you have read the Worked Example carefully.

   a. Let's see how things would change in Figures 3-1 and 3-2 if the labor force in Machismo grew to 1,200. Start with all 1,200 workers placed in the agricultural sector.

   _____ million pounds of bananas per year.
   (ii) Assuming that everyone eats an equal amount, this level of

      farm output permits each worker to consume _____ pounds of bananas per year. [Be careful with the units.]
   (iii) Suppose that the increased number of mouths in Machismo causes the price of bananas to rise to 16 pesos per pound. The bananas consumed by each agricultural worker therefore have

      a money value of _____ pesos per year.

(iv) Study Figure 3−1 carefully. How many of the 1,200 workers could be withdrawn from agriculture before total banana production begins to decline?

_____ workers.

(v) If this number of workers plus 100 more were withdrawn from agriculture, then the level of banana production would

drop to _____ million pounds, enough for each worker

in the economy to consume _____ pounds per year.

(vi) Suppose this drop in production causes the price of bananas to rise to 20 pesos per pound. At this price each worker's

banana consumption has a money value of _____
pesos per year.

b. Now consider these conditions from the perspective of the industrial sector. To attract workers from agriculture, industry has to pay an annual wage high enough to permit urban workers to eat as well as their farm pals.

(i) Starting with all 1,200 workers in agriculture, industry must

pay a wage of _____ pesos per year to attract labor
from agriculture.

(ii) As many as _____ workers can be supplied to industry without causing banana production to drop. Since total banana production and consumption remain in balance as these workers move to industry, there is no upward pressure on banana prices or on urban wages.

(iii) If an *additional* 100 workers move to industry, banana output

drops to _____ pounds per worker [you calculated this above] and the price of bananas rises to 20 pesos per pound.

Then urban wages must rise to _____ pesos per year
to prevent workers from moving back to the farm.

(iv) Based on your answers to the last three questions, carefully draw in Figure 3−2 the labor-supply curve to the industrial sector, and label it S_1S_1. [Hint: the horizontal portion now will lie above that for the original labor-supply curve, and will extend further to the right.]

c. Figure 3−2 now depicts two labor supply curves: S_0S_0, showing conditions when only 1,000 workers were in the labor force, and S_1S_1, showing conditions with 1,200 workers and no improvements in agricultural productivity.

(i) Given the same labor demand curve, *DD*, show the new equilibrium in the industrial labor market. Label the equilibrium point as point *B'*. Comparing point *B* and point *B'*, how has the increase in labor force from 1,000 to 1,200 workers affected:

−job creation,

—output,

—real wages, and

—profits

in Machismo's industrial sector?
(ii) Can you explain why these differences occur, with reference to the terms of trade between agriculture and industry?

d. Still assuming a labor force of 1,200 workers, suppose that productivity in agriculture increased by 50%.
(i) Briefly explain how this would change the agricultural production function in Figure 3–1 and the supply-of-labor curve in Figure 3–2.

(ii) Given the same labor-demand curve in industry (DD), how would the increase in agricultural productivity affect conditions in Machismo's industrial sector?

2. Measuring Gross National Product (GNP)
   Begin this exercise by looking back over textbook Table 3–1. The top half of that table is reproduced in Table 3–1 here, but with new data showing prices and quantities one year later (call it year 1). Also, you will need to fill in some of the blanks.

   a. Start by calculating GNP for the two countries. First, for the United States, the market value of:

   (i) steel output is $_____ billion.

Table 3–1

GNP for United States and India, Year 1

	United States			India		
	Quantity	Price ($)	Value of output (billion $)	Quantity	Price (Rs)	Value of output (billion Rs)
Steel (millions of tons)	105	$210 per ton	————	12	Rs 2,000	————
Retail sales services (millions of personnel)	2.1	$5,100 per person per year	————	5	Rs 4,200	————
Total GNP (in local currency)			————			————

(ii) retail sales services is $_____ billion.

So the total value of goods and services produced in the United States during year 1 is:

(iii) $_____ billion. This is GNP for the United States.

(iv) Fill this information into the column of blank spaces for the United States in Table 3−1. Then, in the same manner, calculate the value of India's steel output, retail sales services, and total GNP (in billions of rupees), and fill in the column of blank spaces for India in the table.

b. You now have GNP figures for each country in local currency units (dollars and rupees). To do a GNP comparison for the two countries for year 1, the GNP figures must be expressed in common currency units. Let's convert India's GNP to U.S. dollars using the exchange rate. Assume here that the Indian government has maintained the exchange rate at Rs 8 = $1. You have calculated that India's GNP for year 1 is:

(i) Rs_____ billion (in rupee units).

At the prevailing exchange rate this is equivalent to:

(ii) $_____ billion (in dollar units).

(iii) The resulting ratio of GNP in the United States to GNP in India (both expressed in dollars) is:

(U.S. GNP)/(Indian GNP) = _____ .

c. Rather than use the exchange rate to convert rupees into dollars, one can directly value each of India's goods and services using its dollar price. At $210 per ton, India's total steel output has a dollar value of:

(i) $_____ billion.

At $5,100 per person per year, the dollar value of India's retail sales services totals:

(ii) $_____ billion.

Adding these two together gives India's total GNP, converted to dollars using the individual price method:

(iii) $_____ billion.

The resulting ratio of GNP in the United States to GNP in India (both expressed in dollars) is:

(iv) (U.S. GNP)/(Indian GNP) = _____ . [Note: in terms of income per capita, the ratio would be far higher, since the United States has far fewer people.]

(v) Briefly explain why switching from the exchange-rate conversion to the individual-price conversion caused such a change in the GNP ratio.

d. Table 3–1 in the textbook shows GNP for India of Rs 29 billion during the year we will call year 0. You have found that India's GNP in year 1 is:

(i) Rs _____ billion.

These two figures show India's **nominal** GNP for the two years. To measure the **real** change in GNP over this period it is necessary to compute the value of the different outputs using a constant set of prices. Let's choose year 0 as the "base" year. For this base year, real GNP is simply the same as nominal GNP: Rs 29 billion. For year 1, however, things are a bit different. Using the base-year steel price (Rs 1,600 per ton), India's steel output for year 1 has a value of:

(ii) Rs _____ billion.

Using the base-year retail services price (Rs 4,000 per person per year), the value in year 1 of retail services in India is:

(iii) Rs _____ billion.

So India's total GNP for year 1, valued at constant year 0 prices, is:

(iv) Rs _____ billion.

This is *real* GNP for year 1. Since India's real GNP for year 0 was Rs 29 billion, real GNP increased from year 0 to 1 by:

(v) _____ %.

3. This exercise applies the Harrod-Domar growth model.

   a. In Indonesia during the 1970s the incremental capital-output ratio (ICOR) averaged 2.50. Using the Harrod-Domar growth equation, what savings rate would Indonesia have required to achieve an

   aggregate growth rate of 8% per annum? $s = $ _____ %

   b. With the same ICOR, what growth target would be attainable if

   the savings rate were projected to be 27%? $g = $ _____ %

   c. Suppose a country's government fears political upheaval unless a growth rate of 4% per annum can be achieved. The ICOR and the savings rate are projected to be $k = 5.0$ and $s = 14\%$, respectively.
      (i) Prove that the 4% growth rate cannot be achieved under these circumstances.

      (ii) Given the savings rate, what ICOR would be required to achieve the growth target?

(iii) How can government policy influence the ICOR in the right direction?

d. Over the period 1973−1983, the GNP growth rate for Jamaica was $g = -1.7\%$ per annum, while gross savings (s) averaged over 20% of GNP. Briefly discuss these figures in relation to the Harrod-Domar growth model.

4. Isoquants and production functions

Brrravia is a highly specialized economy. The only product is chicken soup. The aggregate production function for Brrravia shows the quantity of chicken soup that can be produced for any given quantity of labor (L) and capital (K). This relationship can also be expressed in the form of isoquants, showing various combinations of L and K that will produce a given quantity of chicken soup.

a. Figure 3−3 shows a set of fixed coefficient isoquants for chicken-soup production. The label for each isoquant shows the respective quantity (Q) of chicken soup.
   (i) With 400 units of K and 60 units of L, Brrravia could produce

   _____ barrels of chicken soup. The value of the

   capital-output ratio would be $K/Q =$ _____.
   (ii) With 600 units of K and 90 units of L, Brrravia could produce

   _____ barrels of soup. The incremental capital-output

   ratio for Brrravia is ICOR = _____.

   (iii) If Brrravia had $K = 600$ and $L = 120$, _____ barrels of soup could be produced. The capital-output ratio would be

   $K/Q =$ _____.
   (iv) In the latter case, is there labor surplus in Brrravia? Explain.

b. The isoquants in Figure 3−4 represent a neoclassical production function.
   (i) With 400 units of K and 60 units of L, Brrravia could produce

   _____ barrels of chicken soup. The value of the

   capital-output ratio would be $K/Q =$ _____.

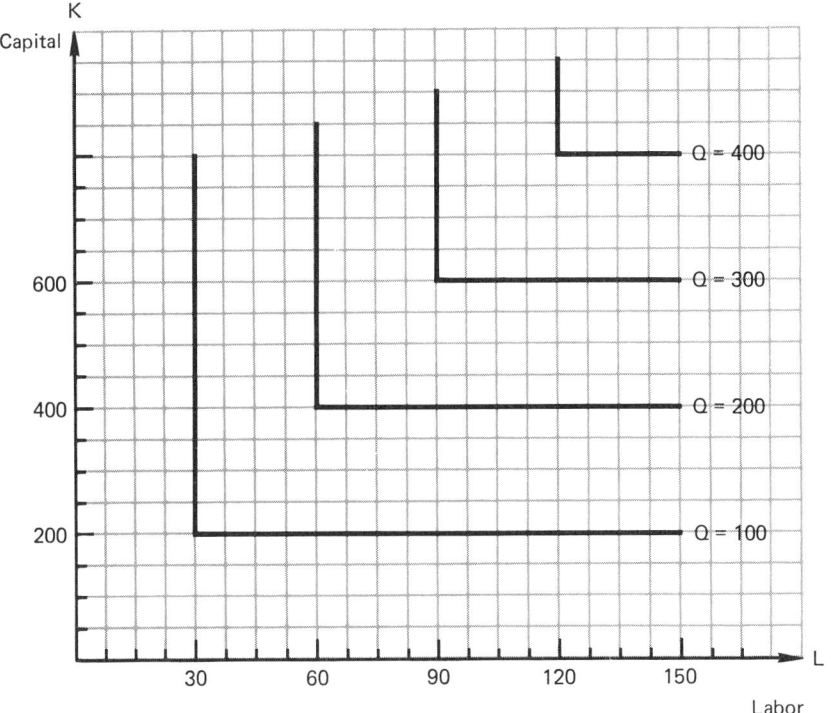

Figure 3–3

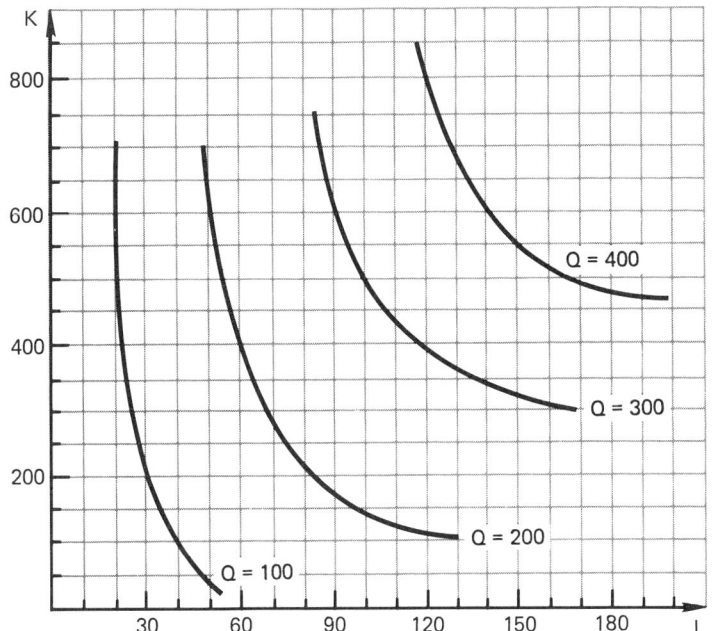

Figure 3–4

(ii) With 600 units of K and 90 units of L, Brrravia could produce

_____ barrels of soup. Comparing this outcome with the one just above, the incremental capital-output ratio for

Brrravia is ICOR = _____ .

(iii) If Brrravia had K = 600 and L = 120, _____ barrels of soup could be produced. The capital-output ratio would be

K/Q = _____ .

(iv) In the latter case, is there labor surplus in Brrravia? Explain.

(v) If Brrravia went from K = 400 and L = 60 as in part (i), to K = 600, L = 120 as in part (iv), the incremental capital-

output ratio would be ICOR = _____ . Why does this ICOR differ from the one calculated in part (ii) above?

c. In Figure 3–5, the vertical axis shows the level of chicken-soup production, while the horizontal axis shows the amount of labor

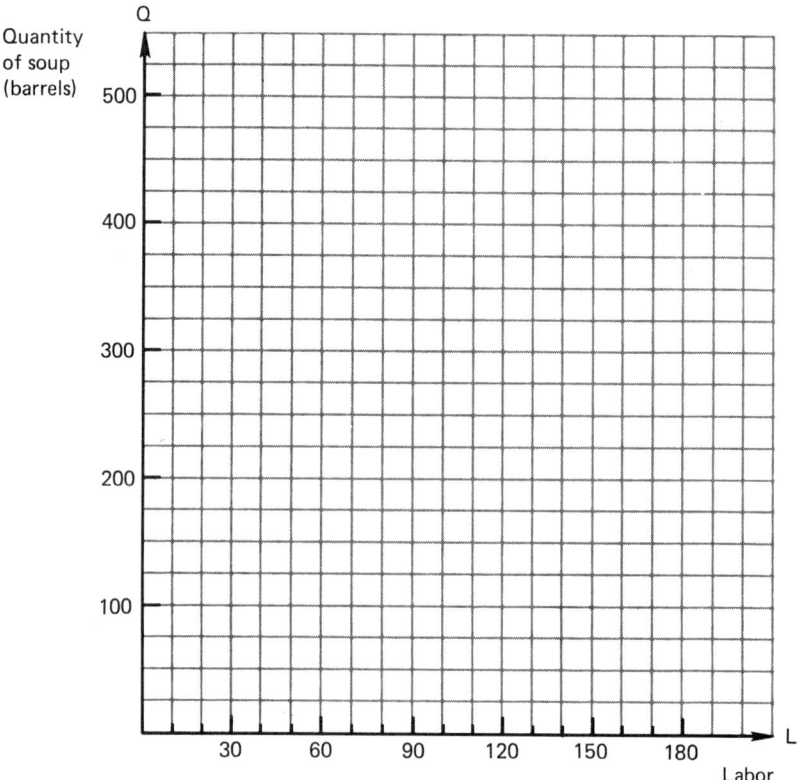

Figure 3–5

-46-

input. Use the information embodied in Figure 3-4 to plot carefully in Figure 3-5 the various combinations of L and Q consistent with a fixed capital stock of $K = 600$. Explain how this neoclassical production function reflects diminishing returns to labor.

d. Still assuming $K = 600$, plot in Figure 3-5 the various combinations of L and Q observed in Figure 3-3, and explain how the marginal product of labor behaves with a fixed coefficient production function.

5. This exercise is an application of the sources-of-growth analysis. Neglecting land and resources (for simplicity), the sources-of-growth equation from the textbook is:

$$g = a + W_K g_K + W_L g_L,$$

where
    g = growth rate of national product;
    a = a mystery variable—call it "the residual";
    W_K, W_L = the shares of national income going to capital and to labor, respectively;
    g_K, g_L = growth rate of the capital stock and the labor force, respectively.

a. Consider an economy in which the labor force is growing at a rate of 2.7% per annum, while the capital stock is growing by 4% per annum. Suppose 55% of national income goes to labor and 45% goes to capital.
(i) If the residual were $a = 0$, what rate of growth would the economy achieve? [Hint: plug the appropriate numbers into the growth equation and solve for g.]

$g = $ _____ %

This is the growth rate accounted for by the weighted growth of capital and labor inputs.

(ii) The actual rate of economic growth, though, has been 4.5% per annum. This is faster than what could be accounted for by the growth of capital and labor inputs. Explain the economic meaning of the "residual." In other words, what economic forces would account for growth over and above what is warranted by the growth of the capital stock and the labor force?

b. Consider a second economy in which labor's share of national income is 60%; the remainder is capital's share. The capital stock is growing by 5% per annum and the labor force is growing at 3% per annum, while national product is growing by only 1% per annum.

(i) Calculate the residual for this economy.

$a =$ _____

(ii) You should find that the value of the residual is rather low this time! Explain what economic conditions might generate the conditions observed in this country.

c. Suppose that the growth equation were applied to data for all the low-income LDCs to measure which element—capital formation, labor force growth, or the residual—actually makes the largest contribution to growth. What do *you* think the results would show? How important do you think these three components are empirically?

6. This exercise explores an empirical "pattern of development."

The solid line in the bottom half of textbook Figure 3–3 shows how, on average, the share of industry in GNP (IND/GNP) is related to levels of per-capita GNP for large countries. Let's examine the same relationship for smaller countries. Table 3–2 shows the data on IND/GNP and per-capita GNP for twelve LDCs with populations under 20 million (in 1983).

a. Carefully plot on Figure 3–6 the twelve points corresponding to the data in Table 3–2. Then use a straightedge to draw in the "best-fit" line summarizing as nearly as possible the "pattern" relating IND/GNP to per-capita GNP.

Table 3-2

Country	1983 per-capita GNP ($)	Industry share of GNP (%)
Nepal	160	14
Niger	240	31
Kenya	340	20
Liberia	480	26
Bolivia	510	26
Honduras	670	26
Ivory Coast	710	24
Cameroon	820	32
Costa Rica	1,020	27
Peru	1,040	41
Tunisia	1,290	36
Dominican Republic	1,340	29

Source: *World Development Report 1985.*

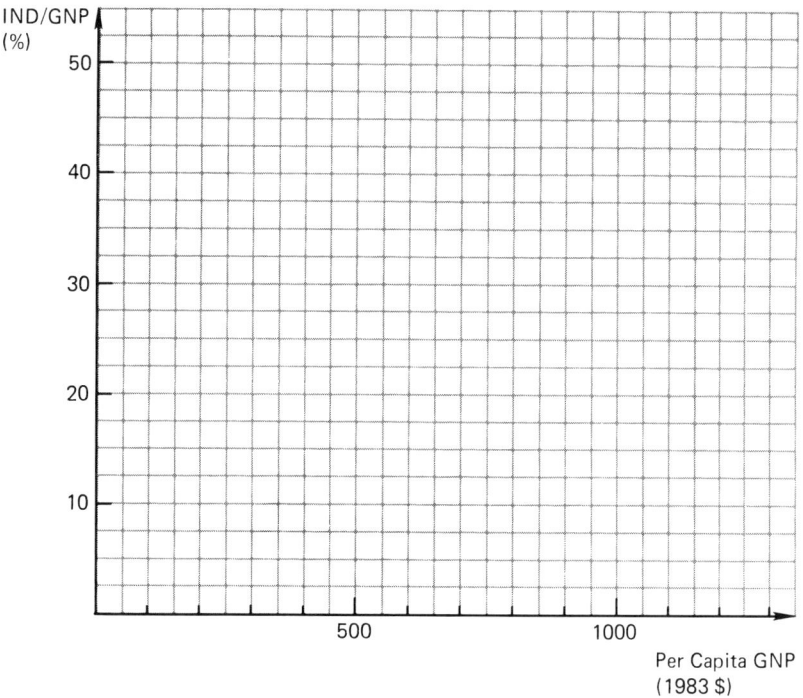

Figure 3-6

b. Niger's level of IND/GNP clearly lies well above the best-fit line, whereas IND/GNP for Costa Rica is below the line. What factors might account for these deviations from the underlying "pattern"? Should the results be interpreted as meaning that Niger has done particularly well and Costa Rica has not performed well? Briefly explain.

Answers to Self-Test

Completion

1. value-added
2. $3,000
3. lower
4. incremental capital-output ratio
5. capital
6. isoquants
7. Indonesia
8. average
9. labor
10. average
11. real
12. early

True-False

1.	F	7.	F
2.	T	8.	T
3.	F	9.	T
4.	T	10.	T
5.	F	11.	T
6.	F	12.	F

Multiple Choice

1.	a and d	6.	b
2.	d	7.	b
3.	a	8.	b
4.	c	9.	c
5.	a	10.	b

CHAPTER 4   Development and Human Welfare

Overview

The previous chapter discussed the changes in economic structure that characterize the development process. This chapter examines the fundamental question of how growth and structural change are related to improvements in human welfare for the billions of citizens of the third world. The problems of income inequality, poverty, and satisfaction of basic human needs are examined.

The chapter defines basic income distribution concepts and presents a number of methods for measuring the human welfare dimension of economic development. The empirical record is discussed and some important theoretical approaches are then examined. These theories help one to understand the determinants of poverty and inequality, including the tendency for income inequality to worsen during the early stages of development. The chapter concludes with a discussion of strategies for more equitable growth. Concern with equity and human welfare will be a recurrent theme in later chapters of the text.

Main Learning Objectives

After studying this chapter you ought to understand and be able to explain:

1. The connection between economic development and improvements in human welfare.

2. The **Lorenz Curve** and **Gini concentration ratio** (also called the Gini coefficient), as well as the use of **income quintiles** for describing the **size distribution** of income.

3. The distinction between income **inequality, poverty** and **equity**, as well as the relationship between changes in inequality and changes in poverty.

4. The use of **social indicators** as measures of welfare and progress towards satisfying **basic human needs**.

5. The **inverted U** relationship between the pattern of income inequality and the level of per-capita GNP (**Kuznets' Law**), and the factors that help to explain variations in the degree of inequality across countries.

6. The basic theoretical determinants of inequality and poverty in the **Ricardo model**, in **Marx' theory of distribution**, in the **labor-surplus model**, and in the **neoclassical model**.

7. Three **strategies** for promoting growth with equity: **redistribute first, then growth; redistribution with growth** (RWG); and **Basic Human Needs** (BHN). [Note: BHN sometimes refers to a set of social indicators, and sometimes to a strategy for equitable growth.]

Additional Key Terms, Concepts, and Institutions

Can you identify and explain each of the following?

functional distribution of income
relative versus absolute poverty
poverty line
PQLI
income weights, population weights, and poverty weights
reserve army of the unemployed
marginal productivity theory
dynamic redistribution of assets
trickle down

Economic Tools and Techniques

From what you have learned in this chapter, can you:

1. Draw a Lorenz Curve from income distribution data?

2. Calculate a Gini coefficient from Lorenz Curve data?

3. Calculate income shares by quintile from data on income distribution (e.g., the share of income earned by the poorest 20% of households)?

4. Calculate GNP growth rates using distribution weights?

5. Use the Lewis-Fei-Ranis model (developed in Chapter 3) to explain the inverted-U pattern of changes in income inequality?

Self-Test

Completion

1. The _____ distribution refers to how income is divided among the factors of production, i.e., the shares of income accruing to land, labor, and _____.

2. The _____ distribution refers to the distribution of income among individuals or families.

3. The curve showing the percentage of total income that goes to any cumulative percentage of recipients is called the _____ curve.

4. The World Bank used a single global poverty line of $75 per capita in 1975 to measure the amount of _____ poverty in the world.

5. Economic growth and welfare can be integrated by use of "_____ weights" in calculating GNP growth.

6. Kuznets's Law states that as per-capita income rises, income inequality first _____, and then _____.

7. Marx contended that with capitalist development, wages would be held to the subsistence level by a "reserve army of _____."

8. The theory stating that competitive-factor markets will determine a return to each factor of production equal to its marginal product is called the _____ theory of distribution.

9. In the labor-surplus model, the most promising way to achieve greater equity is to eliminate the labor surplus through emphasis on _____ creation.

10. The so-called "radical model" of growth with equity can be summarized by the phrase "_____ first, then _____."

11. The basic idea of the _____ strategy is that government policies should influence the structure of development so as to improve earning opportunities for low-income people.

12. In Adelman and Robinson's model of the South Korean economy, the best policies for bettering the income distribution were those that improve the internal terms of trade for _____, and those that encourage _____ migration.

True-False If false, you should be able to explain why.

_____ 1. Without economic growth, one group of people can be made better off only at the expense of another group.

_____ 2. If all income recipients had exactly the same level of income, the Lorenz curve would lie along the 45-degree line, which indicates perfect equality.

_____ 3. From the Gini coefficients for South Korea (= 0.34) and for Peru (= 0.59), one can see that income was distributed more equally in Peru.

_____ 4. The bottom quintile (poorest one-fifth) generally receives about 15% of total income in most LDCs.

_____ 5. Worsening of the size distribution of income in a country does *not* necessarily mean that the poor are getting poorer.

_____ 6. On average, countries with higher per-capita income have higher performance in terms of social indicators.

_____ 7. All low-income countries have very low PQLI scores.

_____ 8. Countries with higher primary school enrollment rates tend to have less income inequality.

_____ 9. The poverty line is another name for the Lorenz curve.

_____ 10. In the Fei-Ranis-Lewis model, the tendency toward increasing inequality is reversed only when governments begin to provide welfare benefits to the poor.

_____ 11. According to Lewis, inequality during the early stages of development makes growth easier to achieve.

_____ 12. The textbook cites Burma, Ghana, and Jamaica as countries that successfully achieved equitable growth by pursuing the socialist approach of redistribution first.

Multiple Choice

1. Higher per-capita GNP does not necessarily mean higher incomes for most citizens because:
   a. gains from growth may be used for expensive "glory" projects that provide few concrete benefits to the people.
   b. gains from growth may be heavily reinvested, so consumption gains are postponed.
   c. those who are already relatively well off may get all or most of the benefits.
   d. all of the above.

2. To derive the Gini coefficient from the Lorenz curve drawn in Figure 4–1, one would calculate the ratio:
   a. $A/(A + B)$
   b. $B/(A + B)$
   c. $C/(A + B)$
   d. A/B

3. Most lists of basic human needs include all of the following items *except*:
   a. basic transportation, such as bicycles.
   b. minimal levels of nutrition.
   c. minimal provision of shelter.
   d. provision of basic health care.

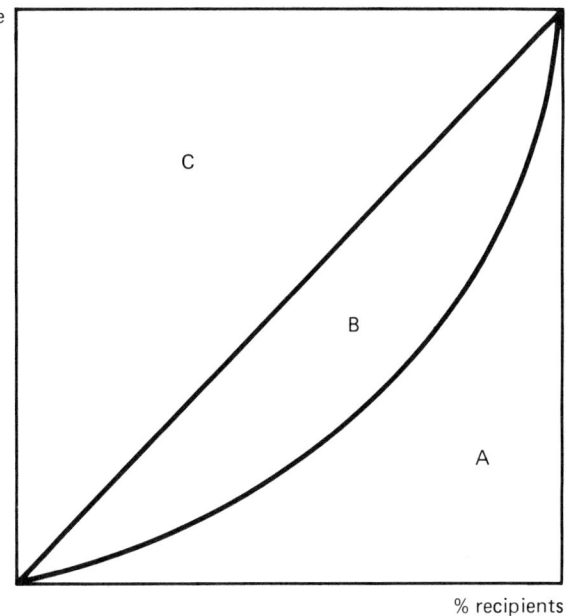

Figure 4-1

4. The PQLI is an aggregate of three widely available indicators of basic human needs. Which of the following is *not* a component of the PQLI?
   a. life expectancy at age one.
   b. per-capita income.
   c. infant mortality rate.
   d. literacy rate.

5. Brazil's growth rate during the 1960s averaged 6.9% per annum using normal "income weights." Using "poverty weights," the average growth rate was 5.4% per annum. From these figures one can conclude that in Brazil:
   a. the poor were getting poorer.
   b. incomes were growing faster for the rich than for the poor.
   c. the size distribution of income inequality improved.
   d. the change in *welfare* was negative.

6. From the case studies in Chapter 4, which country experienced rapid growth with very high inequality?
   a. South Korea   c. Sri Lanka
   b. Brazil   d. India

7. Which of the following policy instruments is *not* a standard part of a redistribution with growth (RWG) strategy?
   a. confiscation of property from the rich
   b. development of appropriate technologies to make low-income workers more productive
   c. "dynamic redistribution" involving investments in small farms and small businesses
   d. measures to alter prices of labor and capital to encourage more employment of unskilled labor

8. The basic human needs (BHN) strategy differs from the RWG strategy in that it:
   a. is concerned with equity as well as growth.
   b. is concerned with equity rather than growth.
   c. emphasizes direct provision of basic commodities and services for the poor.
   d. is revolutionary rather than reformist.

Applications

Worked Example: Income Distribution Measures

Data on the size distribution of income (by quintile) in Mexico (for 1977) and Yugoslavia (for 1978) are shown in Table 4−1:

Table 4–1

Percentage share of household income going to:

	Poorest 20%	Second Quintile	Third Quintile	Fourth Quintile	Richest 20%
Mexico	2.9%	7.0%	12.0%	20.4%	57.7%
Yugoslavia	6.6%	12.1%	18.7%	23.9%	38.7%

Source: World Development Report 1984

Derivation of the Lorenz curve and Gini concentration ratio for Mexico will be worked out here. The corresponding derivations for Yugoslavia will be used in Exercise 1, which follows.

The first step in constructing a Lorenz curve is to calculate the *cumulative* income share accruing to any given percentage of households. Lining up the households from poorest to richest, we find that for Mexico:

20% of the households receive	2.9% of total income;
40% of the households receive	9.9% of total income;
60% of the households receive	21.9% of total income;
80% of the households receive	42.3% of total income;
100% of the households receive	100.0% of total income.

The Lorenz curve is then simply a graph showing these data points. The horizontal axis measures the cumulative percentage of recipient units (households here) covered, and the vertical axis shows the cumulative share of total income earned. Figure 4−2 shows the Lorenz curve drawn from the data for Mexico. For simplicity, the data points are connected by straight lines.

How can a Gini concentration ratio be calculated from these data? We must apply the formula: Gini $= A/(A + B)$, where B is the area under the Lorenz curve, and A is the area between the Lorenz curve and the diagonal line.

First, consider all the percentages as decimal units. In other words, consider 40% as being 0.40. In this way data values on both the horizontal and vertical axes range from 0.00 (i.e., 0%) to 1.00 (i.e., 100%). The box in which the Lorenz curve is drawn is thus a "unit square," which

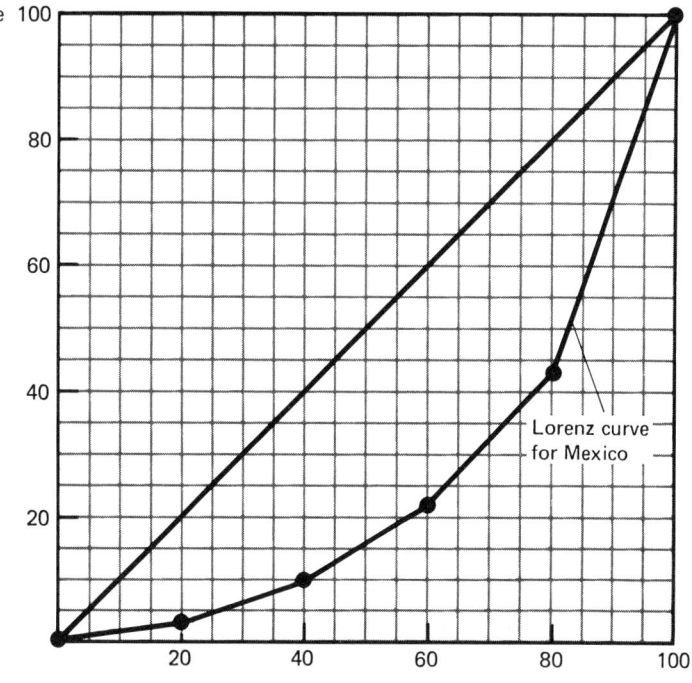

Figure 4-2

always has an area of 1.00 (length times width = 1 × 1 = 1). The value of the area under the diagonal is always half of this, or 0.50. This means that the area A plus area B always equals 0.50.

Area B can be computed geometrically, using the formulas for the area of rectangles and triangles. In this case, area B is 0.254. Knowing B, we can easily find area A from the relationship $A + B = 0.5$, or $A = 0.5 - B$. This gives $A = 0.246$. Then we can calculate the Gini coefficient from the formula:

$$\text{Gini} = A/(A + B) = 0.246/0.5 = 0.492.$$

Exercises

1. It is your turn to derive a Lorenz curve and calculate a Gini concentration ratio.

   a. From the data for Yugoslavia presented in Table 4–1, calculate the *cumulative* income shares. Taking the poorest households first, we find that for Yugoslavia:

   20% of the households receive _____% of total income;

   40% of the households receive _____% of total income;

   60% of the households receive _____% of total income;

   80% of the households receive _____% of total income;

   100% of the households receive _____% of total income.

b. Plot the points corresponding to these data observations on Figure 4–2, and draw in the Lorenz Curve for Yugoslavia.

c. The area under the Lorenz curve for Yugoslavia can be found geometrically; it is $B = 0.348$. Knowing the area under the Lorenz curve, find the value of area A and the value of the Gini concentration ratio.

area A = _____

Gini concentration ratio = _____

d. Compare the Lorenz curve for Yugoslavia with that for Mexico and discuss what these curves show about the size distribution of income in the two countries.

e. Compare the Gini concentration ratios of the two countries. Do the Gini coefficients reflect the differences observed in the Lorenz curves?

2. This exercise covers the measurement and interpretation of income distribution statistics.

a. Pauvritania contains five families, with respective income levels in 1986 as shown:

Family A: family income = 500 rupees
Family B: family income = 700 rupees
Family C: family income = 900 rupees
Family D: family income = 1,100 rupees
Family E: family income = 3,000 rupees
Total income of all families = 6,200 rupees

Defining each family as an income-recipient unit, what is the income share of the poorest 20% (call this P20)? What is the income share of the richest 20% (call this R20)?

P20 = _____ percent

R20 = _____ percent

b. Suppose that in 1976, the income levels of the five families (in constant 1986 prices to control for any inflation effects) were:

Family A: 400 rupees
Family B: 500 rupees
Family C: 600 rupees
Family D: 800 rupees
Family E: 1,500 rupees

(i) What were the values for P20 and R20 in 1976?

$$P20 = \underline{\hspace{2cm}} \text{ percent}$$

$$R20 = \underline{\hspace{2cm}} \text{ percent}$$

(ii) The absolute poverty line in Pauvritania is 650 rupees (again, in constant 1986 prices). Comment on how the size distribution, the extent of absolute poverty, and welfare levels in the country have changed during the past decade.

c. Measures of the size distribution of income can depend greatly on how recipient units are defined. To illustrate this, suppose that families A through E contained two, three, four, five, and six people, respectively.
   (i) One can then convert the 1986 family-income levels into levels of income *per capita* as follows.

   Family A: per-capita income = _____ rupees

   Family B: per-capita income = _____ rupees

   Family C: per-capita income = _____ rupees

   Family D: per-capita income = _____ rupees

   Family E: per-capita income = _____ rupees

   (ii) Ranking families by per-capita income, the poorest recipient unit is now:

   Family _____ .
   (iii) There are twenty individuals in these families. The four poorest individuals (i.e., the poorest 20%) belong to:

   Family _____ .
   The four richest individuals (i.e., the richest 20%) belong to:

   Family _____ .
   (iv) So if we consider each individual as a distinct recipient unit, what are the income shares of the poorest and richest 20% of individuals (assuming that income is equally shared within any given family)?

$$P20 = \underline{\hspace{2cm}} \text{ percent}$$

$$R20 = \underline{\hspace{2cm}} \text{ percent}$$

(v) Comment on how differences in the definition of recipient units can affect income distribution comparisons.

d. Now consider the effect of life-cycle income patterns on the measurement of inequality. Suppose that in each family in Pauvritania, just one person is an income earner, and that these five workers are identical to each other in that each gets married at age 20 and follows an identical pattern of earnings and child rearing.

Age	Children	Income
20	0	500 rupees
25	1	700 rupees
30	2	900 rupees
35	3	1,100 rupees
40	4	3,000 rupees

How does this information affect your interpretation of the 1986 data on the income distribution in Pauvritania?

3. In this exercise you will do some work with distribution weights. In the previous exercise, incomes in Pauvritania were seen to change in the following manner between 1976 and 1986:

Family	1976 Income	1986 Income
A	400	500 rupees
B	500	700 rupees
C	600	900 rupees
D	800	1,100 rupees
E	1,500	3,000 rupees
Total Incomes	3,800	6,200 rupees

These data will now be used to calculate the growth of the Pauvritanian economy over the decade.

a. The standard method for calculating growth uses total income. What is the percentage change in total income between 1976 and 1986 from the above data?

percentage change = _____ %

This ordinary method of calculating growth corresponds to what the text calls "income weights."

b. Instead, one can calculate the growth of income for each income group separately. To simplify the calculations, let's lump together the incomes of families A and B (the lowest 40%); also lump together the incomes of families C and D (the middle 40%). Family E will stand alone (the upper 20%). The growth of income over the decade for the poorest 40% (families A + B) is shown below. Fill in the growth of income over the decade for the other two income groups.

Family	1976 Income	1986 Income	Percentage change in income	Share of population
A + B	900	1,200	33.3%	40%
C + D	_____	_____	_____ %	40%
E	_____	_____	_____ %	20%

c. You can now calculate the growth rate of the Pauvritanian economy using a weighted average of the percentage changes for the three income groups. Using weights that correspond to each group's share of the population (i.e., 0.4, 0.4, and 0.2, respectively), the result is the "population weighted" growth of national income. The population weighted growth rate for Pauvritania from 1976 to 1986 was:

growth using population weights = _____ %

[Hint: (0.4) × (rate of growth for the poorest 40%) plus (0.4) × (rate of growth for the middle 40%) plus . . . .]

d. One can also combine the growth rates for each group using other sets of weights (as long as they add up to 1.0). The text defines "poverty weights" as follows: a weight of 0.6 for the lower 40%; a weight of 0.3 for the middle 40%, and a weight of just 0.1 for the upper 20%. Use these weights to calculate the "poverty weighted" growth of income in Pauvritania during the past decade.

poverty weighted growth of income = _____ %

e. You now have calculated the growth of income in Pauvritania over the period 1976 to 1986 in three different ways. Explain why these three growth rates differ as they do.

f. Referring to Table 4–6 in the textbook, explain precisely what calculation was used to obtain the population-weighted growth rate and the poverty-weighted growth rate for Brazil. [Note: These are growth rates per annum, whereas in the exercise above you have been calculating changes over a decade.]

4. This exercise investigates how the inverted-U pattern can come about during the process of development.

a. Indozania is a country of five dreadfully poor subsistence farmers. Each has an income level of just $75. The income of the five workers will be summarized using the following notation: (75, 75, 75, 75, 75), where each number represents the income of one person. Under these conditions, what are the income shares of the poorest and the richest quintiles (P20 and R20) of the population?

P20 = _____ percent

R20 = _____ percent

b. Now the country starts to experience growth and structural change. A factory opens up in the city, employing one worker. To lure a worker away from the farm, the factory pays a wage of $200. Everyone else's income stays the same. The income levels of the Indozanian workers are now (75, 75, 75, 75, 200). Find the income shares of the richest and poorest 20% now.

P20 = _____ percent

R20 = _____ percent

c. The following year a second factory opens up employing one worker at a wage of $200. The income levels then become (75, 75, 75, 200, 200).
(i) At this stage in the country's development:

P20 = _____ percent

R20 = _____ percent

(ii) And then a third factory opens up, employing one worker at a wage of $200. Incomes now are (75, 75, 200, 200, 200), so:

P20 = _____ percent

R20 = _____ percent

(iii) And then a fourth factory opens up, similar to the others, so incomes are (75, 200, 200, 200, 200) and:

P20 = _____ percent

R20 = _____ percent

(iv) Finally, a fifth factory opens up so that every worker has moved out of subsistence agriculture and is now earning an income of $200. At this point:

$$P20 = \underline{\hspace{3cm}} \text{ percent}$$

$$R20 = \underline{\hspace{3cm}} \text{ percent}$$

Look familiar?

d. Let's add five spouses for the five workers. These spouses would join the labor force, but only if wages were to rise to $300.
   (i) In Figure 4–3, draw the modern sector's labor-supply curve. The curve should show that as many as five workers would supply their labor at a wage of $200, but a wage of $300 is then necessary to attract additional labor supply.
   (ii) As long as there remained "surplus labor" in the form of workers who were willing to supply their labor for $200, new factories could be opened without any change in the real wage. What happens to the equilibrium real wage once a sixth factory is built?

   (iii) How would your last answer change if the population of workers were growing faster than the number of factory jobs?

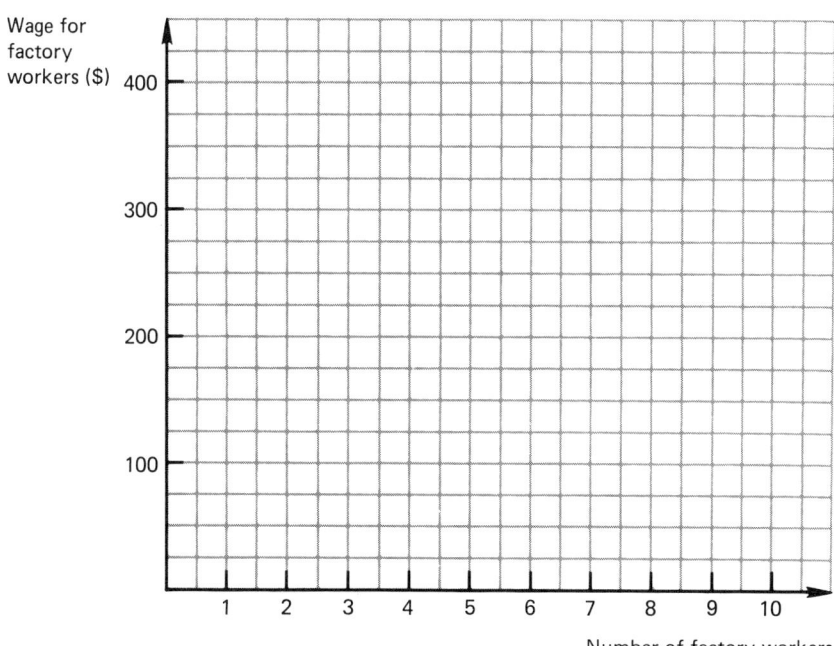

Figure 4–3

e. Let's introduce one capitalist who owns all these factories and makes a large profit on each of them. Taking the capitalist into account, explain how the growth of the modern sector in Indozania produces an inverted-U pattern of income inequality.

5. This exercise examines the relationship between economic growth and basic human needs. The textbook contains a table showing the PQLI for fourteen LDCs. These PQLI figures are reproduced here in Table 4–2 (excluding the four richest to make it easier to graph). Table 4–2 also shows each country's level of per-capita income (in 1970) and the rate of growth of per-capita income (1970–1981).

Table 4–2

Country	PQLI (1970–75 average)	Per-capita income (1970)	Growth of per-capita income per annum (1970–81)
Bolivia	43	$500	1.7%
Ghana	35	579	−3.2
Kenya	39	333	2.1
Tanzania	31	259	0.8
China	69	200	3.8
India	43	217	1.5
Indonesia	48	300	5.3
South Korea	82	791	7.2
Pakistan	38	287	1.9
Sri Lanka	82	215	3.0

Source: PQLI from textbook Table 4–5; growth of per-capita income from World Bank: *World Tables* (3rd ed., 1983); 1970 per-capita income derived from above source.

a. In Figure 4–4, plot the ten points representing the data on PQLI and the per-capita income level for each country. Do the data suggest that the satisfaction of basic human needs improves systematically as per-capita income increases? Explain.

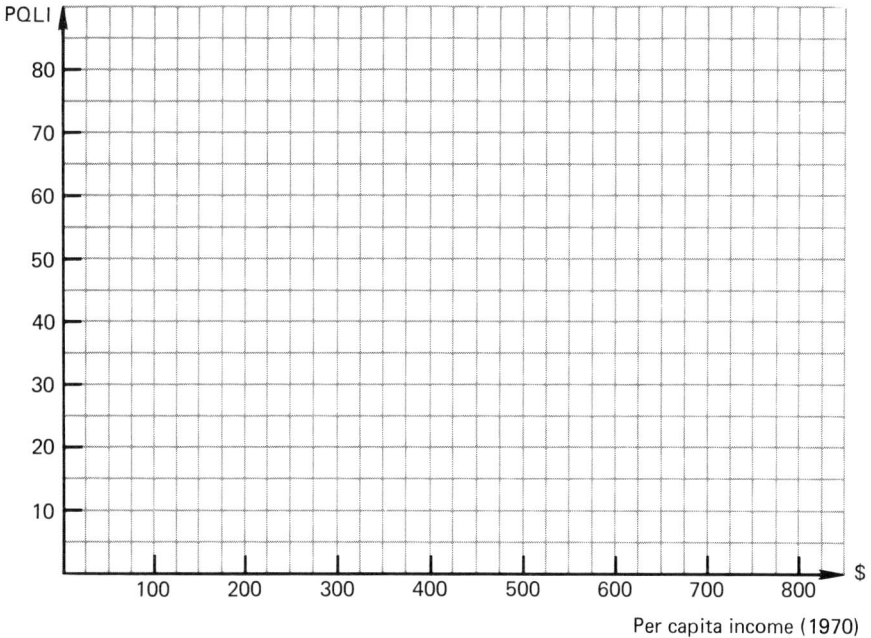

PQLI

80
70
60
50
40
30
20
10

100   200   300   400   500   600   700   800 $

Per capita income (1970)

Figure 4–4

b. If there were a trade-off between growth and equity, one would expect to find that high growth rates are associated with weak PQLI performances. For a crude test of this hypothesis, fill in Table 4–3. Does it appear to be true that countries which perform best in fulfilling basic human needs are sacrificing economic growth? Explain.

Table 4–3

	Country	Rate of growth of per-capita income (1970–81)
PQLI >45		
1.	_____	_____ % per annum
2.	_____	_____
3.	_____	_____
4.	_____	_____
PQLI <40		
1.	_____	_____
2.	_____	_____
3.	_____	_____
4.	_____	_____

c. From these observations, would you conclude that it is practical or not for a country with low income and a great need for growth to concern itself with basic-human-needs problems? How can such a country go about dealing with BHN problems without sacrificing economic growth?

Answers to Self-Test

Completion

1. functional, capital
2. size
3. Lorenz
4. absolute
5. distribution
6. rises, falls
7. unemployed
8. neoclassical
9. employment
10. redistribute, grow
11. redistribution with growth
12. agriculture, rural-urban

True-False

1. T	7. F
2. T	8. T
3. F	9. F
4. F	10. F
5. T	11. T
6. T	12. F

Multiple Choice

1. d	5. b
2. a	6. b
3. a	7. a
4. b	8. c

CHAPTER 5   Planning, Markets, and Politics

Overview

This chapter broadly examines the why, what, and how of development planning, with special emphasis on political factors that permeate the formulation and implementation of development plans. Chapter 6 will discuss the economic models used in formulating plans. In socialist economies, planning is fundamental to economic policy; in mixed economies, planning is a valuable tool to improve government policy and budget decisions. The planning *process* serves a very important role in coordinating government activities and highlighting economic aspects of political decisions. These functions are best served when the process is to a degree decentralized and participative.

The process culminates in a published plan that includes a statement of goals, targets, and policy intentions. These plans are rarely carried out in detail due to the inherent uncertainties of forecasting, as well as political and bureaucratic snags. The implementation problems are accentuated when plans place heavy demands on public administration—one of the scarcest resources in many LDCs. Nonetheless, the plan serves as a guide for government programs, supplies valuable information to the private sector, and provides a framework for discussions with foreign aid agencies. In reaction to the problems encountered in planning, many LDCs (capitalist and socialist alike) have shifted toward more reliance on markets and less dependence on central controls.

Main Learning Objectives

After studying this chapter you ought to understand and be able to explain:

1. The advantages of market allocations compared to direct government controls, and the **market failure** problems that justify government interventions in a **mixed economy**.

2. The role and limitations of **national planning** in both mixed and **centrally planned** economies.

3. The **process** and the politics of planning, including the role of the **national planning agency**, and the reasons for a degree of **decentralization** and **participation** in planning.

4. The contents and the uses of a typical **development plan**.

5. The reasons for the poor record of plan **implementation**, including **bureaucratic politics**, and the lack of administrative capacity.

6. The trend toward **liberalization** involving a better balance between markets and government controls.

Additional Key Terms, Concepts, and Institutions

Can you identify and explain each of the following?

socialism
monopoly power
external economies and diseconomies
infant industry
goals, targets, constraints, and instruments
Ministry of Finance
welfare function
the current or operating budget versus the capital or development budget
absorptive capacity
getting prices right

Economic Tools and Techniques

From what you have learned in this chapter, can you:

1. Define **economic rents** and explain the emergence of **parallel markets** and **rent-seeking** behavior in response to government interventions?

Self-Test

Completion

1. _____ is defined as government ownership and control of the means of production.

2. A mathematical measure of the extent to which a plan satisfies national goals, with the various goals weighted according to priority, is called a _____ function.

3. The annual government budget has two parts: recurrent expenditures are detailed in the _____ budget, while government investments are specified in the _____ budget.

4. An industry that cannot compete initially against imported products, but is expected to become competitive after an initial break-in period, is referred to as an _____ industry.

5. LDC governments may be unable to make use of additional resources or aid for development projects because administrative systems lack _____ capacity.

6. In most countries, the annual government budget is prepared under the control of the Ministry of _____ .

7. In the case of Kenya's 1979–1983 Development Plan, the most severe constraint was stated to be the country's _____ .

8. The text contends that markets are _____ flexible than governments in reallocating resources as economic conditions change.

9. The Ministry of Public Works places a low priority on an irrigation project being promoted by the Ministry of Agriculture. This is an example of _____ politics.

True-False If false, you should be able to explain why.

_____ 1. One reason government intervention is required in market economies is that some national goals would not be satisfied even with well-functioning markets.

_____ 2. Minimum-wage laws, interest-rate ceilings, and food-price controls are examples of government interventions that generally promote the objective of "getting prices right."

_____ 3. The text explains that planning can be a useful tool in both socialist economies and mixed economies.

_____ 4. In practice, development plans are usually built upon a well-defined welfare function that reflects a clear statement by political leaders on goals and priorities.

_____ 5. When unexpected external events alter an economy's prospects shortly after a plan has been published, the entire planning process proves to be fruitless.

_____ 6. Once goals and priorities are defined, the whole planning process—from setting targets to implementing projects—is largely a technical and administrative exercise in which politics plays little part.

_____ 7. It is not uncommon for the list of projects in a development plan to include many that have never been appraised carefully, and many that will never see the light of day.

_____ 8. State-owned enterprises produce a greater share of industrial output in South Korea than in India.

_____ 9. The term "mixed economy" refers to an economy in which there is a good balance between development of agriculture and industry.

_____ 10. The phrase "rent-seeking" behavior refers to the problems landlords have in securing tenants after an excess of construction activity due to planning mistakes.

Multiple Choice

1. All of the following are clear market-failure conditions except one. Which is the exception?
   a. A few large firms dominate a market.
   b. Private middlemen provide the outlet for farmers to sell their crops.
   c. External economies are present, such as downstream flood prevention due to construction of a dam.
   d. External diseconomies are present, such as environmental deterioration from overcutting forests.

2. The national planning agency in a mixed economy usually has the primary responsibility for:
   a. administering the implementation of development programs such as irrigation schemes.
   b. determining prices of important products such as food grains.
   c. putting together annual current and capital budgets.
   d. assuring that planning targets are consistent with macroeconomic resource constraints.

3. If you were to read a country's development plan you would very likely see all of the following except:
   a. a mathematical analysis of the economy using a detailed macro-economic model.
   b. a general statement of goals, along with specific targets to be achieved during the plan period.
   c. an analysis of each of the major sectors of the economy.
   d. a list of projects the government would like to undertake during the planning period.

4. Which of the following would appear in the government develop-ment budget rather than the current budget?
   a. Salaries of school teachers.
   b. Pension payments to civil servants.
   c. Construction costs for building rural health centers.
   d. All of the above belong in the development budget.

5. A protective tariff or a subsidy to an infant industry is justified only if:
   a. the industry is state-owned.
   b. the protection or subsidy can be phased out after a period of time.
   c. the industry is a monopoly.
   d. the industry involves external diseconomies such as pollution.

6. According to the textbook, the trend toward liberalizing developing economies has been motivated by:
   a. conditions set by the World Bank and the IMF for LDCs to obtain loans and assistance.
   b. the difficulties LDCs have encountered in administering central planning.
   c. the observed success of a number of market-oriented LDCs.
   d. all of the above.

7. Indonesia's Second Development Plan stated that "production in agriculture must increase by around 4.6 percent per year." This is an example of a planning:
   a. goal.
   b. target.
   c. constraint.
   d. instrument.

Applications

Worked Example: Rent-Seeking Behavior

The textbook explains that government interventions can create **rents**—abnormally high returns—that lead to parallel markets and rent-seeking behavior. Let's use supply-and-demand analysis to see how this works. Figure 5–1 shows the supply-and-demand curves for flowers in Gardenia. Suppose that the government adopts a policy to control the price of flowers at $0.50 for the benefit of urban consumers. As shown by the supply curve, this controlled price provides rural flower growers the incentive to market only 100 bouquets (point *A*). At this price, the urban consumers demand 500 bouquets (point *A′*). Clearly, there will be a serious shortage at the government flower shops.

Not surprisingly, a parallel market will flourish outside the government shops. If the supply of flowers were indeed held to 100 bouquets, the demand curve shows that there will be unsatisfied consumers willing to

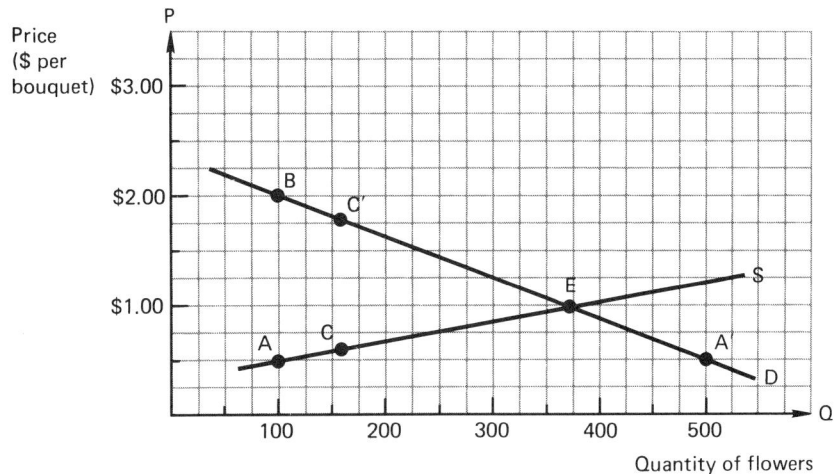

Figure 5–1

pay as much as $2 per bouquet (point *B*). Before long, some clever entrepreneur will figure out that a high profit could be made by offering growers $0.60 per bouquet. At this offer-price, growers have an incentive to boost production to 160 bouquets (point *C*), selling the extra output on the parallel market. The entrepreneurs, in turn, can sell these flowers for $1.78 per bouquet (point *C'*).

Moreover, growers have an incentive to divert some of the original 100 bouquets to the parallel market, where they can earn $0.60 each. Even some of Gardenia's government officials begin diverting flowers from their stores to the parallel market—seeking to share the rents created by the government price controls. Other government officials are accepting bribes to ignore the entrepreneurs who procure flowers in the countryside and sell them in the city—again, seeking a share of the rents.

The diagram suggests that competition can eventually drive the price in the parallel market down to its equilibrium value of $1.00 (point *E*), where excess profits are no longer earned. This is possible. But because of the illegality of the parallel market in Gardenia (in some countries "profiteers" can be sentenced to death) and the need to pay bribes, entrepreneurial activity stops well short of pushing excess profits down to zero. Ironically, if the price controls were removed, the average price paid paid by consumers for flowers would actually drop—to point *E*.

The outcome of the price-control policy is not very efficient: a large government bureaucracy runs a chain of flower shops with bare shelves; furtive parallel markets sell flowers at inflated prices while production wilts in the face of poor price incentives to the growers. The government could supplement its supply of low-priced flowers through imports, but only at a high cost in terms of scarce foreign exchange.

Why did the government adopt the price controls? It was part of a plan to promote the urban industrial sector by holding down the cost of living for urban workers—and for urban government officials, who happen to be very fond of flowers. Why is the policy not reversed now that it has been overrun by market forces? Might the answer have something to do with those government officials who are sharing the rents?

Exercises

1. This exercise explores goals, targets, constraints, and politics. To understand the politics in Pumpernickel, it is helpful to know that the population is 70% farmers, who consume only maize (the traditional crop) and 30% urban workers, who consume only bread (the product of modern industry). A majority of the urban workers are government employees. In addition to maize, farmers grow rye, which is used for bread production.

    a. The welfare function underlying the country's development plan places a high priority on the goal of industrialization.

        (i) Given the stated priority of the industrialization goal, the planners calculate that welfare would be maximized by the following tentative plan targets:

10% per year growth of production for _____

and for _____ .

0% per year growth of production for _____ .

[Remember: the country's three products are maize, rye, and bread.]

(ii) Which group's interests seem to be most heavily weighted in the welfare function used in this initial planning exercise? Explain briefly.

b. After consulting with other ministries about these targets, the planners find that some additional constraints have to be taken into account.

(i) First, the estimated savings rate is revised; it turns out that production capacity in the modern sector cannot grow by more than 7% per year. Explain how this constraint will affect the plan targets for maize and rye production.

(ii) There is also a political constraint. To avoid riots by farmers (who eat only maize), the government must plan for maize consumption to grow by at least 4% per year. Explain how this constraint will affect the plan targets for the other two products.

c. The 4% minimum growth of maize production is a figure based on political compromise. Experts of Ministry A had argued for a minimum 6% growth. Experts of Ministry B had argued for 2%. Which ministry is staffed by experts who come from farm families?

Ministry _____ .

Briefly discuss how this disagreement on a planning constraint reflects bureaucratic politics at work in the formulation of a plan.

d. Although the final plan sets a target of 4% growth of maize production, everyone at the Ministry of Agriculture is an urban bread eater, from the minister down to the agricultural extension officers. In view of this fact, briefly discuss how bureaucratic politics might affect implementation of the plan and achievement of the plan's target for maize.

e. It turns out that maize production fails to grow 4% per year. A populist revolution ensues and a coalition of farmers takes over the government.
   (i) When the revolutionary government formulates a new development plan, how are the goals and targets likely to differ from those of the former government?

   (ii) The Minister of Agriculture is now a farmer. But the people qualified to fill all the other positions at the ministry are still urban bread eaters. How might the interests of these bureaucrats affect implementation of the new plan and achievement of the new targets?

2. Let's continue looking at the situation in Pumpernickel, focusing now on the question of the market versus controls.

   a. Suppose that the prerevolutionary government had permitted the market to determine how much land would be allocated to growing maize and how much to rye.
      (i) Explain briefly how the market allocation of land would work.

(ii) How would the market allocation of land have changed if the salaries of government employees (all of whom are urban bread eaters) had been doubled and paid for from higher taxes on farm products?

(iii) How might the presence of **market failure** problems in the bread industry distort the allocation of land resources in Pumpernickel? Give an example of a market failure that would lead to *more* than optimal rye production. Explain briefly.

(iv) Then give an example of a market failure that would lead to *less* than optimal rye production. Explain briefly.

b. The revolutionary government is firmly committed to shifting resources into maize production.
  (i) Suppose that direct controls are used to shift resources into maize production. Is it possible that maize output ten years after the revolution is actually lower than it would have been under a market system? [Hint: yes]. Explain how this perverse outcome might occur when direct controls are used.

  (ii) By what means could the revolutionary government utilize market forces, rather than direct controls, to increase maize output?

3. In this exercise, it is your turn to examine how government interventions can create rents that lead to parallel markets and rent-seeking behavior. Figure 5–2 reproduces the supply-and-demand curves for flowers in Gardenia (see the Worked Example). This time, let's assume that the supply curve (S) represents flowers *imported* from a neighboring country.

   a. What is the initial equilibrium market price and quantity of flowers in Gardenia (point E)?

   $$P^E = \$\underline{\hspace{2cm}}$$

   $$Q^E = \underline{\hspace{2cm}} \text{ bouquets}$$

   b. Gardenia does not yet produce flowers. But the flower industry is considered to be an infant industry that should become competitive after a breaking-in period. Initially, domestic costs are very high. So the industry cannot develop without protection.
      (i) Draw a straight line that goes through points F and G in Figure 5–2. Label this line S'. This is the initial **domestic** supply curve (i.e., supply from domestic producers).
      (ii) Suppose the government bans flower imports in order to protect the domestic industry. Given the domestic supply curve S', what will be the new equilibrium market price and quantity of flowers?

   $$P' = \$\underline{\hspace{2cm}}$$

   $$Q' = \underline{\hspace{2cm}} \text{ bouquets}$$

      (iii) The ban on imports succeeds in putting domestic flower producers in business. But how are flower consumers in Gardenia affected by the ban on imports?

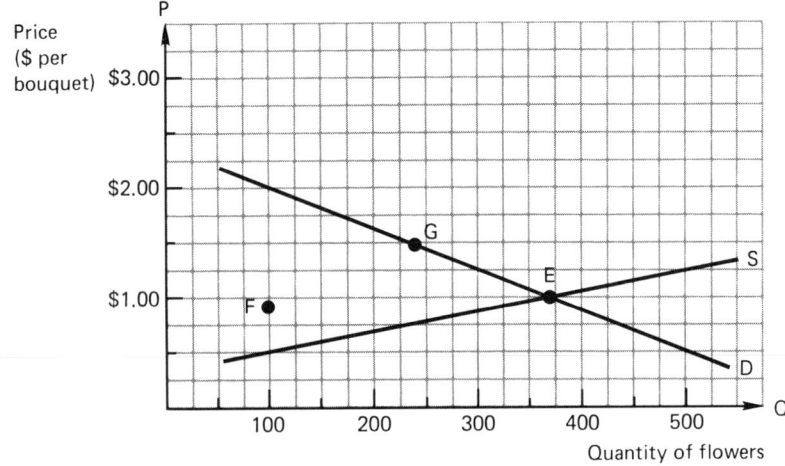

Figure 5–2

c. Before long some traders figure out that a high profit could be made by smuggling.
   (i) Look again at supply curve S in relation to the market price (P') in Gardenia. Explain how potential "rents" have been created by the government intervention in the flower market.

   (ii) As an example, calculate how much rent could be earned by smuggling 100 bouquets across the border, assuming that the smugglers sell the contraband at $1.40 per bouquet to assure a quick sale.

d. How will such smuggling affect the development of the domestic flower industry? Explain.

e. What sort of "rent-seeking" behavior might arise among government personnel in response to the profit opportunities created by the import controls?

Answers to Self-Test

Completion

1. Socialism
2. welfare
3. current or operating; capital or development
4. infant
5. absorptive
6. Finance
7. balance of payments
8. more
9. bureaucratic

True-False

1.	T	6.	F
2.	F	7.	T
3.	T	8.	T
4.	F	9.	F
5.	F	10.	F

Multiple Choice

1.	b	5.	b
2.	d	6.	d
3.	a	7.	b
4.	c		

CHAPTER 6   Planning Models

Overview

Chapter 6 examines some of the major economic tools used in development planning. Introduced first is a macroeconomic growth model based upon the Keynesian theory of aggregate demand and the Harrod-Domar equation for determining supply. This model incorporates both foreign exchange and savings constraints in determining the growth of an economy. The text then examines input-output analysis. Input-output models provide a tool for disaggregated analysis of sector-by-sector output requirements implied by a given set of final demand targets. A recent generalization of input-output, called the social-accounting matrix (SAM), is also discussed. These tools are used for consistency planning—for testing the feasibility of growth targets and for exploring the effects of alternative planning strategies.

Linear programming models, on the other hand, can be used for studying optimality: what is the best plan, or the best project to maximize an explicit objective function, subject to specified constraints. A newer model—the computable general equilibrium (CGE) model—is then discussed. CGE models are not bound to linear equations and permit the simulation of market responses to development policies, including substitution effects caused by relative price changes.

Project appraisal, the final tool introduced, is widely used to evaluate specific development projects. Project benefits and costs are measured using shadow prices that reflect social values and opportunity costs. The net present value (NPV) of alternative projects can then be compared to select the best set of investments. If market prices more closely reflected shadow prices, more efficient and equitable results would be generated by market interactions.

Main Learning Objectives

After studying this chapter you ought to understand and be able to explain:

1. The difference between a **consistent plan** and an **optimal plan**.

2. How economic growth can be analyzed using a **macroeconomic growth model**.

3. The structure of an **input-output table** and an **input-output coefficients matrix**, as well as the limitations of the input-output model.

4. The basic characteristics of the **social-accounting matrix** (SAM).

5. The structure of a **linear-programming model,** including the key differences between linear programming and input-output models.

6. The broad features and the advantages of the **computable general equilibrium (CGE) model.**

7. The basic elements of **project appraisal,** and in particular the use of **shadow prices** reflecting social **opportunity costs.**

8. The applications and the weaknesses of each of these six economic models as tools for development planning.

Additional Key Terms, Concepts, and Institutions

Can you identify and explain each of the following?

welfare function, or objective function
fixed coefficients
final versus intermediate uses
flow of funds matrix
welfare weights in project analysis
net cash flow
discounting
shadow wage and shadow exchange rate
commercial, economic, and social project appraisal
"getting prices right"

Economic Tools and Techniques

From what you have learned in this chapter, can you:

1. Use **community indifference curves** and a **production possibilities frontier** to distinguish between consistent and optimal plans?

2. Solve the **two-gap** macroeconomic consistency model for Y_t when saving is the **binding constraint?** When foreign exchange is the binding constraint?

3. Explain how to solve a simple input-output model to find the sectoral outputs consistent with a given set of final demands?

4. Explain how a welfare function is specified and incorporated into a linear programming model to find the optimal plan?

5. Calculate the **net present value** (NPV) and the **internal rate of return** (IRR) from a given time profile of net benefits for a project?

6. Illustrate the use of shadow prices in project appraisal? (Do you understand text Table 6-4 thoroughly?)

Self-Test

Completion

1. A plan that involves the best feasible use of resources is called an

    _____ plan.

2. Let sector 1 equal agriculture and sector 3 equal manufacturing. The manufacturing sector uses $200 million of agricultural goods to produce $500 million of output. The symbol for the input-output coefficient showing agricultural input per unit of manufacturing

    output is _____ and its numerical value is _____ .

3. The acronym SAM stands for _____ .

4. By adding a _____ matrix to a SAM, one can identify the sources of saving and the resulting allocation of investment in the economy.

5. A linear programming model determines the allocation of resources

    that maximizes the value of a _____

    function, subject to _____ such as the
    availability of resources.

6. The discount rate for which the net present value of a project would

    equal zero is called the _____ .

7. The World Bank differentiates between: _____

    project appraisal using cash flows; _____

    project appraisal using shadow prices; and _____
    project appraisal using welfare weights in addition to shadow prices.

8. The process of calculating the present value of a given future cash

    flow is called _____ .

9. Economists have developed _____
    models to simulate the mixed economies in which policies influence
    individual decisions via markets, with individuals responding to price
    signals.

10. The assumption of _____ coefficients in input-output
    models rules out substitution effects that may in reality be very
    important elements of any economic adjustment.

True-False If false, you should be able to explain why.

_____ 1. For a plan to be *consistent*, it must be feasible and it must represent the best use of available resources.

_____ 2. Planning models are too abstract to be of any use to development planners.

_____ 3. Each column of an input-output coefficients matrix defines a fixed-coefficient production function for a certain sector.

_____ 4. In a poor country with low savings and abundant labor, a strategy of "getting prices right" would tend to encourage more labor-intensive development in the private sector.

_____ 5. The coefficient a_{ij} shows the amount of j input used per unit of i output.

_____ 6. Input-output models are optimality models, not consistency models.

_____ 7. For each sector, the basic input-output equation says that total output must equal the sum of intermediate uses plus final uses of the product.

_____ 8. If a project is commercially profitable, then it must also be desirable when evaluated using shadow prices.

_____ 9. By providing a detailed picture of income and expenditure flows for different types of households, a SAM can permit planners to study how various policies will affect the distribution of income.

_____ 10. If the textiles used as an input in a clothing factory project are imported, then the shadow price of the textiles is zero.

Multiple Choice

1. In the accompanying figure (top of facing page), which target point would represent a consistent plan?
   a. _A_
   b. _B_
   c. _C_
   d. All of the above are consistent plans.

2. In the equation $\Delta Y_t = (1/k)(I_{t-1} - \delta K_{t-1})$, the parameter δ stands for:
   a. the ICOR.
   b. the rate of depreciation of capital stock.
   c. the savings rate.
   d. the rate of growth of the capital stock.

3. A major problem with input-output models is that they:
   a. can distinguish only four sectors.
   b. capture intermediate linkages but ignore final demands.
   c. do not easily handle changes in input-output coefficients due to technological change or input substitution.
   d. are subject to all of the above criticisms.

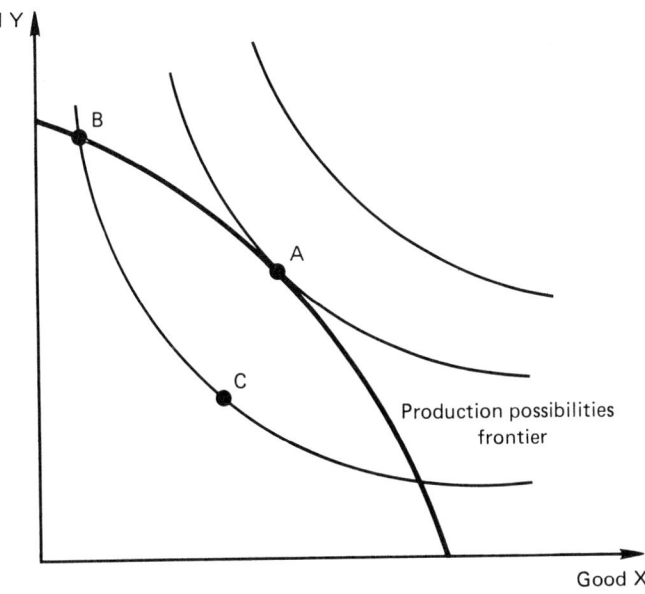

Good Y

B

A

C

Production possibilities
frontier

Good X

4. With a discount rate of 15%, the present value of $100 to be received
   ten years from now is:
   a. $100/(1.15)^{10}$
   b. $100/(0.15)^{10}$
   c. $100 \times (1.15)^{10}$
   d. $100/(10 \times 0.15)$

5. A road project pays $50 per month to workers who would otherwise
   be earning only $30 per month. The opportunity cost of using these
   workers for the project is:
   a. $50 per month
   b. $20 per month
   c. $80 per month
   d. $30 per month

6. Given the final demands for the output of each sector, input-output
   analysis can be used to:
   a. compute the total (direct plus indirect) demand for each sector's
      output.
   b. identify sectors requiring capital investment to increase produc-
      tion capacity.
   c. compute skilled manpower requirements.
   d. do all of the above.

7. If the shadow foreign exchange rate is 40% higher than the official
   exchange rate (local currency per dollar) then shadow pricing will
   favor projects that:
   a. reduce reliance on export markets.
   b. heavily depend on imported inputs.
   c. earn or save foreign exchange.
   d. depend on high levels of protection from imports.

8. If $a_{35} = 0.09$, then:
   a. 0.09 unit of sector 5 goods are required as an input for every unit of output of sector 3.
   b. 0.09 unit of sector 3 goods are required as an input for every unit of output of sector 5.
   c. one unit of sector 5 output is required as an input for every 0.09 unit of output of sector 3.
   d. one unit of sector 3 output is required as an input for every 0.09 unit of output of sector 5.

9. In a standard input-output model, the final demand (F_i) for each sector's product is generally:
   a. estimated based on a predetermined target growth rate for the economy.
   b. calculated within the model as part of the solution.
   c. measured directly from national-income accounts data.
   d. known by seeing which point on the country's production frontier is tangent to an indifference curve.

10. Which of the following is *not* true of SAMs?
   a. An input-output matrix can be embedded within a SAM.
   b. SAMs can integrate data from household surveys together with data from national-income accounts.
   c. Unlike input-output models, SAMs are not based upon linear, fixed-coefficient relationships.
   d. From the respective row and column totals in a SAM, one can identify data inconsistencies.

Applications

Worked Example: *Input-Output Analysis*

Planland is an economy with three sectors: (1) agriculture, (2) manu-facturing, and (3) services. The interindustry flow matrix for the year 1985 is shown in Table 6–1. Looking across any row will show where the sector's output was sold, while each column shows the breakdown of sector output according to cost. Study these data.

Notice the dominance of agriculture in final demand and labor income. Intermediate inputs, rather than value-added payments, account for the bulk of total cost in manufacturing and services. And, the manufacturing sector is far less labor intensive than agriculture and services. Notice that GNP in Planland was $300 (not $530!). The input-output table is simply an accounting framework showing these relationships. Table 6–2 converts this information into an input-output coefficients matrix. Each inter-industry flow is expressed as the input required **per unit of output** in the sector (by column).

How is the input-output table used in planning? Suppose that the target for GNP growth is 7%. More specifically, final demand for agricultural products is targeted to increase to $166.40 (4% growth); final demand for manufactured goods is targeted to grow to $100.80 (12% growth); and final demand for services is targeted to grow to $54.00 (8%

Table 6-1
Interindustry Flow Matrix for Planland (values in dollars)

	Agriculture (1)	*Using Sectors* Manufacturing (2)	Services (3)	Total intermediate use	Final use	Total use
1. Agriculture	20	40	30	90	160	250
2. Manufacturing	10	80	20	110	90	200
3. Services	0	20	10	30	50	80
4. Total purchases, (1–3)	30	140	60	230		
5. Payments to labor	200	30	16 }		value-added = 300	
6. Payment to capital	20	30	4 }			
7. Total output	250	200	80			530

Table 6-2
Input-Output Coefficients Matrix for Planland

	X_1 Agriculture (1)	X_2 Manufacturing (2)	X_3 Services (3)
1. Agriculture (X_1)	0.08	0.20	0.375
2. Manufacturing (X_2)	0.04	0.40	0.25
3. Services (X_3)	0.00	0.10	0.125
4. Total purchases (1–3)	0.12	0.70	0.75
5. Payments to labor	0.80	0.15	0.20
6. Payments to capital	0.08	0.15	0.05
7. Total output	1.00	1.00	1.00

growth). The corresponding required output levels (X_1, X_2, and X_3, respectively) can be found using this key: each sector's total output must be large enough to meet demand for the product as an intermediate good, plus the projected final demand. Expressed algebraically:

$$X_1 = .08\ X_1 + .20\ X_2 + .375\ X_3 + 166.4 \qquad [6.1]$$

$$X_2 = .04\ X_1 + .40\ X_2 + .25\ X_3 + 100.8 \qquad [6.2]$$

$$X_3 = .00\ X_1 + .10\ X_2 + .125\ X_3 + 54 \qquad [6.3]$$

The problem now amounts to solving these three equations for the three unknown Xs. Various methods for doing this are taught in algebra classes. With minor rounding error, the solution (found here by substitution) is:

$$X_1 = \$265$$

$$X_2 = \$222$$

$$X_3 = \$\ 87.$$

Although final demand for agricultural products is to grow by only 4%, total agricultural output must grow by 6% (from $250 to $265). The reason? Because rapid growth in the other sectors requires agricultural products as inputs. The importance of input-output analysis is precisely due to the fact that the pattern of final demands may be a very poor indicator of the ultimate sectoral production requirements.

Knowing the sectoral output levels required to achieve the target growth rate, one can compute both the investment and labor requirements for each sector. Will adequate savings be available? Will labor supply be expanding rapidly enough? In other words, is the plan consistent?

Exercises

1. It is your turn to try a simple input-output analysis.

  a. Table 6–3 presents the 1980 interindustry flow table for a simple economy with only two sectors: (1) agriculture and (2) industry. But some data are missing.
  (i) From your understanding of the format of the table, supply the missing numbers.
  (ii) Briefly describe the characteristics of this economy as revealed in the table.

  b. Fill in Table 6–4 with the input-output coefficients computed from the interindustry flow data in Table 6–3.

  c. By the fifth year of the planning period, final demand for agricultural products is projected to grow to $1,500; final demand for manufactured output is projected to reach $500. Fill in the

Table 6-3
1980 Interindustry Flow Matrix for a Simple Economy

| | Using Sectors | | Total intermediate use | Final use | Total use |
	Agriculture (1)	Manufacturing (2)			
1. Agriculture	50	20	___	930	1,000
2. Industry	50	___	___	250	___
3. Total purchases	___	120	220		
4. Value-added	900	___	___	___	
5. Total output	___	400	___		

Table 6-4
1980 Input-Output Coefficients Matrix for a Simple Economy

| | Using Sectors | |
	X_1 Agriculture (1)	X_2 Industry (2)
1. Agriculture (X_1)	___	___
2. Industry (X_2)	___	___
3. Total purchases	___	___
4. Value-added	___	___
5. Total output	___	___

blanks in the following equations, which state that each sector's total output (X_1 and X_2, respectively) equals required intermediate uses plus the projected final demand:

$$X_1 = \underline{\hspace{1cm}} X_1 + \underline{\hspace{1cm}} X_2 + 1{,}500.$$

$$X_2 = \underline{\hspace{1cm}} X_1 + 0.25\, X_2 \quad + \underline{\hspace{1cm}}.$$

d. Solve these two equations for the two unknowns:

$$X_1 = \underline{\hspace{1cm}}, \text{ compared to } \underline{\hspace{1cm}} \text{ in 1980.}$$

$$X_2 = \underline{\hspace{1cm}}, \text{ compared to } \underline{\hspace{1cm}} \text{ in 1980.}$$

e. Each dollar of extra output in agriculture requires $2 of capital stock. Each dollar of extra output in industry requires $7 of capital stock.

(i) How much capital investment will the economy require during the five-year planning period in order for the indicated output growth to be feasible?

Required investment in agriculture = $\underline{\hspace{2cm}}$;

required investment in industry = $\underline{\hspace{2cm}}$;

total investment over the five year period = $\underline{\hspace{2cm}}$; and

average investment requirement per year = $\underline{\hspace{2cm}}$/year.

(ii) In comparison to GNP for 1980, does this investment requirement appear to be feasible? Does the plan appear to be consistent?

f. Explain briefly what would be included in a social-accounting matrix for this economy that is not included in the input-output matrix.

2. This exercise involves consistency planning and optimality planning using an explicit welfare function. You are a planner in Rambonesia, a country that produces bread (B) and weapons (W). The production possibilities frontier in Figure 6–1 shows alternative combinations of B and W that you estimate the economy can produce during the forthcoming five-year planning period. Survival requires that at least 1,000 tons of bread be produced. Otherwise, Rambonesia's goal is to militarize.

a. (i) The initial planning target set by the president is for production of 10,000 tons of weapons and 1,000 tons of bread. You are asked whether this target is consistent with resource

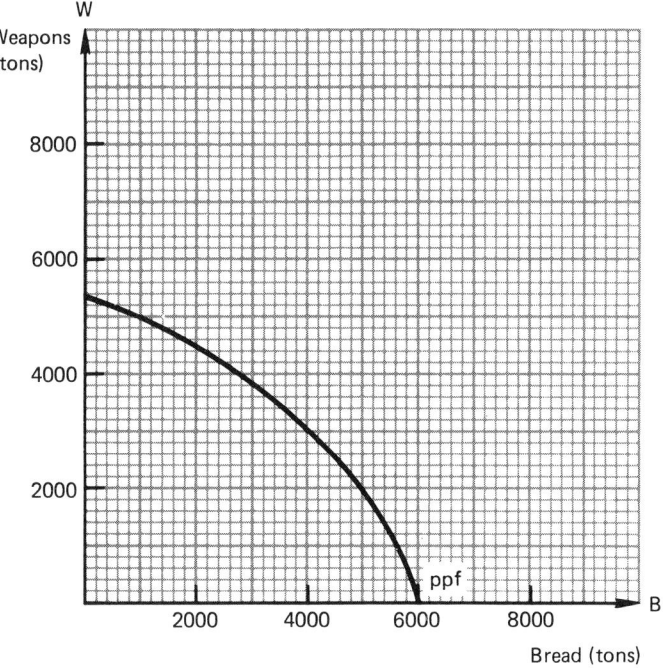

W
Weapons (tons)

8000

6000

4000

2000

ppf

2000   4000   6000   8000   B

Bread (tons)

Figure 6-1

constraints. Give an honest answer, along with a brief explanation. Identify the point in Figure 6–1 corresponding to this target, and label it *point 1*.

(ii) The president offers a revised target consisting of 3,000 tons of weapons and 1,000 tons of bread. You are again asked if this new target is consistent with resource constraints. Give an answer and a brief explanation. Identify the point in Figure 6–1 corresponding to this target, and label it *point 2*.

(iii) In an unusually compassionate mood, the president explores an alternative target consisting of only 1,000 tons of weapons and 5,600 tons of bread. Is this target consistent with resource constraints? Give an answer and a brief explanation. Identify the point in Figure 6–1 corresponding to this target, and label it *point 3*.

b. Back to his normal frame of mind, the president decides to specify an objective function, or welfare function, for Rambonesia. It is very simple: bread has utmost priority up to 1,000 tons; thereafter, bread has a zero priority weight. Given this welfare function, identify the point in Figure 6−1 that would be the optimal set of planning targets. Label it *point 4*.

c. The government settles on point 4 as the target for the plan. But due to inefficiency and bureaucratic impediments, actual production falls short of target levels by 40% in both industries. Identify the point in Figure 6−1 corresponding to the actual production levels. Label it *point 5*.

d. The shortfall in bread production triggers a military coup. The new leadership specifies a new welfare function, giving equal priority weights to bread and to weapons.
  (i) On Figure 6−1, draw in a set of lines representing Rambonesia's new community indifference curves. [Hint: the curves will be straight lines showing that a one-ton drop in weapons production accompanied by a one-ton increase in bread output will not change the level of welfare.]
  (ii) Given this new welfare function, identify the optimal point in Figure 6−1. Label it *point 6*.

3. In this exercise you will see how to apply a simple Keynesian macroeconomic growth model. The following five equations provide a simplified version of the macroeconomic model discussed in the textbook. The consumption equation has been omitted, the import requirement equation has been altered (as explained below), and the depreciation rate of the capital is assumed to be zero:

$Y_t = Y_{t-1} + 0.2\ I_{t-1}$ [Equation 6−4: production capacity]

$S_t = 0.15\ Y_t$ [Equation 6−5: savings behavior]

$I_t = S_t + F_t$ [Equation 6−6: investment capacity]

$M_t = 10 + I_t$ [Equation 6−7: import requirements]

$M_t = E_t + F_t$ [Equation 6−8: import capacity]

Data for year $t = 0$ show that the level of GDP was $Y_0 = \$100$ and gross investment was $I_0 = \$20$.

a. Explain Equation 6−4. In particular, how is this equation related to the Harrod-Domar growth equation?

b. Assume for the moment that export earnings (E) are large, so that growth is not constrained by the economy's import capacity. In this case, savings behavior determines economic growth. Thus we can focus on the first three equations; Equations 6–7 and 6–8 are redundant.

(i) Given the values for Y_0 and I_0, use Equation 6–4 to determine production capacity for year $t = 1$.

$$Y_1 = \$\underline{\hspace{2cm}}.$$

(ii) Assuming that net foreign capital inflow in year 1 will be $F_1 = \$8$, use Equations 6–5 and 6–6 to determine the value of I_1.

$$I_1 = \$\underline{\hspace{2cm}}.$$

(iii) Now plug the figures you have derived for Y_1 and I_1 into Equation 6–4 to find output capacity for year 2:

$$Y_2 = \$\underline{\hspace{2cm}}.$$

(iv) Comparing the value calculated for Y_2 with the value for Y_1, the projected rate of economic growth from year 1 to year 2 is

$$g = \underline{\hspace{1.5cm}}\%.$$

(v) What policies could be used to achieve a higher rate of growth in this savings-constrained example?

c. Now consider the case in which the availability of foreign exchange is the binding constraint on growth. Equations 6–7 and 6–8 can no longer be neglected. In this simple model, Equation 6–7 says that all investment goods plus $10 of consumer goods constitute the country's import requirement.

(i) Using the same Year 0 data as before and again letting $F_1 = \$8$, find the *required* level of imports in year 1:

$$M_1 = \$\underline{\hspace{2cm}}.$$

[Hint: You have already calculated I_1 above.]

(ii) If the level of exports is $E_1 = 20$, use Equation 6–8 to find the economy's import **capacity** (i.e., the availability of foreign exchange).

$$M_1 = \$\underline{\hspace{2cm}}.$$

(iii) You should find that the country, unhappily, is not earning enough foreign exchange to satisfy its import requirements. If imports of consumer goods (= $10) cannot be squeezed further, the import capacity constraint dictates that I_1 must be

reduced to $\underline{\hspace{2cm}}.$

(iv) With this level of investment, Equation 6–4 shows that output

capacity for year 2 will be $Y_2 = \$\underline{\hspace{2cm}}$, and the economy's projected rate of economic growth from year 1 to

year 2 is $g = \underline{\hspace{2cm}}\%.$

(v) What policies could be used to achieve a higher rate of growth in this case of an import capacity constraint?

4. This exercise includes some net present value (NPV) calculations and a project appraisal.

   a. (i) What is the present value of a payment of $600 due in one year, when the interest rate (or discount rate) is 12%?

$$PV = \$_____.$$

     (ii) What is the present value of a payment of $1,500 due in two years when the discount rate is 9%?

$$PV = \$_____.$$

   b. (i) Using a discount rate of 10%, what is the net present value of an investment costing $1,000 today and generating an income of $600 per year for two years? [Consider the income to be paid at the end of each year.]

$$NPV = \$_____.$$

     (ii) What would the NPV on this same investment be if the discount rate were 15%?

$$NPV = \$_____.$$

    (iii) Is this a worthwhile investment when the discount rate is 10%? When it is 15%?

   c. (i) What is the internal rate of return (IRR) to the nearest one percent for the investment described above? Recall that the IRR is the discount rate for which NPV = 0. [Hint: the IRR must lie between 10% and 15%, so test the intermediate values to see which generates an NPV closest to zero.]

$$IRR = _____\%.$$

     (ii) If the proper discount rate exceeds the IRR, then the NPV must be _____ (positive or negative).

   d. The Ministry of Industries of Galaxia has proposed two projects to the planning commission. The relevant financial data are presented in Table 6–5. Using the market interest rate of 5% as the discount rate, the ministry has computed the net present value of projects A and B to be $102 and $73, respectively.

    (i) Hence, the ministry prefers project _____.

Table 6–5

Two Proposed Industrial Projects for Galaxia

	Project A			Project B		
Year	Costs ($)	Benefits ($)	Net benefits ($)	Costs ($)	Benefits ($)	Net benefits ($)
0	100	0	−100	100	0	−100
1	50	0	− 50	50	0	− 50
2	5	10	5	5	125	120
3	5	10	5	5	125	120
4	5	155	150	5	10	5
5	5	155	150	5	10	5

(ii) The planning commission recomputes the NPV using a discount rate of 15%, which is the estimated opportunity cost of capital for the economy. The result is an NPV for project A of $30.10, and an NPV for project B of $35.00. Hence, the planning commission prefers project _____ .

(iii) Study the time pattern of benefits for the two projects. Why does the higher discount rate alter the NPV rankings in this manner?

e. In the Galaxian economy, the shadow foreign exchange rate exceeds the official foreign exchange rate (local currency per dollar) by 25%. Also, an effective minimum-wage law holds the market-wage rate above the equilibrium wage for unskilled labor. Of the two projects proposed by the Ministry of Industries, project B uses fewer imported inputs and is more labor intensive. Explain briefly how the use of shadow prices will affect the planning commission's economic appraisal of the two projects.

5. *Optional* This exercise presents and solves a simple linear programming model. In Zeeland the only factor of production is labor; the economy has 100 workers. There are two industries, cotton (C) and textiles (T). In each industry 2 workers are required per unit of output. In addition, .2 units of cotton are required per unit of textile

output; all the other input-output coefficients are zero. Input-output analysis can find the total outputs corresponding to any given set of final demands and check for consistency. But with linear programming, one can find the *best* output combination for any given objective function.

a. The amount of labor to be used in C plus the amount of labor to be used in T must not exceed 100.
   (i) Letting X_C and X_T represent the total output for each of the two industries, the labor constraint would be violated by any production combination lying beyond the line:

$$\underline{\hspace{2cm}} = \underline{\hspace{2cm}} X_C + \underline{\hspace{2cm}} X_T.$$

   (ii) Draw this line on Figure 6–2. Label it L and shade in the area that is infeasible in terms of this constraint.

b. There is also an interindustry flow constraint which says that the amount of cotton produced must be no less than the amount required as an input to the textile industry.
   (i) This interindustry constraint would be violated by any production combination lying below (in the figure) the line:

$$X_C = \underline{\hspace{2cm}} X_T.$$

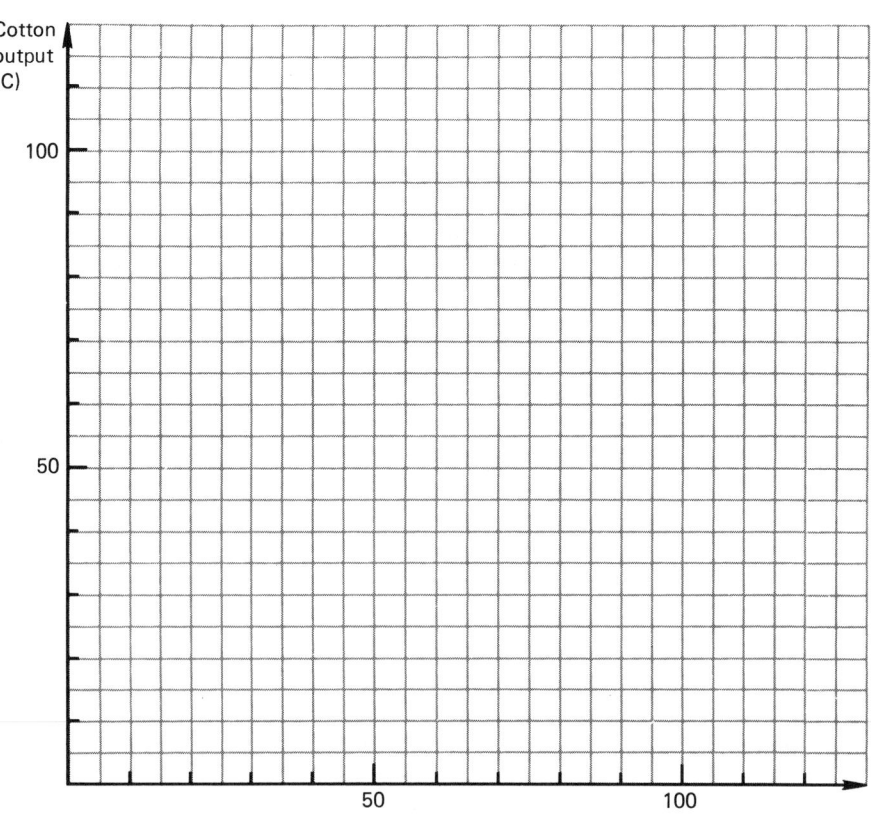

Figure 6-2

(ii) Draw this line on Figure 6-2. Label it I and shade in the area that is infeasible in terms of this constraint.

c. Suppose that each unit of textile final goods (call this FT) is worth 11 happiness points (hp's), while each unit of final cotton goods (call this FC) is worth 5 hp's.
   (i) The welfare function for Zeeland can therefore be written as:

$$W = \underline{\hspace{2cm}} FC + \underline{\hspace{2cm}} FT.$$

   (ii) Notice that for textiles, total output is identical to final output. In symbols, $FT = X_T$. But not for cotton. Gross output (X_C) of cotton only provides

$$FC = X_C - \underline{\hspace{2cm}} X_T$$

   units of final product, since some cotton is required as a textile input.
   (iii) By substituting for FC and FT, you can now express the welfare function in terms of the variables X_C and X_T:

$$W = \underline{\hspace{2cm}} X_C + \underline{\hspace{2cm}} X_T.$$

   (iv) Using this welfare function, draw a number of representative community indifference curves on Figure 6-2. Specifically, draw in and label the curves showing output combinations for which W = 200, W = 400 and W = 600. [Hint: the curves are straight lines here.]

d. Given the welfare function as represented by the set of indifference curves, and the two constraints facing the economy, identify the optimal levels of production of X_C and X_T in Figure 6-2. Label the optimum as *point A*. Briefly discuss the implied resource allocation.

Congratulations. You have just solved a linear programming problem.

Answers to Self-Test

Completion

1. optimal
2. a_{13}, 0.40
3. social accounting matrix
4. flow of funds
5. welfare (or objective), constraints
6. internal rate of return (IRR)
7. commercial, economic, social
8. discounting
9. computable general equilibrium (CGE)
10. fixed

True-False

1.	F	6.	F
2.	F	7.	T
3.	T	8.	F
4.	T	9.	T
5.	F	10.	F

Multiple Choice

1.	d	6.	d
2.	b	7.	c
3.	c	8.	b
4.	a	9.	a
5.	d	10.	c

CHAPTER 7   Population

Overview

   This chapter on population is the first of four chapters that examine the vital role of human resources in development. After defining and explaining a number of basic demographic concepts, the chapter outlines the history of the growth of the world's population. Of particular importance is the sharp acceleration of population growth since World War II, even as the industrial countries were passing through a demographic transition to low rates of population growth. Some signs of a similar transition can be seen taking place in the LDCs. But at present, most LDCs have experienced sharp drops in death rates that have not been matched by similar drops in birth rates. The result has been rapid population growth that is likely to continue for decades. The text then examines the theory of fertility for insight into the factors that can contribute to lower birth rates in the developing countries.

   The effects of rapid population growth on economic development are considered next, with the conclusion that, on balance, less rapid population growth would facilitate more rapid development. Having examined both the causes and the consequences of rapid population growth, the text then turns to population policy. Most LDC governments do favor slower population growth. The policies that have been used to promote this objective include family planning programs, direct population controls, and "selective interventions" that encourage couples to have fewer children.

Main Learning Objectives

After studying this chapter you ought to understand and be able to explain:

   1. Basic demographic terms such as the **birth rate**, the **death rate**, the **rate of natural increase**, the **infant death rate**, **life expectancy**, and the **total fertility rate**.

   2. The major features of world population history, including the **demographic transition**.

   3. The broad characteristics of present demographic conditions in the third world, including the population **age structure** and the rapid pace of **urbanization**.

4. The **economic theory of fertility** that views family size as an economic decision influenced by the costs and benefits of having children.

5. Why most economists and demographers agree that slower population growth would favor more rapid increases in per-capita incomes in most developing countries.

6. The range of attitudes about population policy in the LDCs, and the reasons for such differences.

7. The various types of policies used in developing countries to slow down population growth rates, including **family planning programs, direct population controls**, and **selective interventions.**

8. The fundamental point: that population policy and development policy are mutually supportive; lack of development hinders population control, and vice versa.

Additional Key Terms, Concepts, and Institutions

Can you identify and explain each of the following?

demography
population doubling time
dependency ratio
demographic momentum
Malthusian theory
Coale-Hoover model
capital widening versus capital deepening

Economic Tools and Techniques

From what you have learned in this chapter, can you:

1. Explain the concepts and the implications of Becker's **new household economics** theory of fertility, and distinguish them from Easterlin's theory of fertility.

2. Explain what determines a country's **optimum population** at any point in time, and how it changes over time?

Self-Test

Completion

1. The rate of natural increase of the population is the difference

between the _____ rate and the _____ rate.

2. The number of children the average woman would bear during her lifetime, given prevailing age-specific fertility rates, is called the

_____ fertility rate.

3. The doubling time for a population growing at 2.5 percent per year is approximately _____ years.

4. The term _____ refers to the shift from a pattern of slow population growth with high birth and death rates to a pattern of slow population growth with low birth and death rates.

5. The one continent in which birth rates have not declined significantly since 1960 is _____ .

6. Even if fertility rates were to drop immediately to the replacement level, population would continue to grow for decades. This phenomenon is called demographic _____ .

7. According to Becker's "new household economics," the fall in fertility as incomes rise can be explained primarily by the rising opportunity cost of parents' _____ .

8. Empirical research tends to support the view that rapid population growth _____ private savings.

9. _____ is the study of population.

10. By 1987 the world population surpassed _____ billion people.

True-False If false, you should be able to explain why.

_____ 1. The crude birth rate is defined as the number of births per 1,000 women of child-bearing age.

_____ 2. Some LDCs have crude death rates as low as those in the developed countries despite much higher age-specific death rates.

_____ 3. The sharp increase in the rate of population growth since World War II has caused a sharp increase in death rates in the LDCs.

_____ 4. Studies have found that, on average, rural-urban migrants in LDCs improve their standards of living as a result of moving to the cities.

_____ 5. Changes in tastes are a major determinant of fertility in Easterlin's model of child-bearing decisions.

_____ 6. The empirical record does not in fact establish a clearcut negative correlation between the growth rate of population and the growth rate of per-capita income.

_____ 7. In a country where the population is growing rapidly there may be no capital deepening even though the capital stock is increasing.

_____ 8. The slogan "take care of the people and the population will take care of itself" aptly expresses the consensus view on population policy as presented in the text.

_____ 9. A country's crude birth rate can increase even though age specific fertility rates are stable.

_____ 10. Studies show that most couples in LDCs desire no more than two children, and that large families are primarily the result of inadequate birth control methods.

Multiple Choice

1. In a country of 1 million people, 40,000 babies are born in a year. Of these, 4,000 die within their first year of life. The infant death rate is:
   a. 100
   b. 10
   c. 4
   d. 4,000

2. At the beginning of the Industrial Revolution, the population of the world was roughly:
   a. 100 million people.
   b. 1 billion people.
   c. 10 billion people.
   d. 10 million people.

3. In Africa, Asia, and South America, the average annual rate of population growth over the period 1973−1983 was in the range of:
   a. 1% to 2%.
   b. 2% to 3%.
   c. 3% to 4%.
   d. 4% to 5%.

4. The dependency ratio is defined as the ratio of:
   a. imports to GDP.
   b. children to adults in the population.
   c. unemployed to employed workers in the labor force.
   d. non-working age population to working age population.

5. Viewing child-bearing as an economic decision has several important implications. All have been well verified *except* the inference that fertility should be lower when:
   a. there are fewer opportunities for children to work.
   b. child survival rates improve.
   c. income is lower.
   d. there are more opportunities for women to work outside the home.

6. According to the modern theory of fertility, what is the most important factor in lowering birth rates in LDCs?
   a. increased availability of modern birth-control methods
   b. improved perception of the social problems caused by rapid population growth
   c. changes in the age structure of LDC populations
   d. changes in the balance of benefits and costs of child-bearing at the family level

7. Which of the following would reduce a country's "optimum" population?
   a. capital accumulation
   b. increased labor productivity
   c. depletion of natural resources
   d. establishing an effective social security system

8. Which of the following is not a "selective intervention" policy to reduce population growth rates?
   a. wide distribution of free birth-control devices
   b. compulsory school attendance through age 12
   c. monetary incentives and disincentives for controlling family size
   d. establishing an effective social security system

9. The Malthusian theory included each of the following elements except:
   a. population grows geometrically while food supplies grow arithmetically.
   b. population is controlled largely by disasters such as famines, wars, and epidemics.
   c. strong advocacy of birth control.
   d. improvements in living standards could only be temporary because they would lead to higher birth rates.

10. Which of the following statements best summarizes China's population policy since 1971?
    a. No action is needed since "revolution plus production" will solve all problems.
    b. No action is needed since there is still a large amount of unused arable land.
    c. The government has tried to slow the population growth rate but with no success.
    d. The government has adopted strong and fairly successful policies to reduce the population growth rate.

Applications

Worked Example: Effects of Population Growth on Development

Let's see how rapid population growth can reduce the growth of per-capita income, using the simple Harrod-Domar model from Chapter 3. Recall that the GDP growth rate (g) can be expressed as $g = s/k$, where s is the savings rate and k is the incremental capital-output ratio (ICOR). For simplicity, the ICOR is fixed at $k = 4$ here, so $g = s/4$.

Consider Hobbitshire, a placid country with a population in year 0 of 1,000 workers (over age 10) and 1,000 children (under age 10), giving a dependency rate of $1,000/1,000 = 1.0$. Total GDP is $Y =$ BB1 million (BB stands for Bilbo, the currency). Hence, per-capita income is BB500. The number of deaths, births, and children reaching age 10 are equal, so the population is constant in terms of both size and structure. The savings rate is $s = 28\%$, so GDP grows by $g = 28/4 = 7\%$ per year. Because the population is constant, per-capita income also grows by 7% per year, reaching BB983 $[= 500(1.07)^{10}]$ by year 10.

Suppose that starting in year 0 the population begins to grow by 4% per year. Hobbitshire will then have 80 extra people in year 1, all of whom are children. In year 10 there will be an extra 960 people, still all children. What are the effects on per-capita income? *First*, the "more-mouths-to-feed" effect precedes the "more-hands-to-work" effect by 10 years. During this period, the extra people don't add to output. They simply reduce income per capita. If output were to continue to grow by 7% a year while the population grows by 4% per year, per-capita income would increase by only 3% per year.

Second, with more and more children around, the dependency rate increases steadily. As workers now have more mouths to feed, the savings rate drops by, say, one percentage point each year, hitting 18% in year 10. This causes GDP to grow more and more slowly. Table 7-1 summarizes the trend. *Third*, when the population bulge does enter the labor force, not only will investment be lower (due to lower values for both s and Y compared to the case of zero-population growth), but in addition the available capital stock will be spread among more workers. Consequently, worker productivity will be growing more slowly. More of the available investment will be used for capital widening and less for capital deepening.

As the textbook notes, this kind of analysis, pioneered by the Coale and Hoover model for India, is quite simplistic. The outlook for Hobbitshire would brighten if population pressure induced workers to work harder, or if necessity stimulated more rapid technical progress.

Table 7-1

Hobbitshire, with 4% Population Growth[a]

Year	s (%)	g (%)	Y (million BB)	Population	Y/pop (BB)	Dependency rate
0	28	7.0	1.00	2,000	500	1.00
1	27	6.75	1.07	2,080	514	1.08
2	26	6.50	1.14	2,163	527	1.16
3	25	6.25	1.22	2,250	542	1.25
.	.	.	.	.	.	.
.	.	.	.	.	.	.
.	.	.	.	.	.	.
10	18	4.50	1.77	2,960	597	1.96

[a]An ICOR of 4 is assumed.

1. This exercise examines the demographic transition in the LDCs.
   Table 7–2 shows the 1965 and 1983 crude birth rate (CBR), crude
   death rate (CDR), and per-capita income level for four broad groups
   of countries.
   a. Fill in the blanks in the last column of Table 7–2 by calculating
      the natural rate of population increase implied by the CBR and
      the CDR data.

   b. On Figure 7–1 plot the eight crude birth-rate observations. Draw
      a line connecting these eight points and label it *CBR*. Similarly,
      plot the eight crude death rate observations and connect these
      points with a line labeled *CDR*. [Note: the horizontal axis is
      drawn using a ratio scale.]

   c. Suppose Figure 7–1 is interpreted as showing the broad average
      "pattern" of demographic conditions for different levels of
      development (see Chapter 3). Does the graph reveal any sign of a
      demographic transition taking place in the LDCs? Explain.

   d. Explain why the decline in the birth rate occurs so much later
      than the decline in the death rate as countries proceed to higher
      levels of per-capita income.

Table 7–2

Demographic Data

Country group	Per-capita income (1983 $)	Crude birth rate	Crude death rate	Natural rate of increase (%)
Low-income[a]				
1965	176	46	21	_____
1983	200	43	16	_____
Lower-middle income				
1965	448	45	18	_____
1983	750	36	12	_____
Upper-middle income				
1965	1,048	38	12	_____
1983	2,050	31	8	_____
Industrial				
1965	7,091	19	10	_____
1983	11,060	14	9	_____

Source: World Development Report 1985.
[a]Excluding India and China.

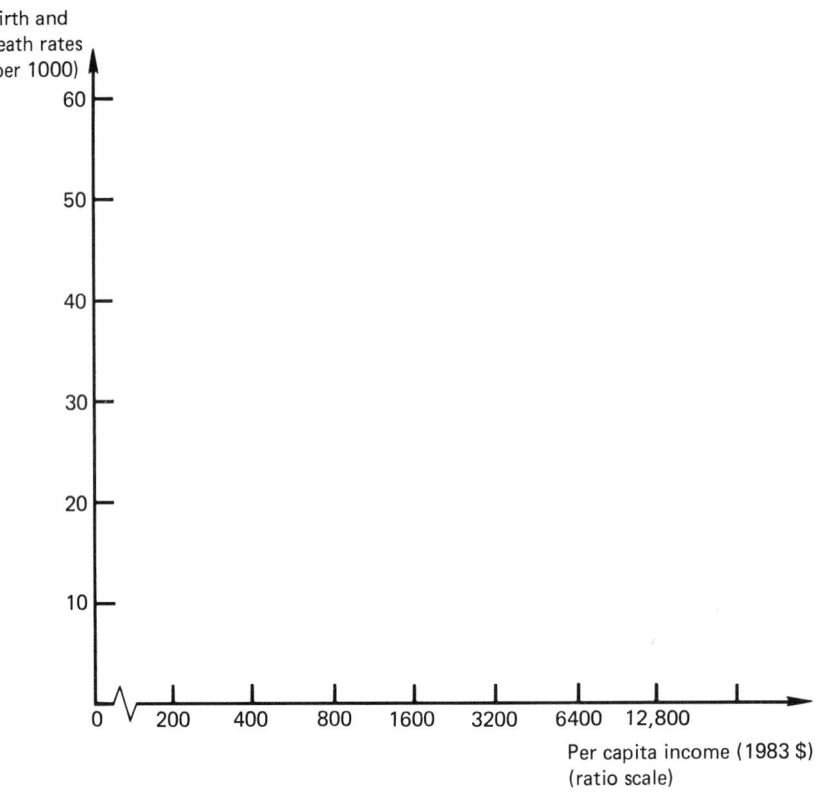

Birth and
death rates
(per 1000)

60
50
40
30
20
10

0   200   400   800   1600   3200   6400   12,800

Per capita income (1983 $)
(ratio scale)

Figure 7–1

e. If countries that are poor today do indeed follow the pattern
revealed in Figure 7–1, when would one expect the rate of
population growth to decline as a result of development? How
long would it take for population growth in these countries to
drop below 1% per annum? Explain briefly.

2. This exercise explores the relationship between infant mortality rates,
the age structure of the population, and demographic momentum.
  Table 7–3 provides a worksheet for tracking demographic
conditions in Fecund, a country in which quadruplets are common.
[A few blanks are already filled in to help you with your calculations.] To simplify matters greatly, suppose that people in Fecund
live just one year as children plus two years as working adults. Only
"young adults" produce babies. Death strikes half the newborn
infants, plus all of the "older adults" at the end of their third year
of life.

-104-

Table 7-3

Demographic Worksheet for Fecund, 1987–1992

Year	Number of children* (1)	Number of young adults (2)	Number of older adults (3)	Total population (4)	Rate of pop. growth (5)	Number of births (6)	Number of infant deaths (7)
1987	100	100	100	300	0%	200	100
1988	100	100	100	300	0%	200	100
1989	___	___	___	___	___	___	___
1990	___	100	___	___	___	___	___
1991	___	___	___	___	16.7%	___	___
1992	___	___	___	___	___	___	___

*Columns 1–4 refer to population at the beginning of the year; column 5 is the rate of growth over the previous year; columns 6 and 7 are the number of births and infant deaths *during* the year.

a. Carefully examine the 1987 and 1988 lines in Table 7–3. Be sure you see how conditions in 1987 determine columns 1–5 for the following year. Notice that the birth rate is *very* high—two babies per young adult. But the population remains stable because the death rate is also high: 100 newborns plus 100 adults die each year. Based on conditions in 1988, fill in columns 1–5 for 1989.

b. Improved health care causes the incidence of infant mortality to drop abruptly from 50% to 20% in 1989. Fertility remains unchanged: there are still two births per young adult.
   (i) Given these conditions, fill in the last two entries for 1989, and columns 1–5 for 1990.
   (ii) In 1990 the birth rate remains at two births per young adult, and the infant mortality rate stays at 20%. Fill in the last two entries for 1990, and columns 1–5 for 1991.

c. (i) In 1991, fertility in Fecund drops to 1.25 births per young adult. Since 20% of the newborns do not survive their first year, the new fertility rate results in one surviving baby per young adult. Does this new fertility behavior stop the population growth? To find out, fill in the remaining columns for 1991 and columns 1–5 for 1992.
   (ii) You should find that the population is still growing. Briefly explain why.

d. The World Bank estimates that *even if* the fertility rate were to drop immediately to the replacement level (i.e., one baby per adult), the population in many LDCs would continue to grow for more than fifty years, almost doubling before it stabilizes. What is the reason for this demographic momentum?

3. This exercise deals with the effects of rapid population growth. The exercise is based on the demographic changes in Fecund that were examined in Exercise 2.

   Review the figures in Table 7–3. If the infant mortality rate had not declined in 1989, Fecund's population size and age structure would have remained stable. Because of the decline in the infant mortality rate, Fecund experienced major demographic changes: a high rate of population growth, together with changes in the population age structure.

a. Will these demographic changes be likely to increase or decrease each of the following items? Briefly explain why.
   (i) The 1990 level of per-capita income.

   (ii) The 1990 domestic savings rate.

   (iii) The 1990 GNP growth rate.

   (iv) The health and education services provided to children in Fecund in 1990?

       [Hint: The first three points are covered in the Worked Example. The fourth one will require some thought.]

b. Examine the figures for 1991 in Table 7−3. State whether each of the following items is likely to be higher or lower as a result of the decline in the infant mortality rate, and briefly explain why.
   (i) The 1991 domestic savings rate.

   (ii) Capital deepening in 1991.

   (iii) The rate of growth of GNP in 1991.

c. Fecund's government must deal with the economic effects of the demographic changes caused by the infant-mortality-rate decline. What types of policies would you recommend to its officials?

4. This exercise examines the concept of optimum population.

Table 7−4 shows a hypothetical relationship between the size of a country's labor force (*LF*) and the level of GNP, given the initial stock of capital and natural resources and the initial level of technology.

a. Assume for simplicity that the labor force equals exactly one-half of the population (POP). It is easy to compute the population size for any given labor force (POP = $LF \times 2$), and you know GNP from Table 7−4. From these figures, you can calculate per-capita income (PCI). Fill in the values for POP and PCI in the last two columns of Table 7−4.

b. On Figure 7−2, draw in the curve showing the relationship between population size and per-capita income. Label this curve *P-P*. Label the optimum population as POP*, and label the corresponding level of per-capita income as PCI*.

c. If the actual population size (POP^0) is less than the optimal population POP*, would the government have any cause to be concerned about reducing the population growth rate?

d. Using a dotted line, draw in a second curve with the following characteristics: the optimum is *lower* than POP*, but the corresponding level of per-capita income is *higher* than PCI*. Label this new curve *P'-P'*. What economic changes could shift the population-income relationship from *P-P* to *P'-P'*?

Table 7–4

Population and Per-Capita Income

Labor force	GNP	Population	Per-capita income
10	10,000	_____	_____
20	28,000	_____	_____
30	48,000	_____	_____
40	72,000	_____	_____
50	98,000	_____	_____
60	118,000	_____	_____
70	134,000	_____	_____
80	148,000	_____	_____

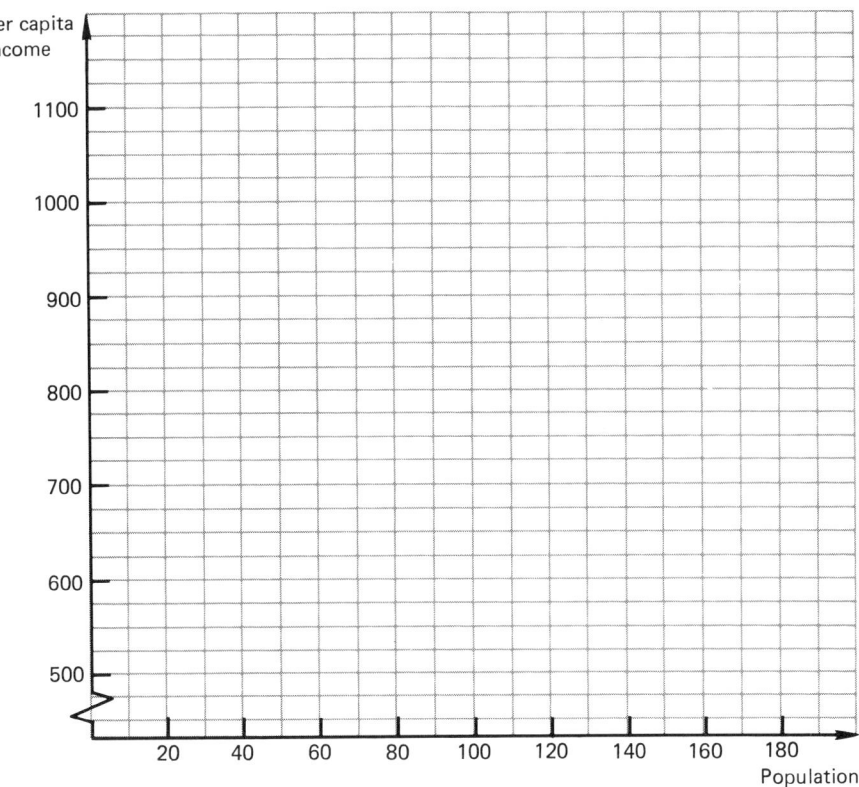

Figure 7–2

e. For each of the economic changes listed below, what is the effect
   (*ceteris paribus*) on optimum POP and optimum PCI? Use the
   symbol "+" to designate a positive effect and the symbol "−" to
   designate a negative effect.

Effect on Optimum:

POP   PCI

    (i) increase in capital stock   _____   _____
   (ii) increase in labor-force
       participation rate   _____   _____
  (iii) a major natural resource
       discovery   _____   _____
  (iv) widespread introduction
       of production robots   _____   _____

5. This exercise deals with the economic theory of fertility.
   According to the theory of fertility, a couple's desired family size
   is influenced significantly by economic conditions that determine the
   private benefits and costs of child-bearing and child-raising.

   a. In the context of the economic theory of fertility, how will each
      of the following changes in economic conditions affect fertility?
      Let "+" = positive, "−" = negative, and "0" = no effect on
      fertility.

(i) primary school made compulsory _____
(ii) a reliable social security system introduced _____
(iii) migration from farms to urban areas _____
(iv) improved opportunities for women to work
    outside the home _____
(v) redistribution of farmland to poor families _____
(vi) a campaign to educate people about social
    congestion effects of high fertility _____
    [Hint: the last one is a bit tricky.]

b. If fertility decisions are the result of fairly rational individual decisions that take into account economic benefits and costs, how can family-planning programs and provision of birth-control devices have any significant effect on fertility rates?

c. If families have children because they perceive net benefits from having children (including the sheer pleasure of raising children), what rationale might justify government action to reduce fertility rates?

d. Since children are certainly not an inferior good, economic theory suggests that the desired quantity of children will increase with family income. Yet the desired quantity of children per family seems to decline with family income. Briefly discuss how economists explain this apparent inconsistency.

Answers to Self-Test

Completion

1. birth, death
2. total
3. 28
4. demographic transition
5. Africa

6. momentum
7. time
8. reduces
9. Demography
10. 5

True-False

1. F	6. T
2. T	7. T
3. F	8. F
4. T	9. T
5. T	10. F

Multiple Choice

1. a	6. d
2. b	7. c
3. b	8. a
4. d	9. c
5. c	10. d

CHAPTER 8   Labor's Role

Overview

This chapter examines the structure of labor markets in the LDCs. A growing population generates a growing labor force. Consequently, most developing countries must contend with a rapidly growing labor force along with already high rates of *labor underutilization*—a term encompassing jobs of low productivity as well as overt unemployment. These countries thus have a pressing need for more rapid employment creation. But even in densely populated, low-income countries, labor surplus in the sense of a zero-marginal product of labor is rarely found. Hence, the need is not just for jobs, but for more productive jobs. Evidence strongly supports the presumption that migration and labor reallocation will respond to changes in employment opportunities and opportunities for higher wages.

Despite its rapid growth, the modern industrial sector in most LDCs has absorbed only a small share of the growing labor force. Productive employment opportunities in this sector could expand more rapidly with policies that reduce factor price distortions that encourage capital-intensive production. Other policies that would help create a more labor-intensive industrial structure include reducing protectionist trade barriers, developing more appropriate technologies, and encouraging small-scale industry. Fundamentally, a strategy of growth with equity hinges on more rapid creation of productive employment.

Main Learning Objectives

After studying this chapter you ought to understand and be able to explain:

1. The characteristic features of the **labor force** in the developing countries.

2. The segmented structure of LDC labor markets, consisting of the **urban formal sector**, the **urban informal sector**, and the **rural labor market**.

3. The problems of defining and measuring **labor underutilization**, as distinct from **visible unemployment**.

4. The various costs and benefits of urban job creation, and the economic factors that motivate **induced migration**.

5. Why **employment creation** in the industrial sector of most LDCs has absorbed only a small fraction of the rapidly growing work force.

6. How employment creation can be accelerated by various policies including reductions in **factor price distortions** and promotion of more **appropriate technology**.

7. The importance of employment as an objective of development policy and planning.

Additional Key Terms, Concepts, and Institutions

Can you identify and explain each of the following?

disguised unemployment
discouraged workers
opportunity cost of labor
expected urban wage
brain drain
indirect, and secondary job creation
factor proportions
wage to rental ratio
elasticity optimists and pessimists
small-scale industry
food for work

Economic Tools and Techniques

From what you have learned in this chapter, can you:

1. Use supply and demand analysis to characterize the three-tiered structure of LDC labor markets?

2. Apply the **Harris-Todaro model** to determine the rate of **rural-to-urban migration** from data on rural and urban wages?

3. Calculate ΔE_i, the employment creation generated by a given rate of output growth in the industrial sector?

4. Use the **elasticity of substitution** and **isoquants** to analyze how factor price distortions affect employment?

Self-Test

Completion

1. In very poor countries more than half of the labor force works in the _____ sector of the economy.

2. The urban _____ sector in most LDCs nearly always has a queue of workers looking for jobs at wages above the market clearing level.

3. _____ unemployment consists of workers who are employed, but in jobs of low productivity and extremely low pay.

4. People who are not in the labor force because they have no expectation of finding a job are called _____ workers.

5. The elasticity of substitution shows the percentage change in the

_____ ratio resulting from a given

percentage change in the _____ ratio.

6. An elasticity pessimist believes that the elasticity of substitution is

very _____ .

7. For countries with abundant _____ labor, international migration of such workers has a low opportunity cost and it generates significant benefits in terms of remittances and training.

8. The emigration of highly educated, skilled workers from LDCs is

often referred to as the _____ .

9. An increase in the wage to rental ratio causes labor intensity to

_____ .

10. An important part of the social cost of using labor is its

_____ ; i.e., the value of labor in its next best alternative use.

True-False If false, you should be able to explain why.

_____ 1. Wage differentials across skill and education levels are generally wider in LDCs than in developed countries.

_____ 2. By the definition of unemployment, all those with jobs in the urban informal sector are counted as unemployed.

_____ 3. Underutilized labor represents a pool of resources that can be put to work on development projects at virtually zero cost to the economy.

_____ 4. A consensus has emerged that the marginal product of labor in LDC agriculture is nearly always zero in densely populated, low-income countries.

_____ 5. Minimum-wage policies generally benefit those with modern-sector jobs while hurting the much larger group of workers in the informal sector.

_____ 6. Domestic producers are more likely to use inappropriate, capital-intensive factor proportions when insulated from import competition by trade barriers.

_____ 7. If the elasticity of substitution is very low, then factor price distortions have a large adverse effect on labor intensity.

_____ 8. Simulation studies have revealed that redistribution of income to the poor can create many jobs as a result of changes that would take place in demand patterns.

_____ 9. Irrigation is one example of investment that may complement labor, rather than substitute for labor.

_____ 10. Economists generally agree that creating appropriate technologies and using appropriate factor proportions cannot occur without a political and social revolution.

Multiple Choice

1. It has been observed that in poor countries unemployment is a "luxury." This remark refers to the fact that:
   a. many people in poor countries prefer not to work.
   b. only the relatively well off can afford to be without work for an extended period while searching for a job.
   c. there are fewer high-paying jobs than low-paying jobs.
   d. for poor people, a period of unemployment is a relief from working long hours at strenuous jobs.

2. Which of the following remarks about unforced, internal migration in developing countries is correct?
   a. Migration from urban areas back to rural areas is rare.
   b. Migrants are generally worse off in the city than they would have been in the rural area.
   c. Economic factors have little effect on migration decisions.
   d. Large wage distortions and congestion effects can cause the social costs of migration to exceed the social benefits.

3. "Inappropriate" technology is commonly characterized by all of the following conditions except:
   a. excessive labor intensity.
   b. large-scale production operations.
   c. need for technical skills that are very scarce in LDCs.
   d. products that are not designed for LDC market conditions.

4. The accompanying figure shows two isoquants. The elasticity of substitution is greater and factor proportions are _____ responsive to changes in the wage to rental ratio along isoquant _____.
   a. more, A
   b. less, A
   c. more, B
   d. less, B

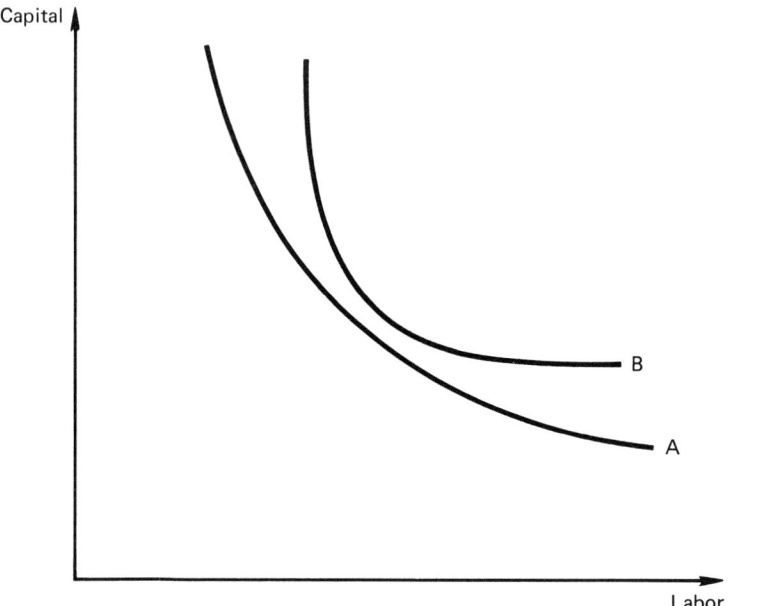

5. The use of more labor-intensive production technologies in LDCs is generally discouraged by policies that:
   a. open domestic industry to more import competition.
   b. hold minimum wages above the market clearing level.
   c. lower interest rates on bank loans.
   d. all of the above.

6. If workers perceive a 10% chance of obtaining an urban job paying 20 shillings per day when the rural wage rate is 5 shillings per day, the Harris-Todaro model would predict:
   a. rural-to-urban migration of workers.
   b. no internal migration; this is an equilibrium.
   c. urban-to-rural migration of discouraged urban workers.
   d. none of the above; additional information is needed.

7. As an empirical average, when value-added in the industrial sector of a low-income country increases by 10%, industrial employment increases by about _____.
   a. 16%
   b. 6%
   c. 0.6%
   d. 60%

8. Which of the following countries has managed to achieve rapid growth of industrial employment through rapid expansion of labor-intensive industrial exports?
   a. Korea
   b. Pakistan
   c. Nigeria
   d. Venezuela

Applications

Worked Example: Factor Prices and Labor Intensity

Urban formal sector employees in Dynamique are paid the legal minimum wage of $w = \$60$ per month. The cost of capital services is $r = \$40$ per month. This cost of capital depends on the purchase price of capital goods, the cost of financing capital formation, and the relevant tax laws. With these initial factor prices the wage to rental rate is $w/r = \$60/\$40 = 1.5$. Knowing the factor prices, one can identify the various combinations of labor (L) and capital (K) that exhaust any given budget (B). For example, with $B = \$900$, a firm can purchase any combination of K and L satisfying the relationship: $900 = 40\ K + 60\ L$. For any given level of B, one can draw a budget line in Figure 8−1. All such lines will have a slope equal to $-w/r$. In the present case, the slopes would equal -1.5, showing that at prevailing factor prices 6 K can be traded for 4 L (or vice versa).

A Dynamiquan zipper producer is considering investing in a new factory to produce 1,000 boxes of zippers per month. Isoquant ZZ in Figure 8−1 shows the alternative combinations of K and L that can be

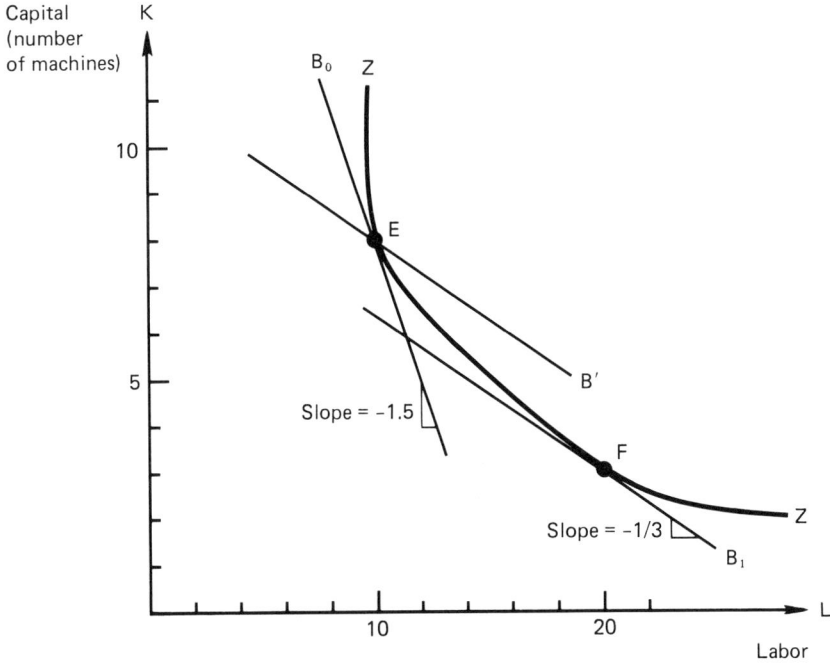

Figure 8–1

used to produce this level of output. To find the least-cost production method, the firm looks for the point on ZZ that lies on the lowest possible budget line, B_0. The firm will choose point E, involving the use of 8 machines and 10 workers—a monthly cost of $B = \$920$. The firm will have a capital to labor ratio of $K/L = 8/10 = 0.8$.

Shortly thereafter the government of Dynamique, concerned that more jobs are needed for the growing labor force, reduces the minimum wage to $w = \$50$. Also, capital subsidies are eliminated, raising the firm's cost of capital to $r = \$150$. Now the wage to rental ratio is $w/r = 50/150 = 1/3$. Reflecting these new factor prices, the budget line through point E in Figure 8–1 now has a slope of $-1/3$, as shown by line B'. Obviously, point E no longer minimizes costs. Instead, point F, tangent to budget line B_1, has become the least-cost production technique. The 1,000 boxes of zippers will be produced using $K = 3$ and $L = 20$. The firm will now operate with a capital to labor ratio of $K/L = 3/20 = 0.15$. The change in factor prices results in more jobs per unit of capital, and more jobs per zipper produced.

The policy reform reduced the wage to rental ratio from 1.5 to 0.33. This is a change of $(0.33/1.5) - 1 = -0.78\%$, or a decline of 78%. As a result, the capital to labor ratio dropped from 0.8 to 0.15. This is a change of $(0.15/0.8) - 1 = -0.8125$, or -81.25%. Hence the elasticity of substitution in Dynamique's zipper industry is:

$$\sigma = \frac{\text{percentage change in } K/L}{\text{percentage change in } w/r} = (-81.25)/(-78) = 1.04$$

The elasticity pessimists are driven out of Dynamique.

Exercises

1. Now it is your turn to examine the effect of relative factor prices on factor proportions.

   a. In Figure 8–2, isoquant SS shows alternative combinations of capital and labor that can be used to produce 100,000 polyester shirts per month in Travail, a country with an abundance of labor. The wage rate in Travail's modern sector is $w = \$400$ per month, and the cost of capital is $r = \$400$ per month. Hence the wage to rental ratio is:

      (i) $w/r =$ _____.

      Any budget line showing combinations of labor and capital that can be purchased on a given budget (B) will have a slope of:

      (ii) slope = _____.
      (iii) Draw the budget line for $B = \$40,000$ in Figure 8–2 and label it B_0. [Hint: B_0 will go through the point $K = 100$, $L = 0$. You already know the slope.]

   b. Given the prevailing wage to rental ratio:
      (i) Identify the minimum cost point on isoquant SS in Figure 8–2; label it *point X*.
      (ii) Draw in the budget line through point X, and label it B_X.

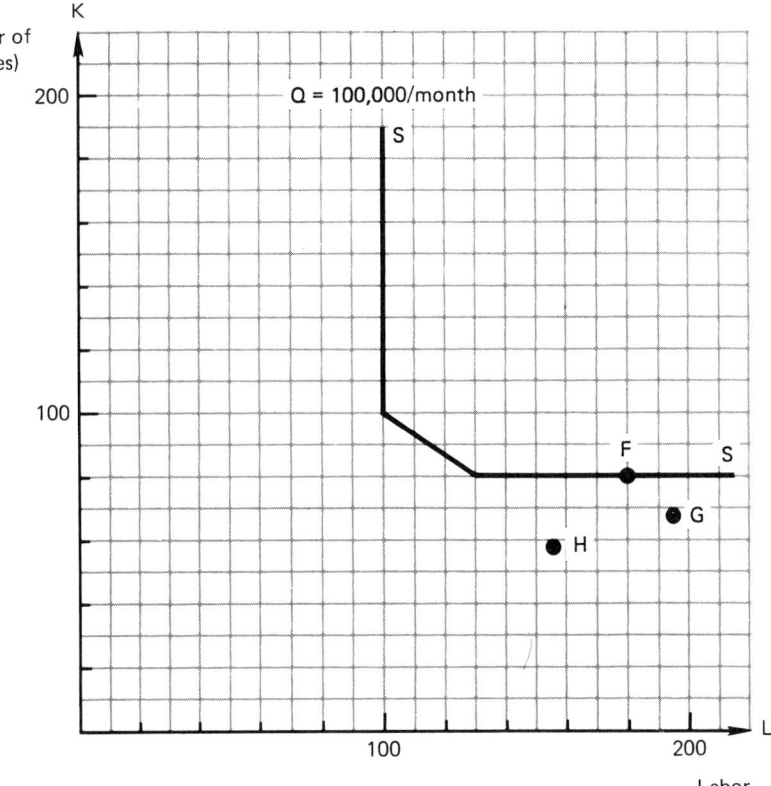

Figure 8-2

(iii) At point X, $L =$ _____ workers employed and $K =$ _____
units of capital used to produce 100,000 shirts.

(iv) At point X, the capital to labor ratio used to produce poly-

ester shirts is $K/L =$ _____.

c. You are hired by the government of Travail to explore policy
changes that might increase labor-intensity in the industrial
sector. Immediately your thoughts turn to factor price distortions.

(i) Industrial production would tend to be excessively capital-
intensive if existing policies caused the wage to rental ratio to

be too _____.

(ii) Name three types of government policies that can produce this
kind of a distortion in the wage-rental ratio:

_____ , _____ ,

and _____ .

d. As suspected, such policies have indeed been distorting the wage
to rental ratio in Travail. You convince the government to try an
experiment that will increase the cost of capital to $r = \$500$ while
keeping $w = \$400$.

(i) Under this policy experiment, the wage to rental ratio is

$w/r =$ _____.

(ii) Given this new wage to rental ratio, identify the minimum cost point on isoquant SS in Figure 8-2; label it *point X'*. [Hint: the result may seem a bit surprising.]

(iii) At point X', 100,000 shirts per month are being produced with:

$$L = \underline{\hspace{2cm}};$$

$$K = \underline{\hspace{2cm}}; \text{ and}$$

$$K/L = \underline{\hspace{2cm}}.$$

e. As a result of the policy experiment that increased the cost of capital to $r = \$500$:

(i) The wage to rental ratio changed from $w/r = \underline{\hspace{2cm}}$ to

$$w/r = \underline{\hspace{2cm}}.$$

(ii) So w/r changed by $\underline{\hspace{1cm}}\%$.

(iii) Prior to this change in the wage to rental ratio, the capital to labor ratio in zipper production was $K/L = \underline{\hspace{2cm}}$; following the change in w/r, the capital ratio is $K/L = \underline{\hspace{2cm}}$.

(iv) So K/L changed by $\underline{\hspace{1cm}}\%$.

(v) The elasticity of substitution observed during this policy experiment is $\sigma = \underline{\hspace{2cm}}$.

(vi) The elasticity $\underline{\hspace{3cm}}$ (optimists/pessimists) claim that the experiment has confirmed their arguments.

f. Nonetheless, your arguments prevail. The government decides to liberalize the labor and capital markets more completely. The formal-sector wage rate is reduced to $w = \$300$ and the rental rate increases to $r = \$600$.

(i) With these factor prices, the wage to rental ratio becomes

$$w/r = \underline{\hspace{2cm}}.$$

(ii) Identify the point on isoquant SS in Figure 8-2 that would minimize production costs given the new set of factor prices; label this as *point Y*.

(iii) Draw in the relevant budget line; label it B_Y.

(iv) At point Y 100,000 shirts are being produced with:

$$L = \underline{\hspace{2cm}}$$

$$K = \underline{\hspace{2cm}}$$

$$K/L = \underline{\hspace{2cm}}.$$

g. Compare the situation after liberalization of the factor markets in Travail (part f) with the initial conditions ($w = \$400$ and $r = \$400$).

(i) After the policy change, the wage to rental ratio has declined by $\underline{\hspace{1cm}}\%$.

(ii) The capital to labor ratio has declined by $\underline{\hspace{1cm}}\%$.

(iii) The observed elasticity of substitution is $\sigma = \underline{\hspace{2cm}}$.

(iv) The same output is being produced using _____% less capital

and _____% more labor.

(v) Explain briefly why the effect of a change in factor prices observed in part f is so different from the effect observed in part e.

2. Factor prices influence not only the factor proportions used to produce a particular product. They also affect employment creation by altering the mix of products that are produced, and to some extent the nature of technical change. This exercise explores these broader repercussions. [Note: it is important that you have completed Exercise 1.]

a. Factor prices affect production costs. Look back at your analysis of polyester-shirt production in exercise 1.
   (i) When factor prices were $w = \$400$ and $r = \$400$ in Travail, you found that 100,000 polyester shirts would be produced

   using $L = $ _____ workers and $K = $ _____ units of capital (your point X in Figure 8−2).
   (ii) At these factor prices the factor cost for producing 100,000

   polyester shirts was $C_p = \$$_____. [Hint: $(wL) + (rK)$]
   (iii) After factor prices became $w = \$300$ and $r = \$600$, you found that the same volume of output would be produced using $L = $

   _____ and $K = $ _____ (your point Y in Figure 8−2).
   (iv) At these new factor prices the factor cost for producing

   100,000 polyester shirts became $C_p' = \$$_____.
   (v) The decline in the wage to rental ratio causes factor costs to

   _____ in the polyester-shirt industry.

b. Polyester, though, is not the only game in Travail. Close competitors, *cotton* shirts, are produced using 50 K and 150 L per 100,000 shirts. Assume that the cotton-shirt industry is characterized by fixed factor proportions: the isoquants are L-shaped, and the elasticity of substitution is zero. [Be sure you understand these terms before proceeding.]
   (i) The capital to labor ratio in cotton shirt production is fixed at

   $K/L = $ _____.
   (ii) When factor prices were $w = \$400$ and $r = \$400$ in Travail, the factor cost for producing 100,000 cotton shirts was $C_c = $

   $\$$_____.
   (iii) After factor prices changed to $w = \$300$ and $r = \$600$, the factor cost for producing 100,000 cotton shirts became $C_c' = $

   $\$$_____.

(iv) The decline in the wage to rental ratio caused factor costs to

_____ in the cotton-shirt industry.

c. (i) Which type of shirt (polyester or cotton) uses more labor-intensive factor proportions in Travail?

_____ shirts

(ii) In terms of production costs, producers of which type of shirt benefit most from a decline in the wage to rental ratio?

_____ shirts

(iii) Assuming that product prices change to reflect factor costs,

one would see the price of cotton shirts _____ relative to the price of polyester shirts when the wage to rental ratio declines. [Hint: supply curves shift when costs change.]

(iv) This change in relative prices is likely to cause sales of cotton

shirts in Travail to _____, while sales of poly-

ester shirts are likely to _____.

(v) How will these market adjustments affect employment creation in the shirt industry? Briefly explain.

d. You should have concluded that polyester shirt producers will see their market share falling following the change in factor prices. But the story need not end there. As a result of competitive pressure they will have a strong incentive to develop new labor-intensive production techniques.

(i) Point F in Figure 8–2 is a feasible production point that is far more labor-intensive than your point Y. Would F be more profitable than point Y for polyester-shirt producers? Briefly explain. [Hint: Think about the budget lines.]

(ii) Suppose that as a result of technology research, point G becomes feasible. This point has a very low capital to labor ratio. Would G be more profitable than point Y for polyester-shirt producers? Briefly explain.

(iii) Suppose research led to point H being feasible. It is less labor-intensive than point G, but would H be a more profitable technology for polyester-shirt producers? Briefly explain.

(iv) Assuming that the opportunity costs of labor and capital are properly reflected by the new factor prices (w = $300 and r = $600), which point—$Y$, F, G, or H—is a more "appropriate" technology for producing polyester shirts in Travail? Briefly explain.

3. Now let's use supply-and-demand analysis to trace the impact of Travail's liberalization policies (from Exercise 1) on the country's labor markets. The three panels in Figure 8–3 show the initial conditions in each of the three labor markets—the urban formal market (F), the urban informal market (I), and the rural market (R).

a. (i) Assume that the supply-and-demand curves for labor in the urban formal market remain fixed. Draw a line in panel F of Figure 8–3 showing a decline in the minimum wage in the formal sector to w_F = $300. Label the resulting quantities of labor supplied and demanded as L_s' and L_d', respectively.
   (ii) How does the decline in the minimum wage affect the size of the queue for jobs in the urban formal market?

b. Assume here that the formal-sector queue consists of people who are working at informal-sector jobs while searching for formal-sector employment.
   (i) How would the increased employment in the formal sector affect the labor supply in the informal market? Draw in the new supply curve in panel I of Figure 8–3 and label it S_I'.

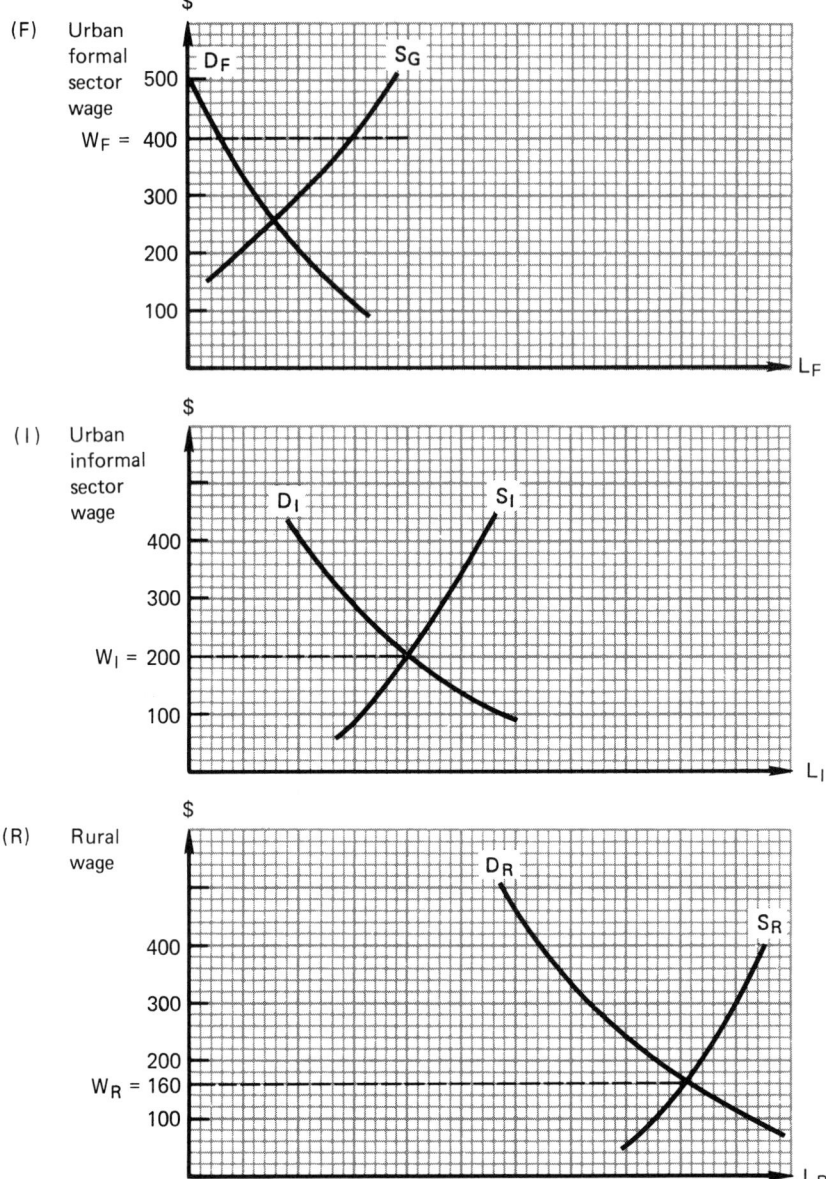

Figure 8–3

(ii) How would this shift in S_I affect the equilibrium wage in the urban informal market? In the figure, label the new wage as W_I'.

(iii) Explain how this change in W_I can induce more **migration** to the cities, and how such migration would affect the two urban labor markets.

c. Assume that some migration to the cities does in fact occur. What would be the effect on the equilibrium in the rural labor market?

4. This exercise applies the analysis of industrial employment growth (Equation 8–5 in the textbook).

   a. The Republic of Kita in 1987 has a labor force of 1,000 workers, of whom 150 work in the industrial sector. Because industrial policy favors growth of capital intensive activities, on average a 10% increase in industrial value-added brings about only a 4% growth in industrial employment.

   (i) This means that the elasticity of industrial employment with respect to value-added in industry is _____. Call this the "employment elasticity," for short.

   (ii) In 1988, value-added in the industrial sector is expected to increase by 15%. If so, then employment in the industrial sector will increase by _____%.

   b. The planning minister is pleased to hear how quickly industrial employment will be growing. She remarks, "Since the labor force is growing by only 2% per year, the industrial sector growth should take care of the employment problem in Kita."

   (i) But in fact only _____ new jobs will open up in the industrial sector in 1988, whereas the labor force will grow by _____ workers.

   (ii) In terms of the Equation 8–5 formula from the text, 1988 industrial-employment growth in Kita can be analyzed as follows:

$\eta =$ _____ (employment elasticity);

$g(V_i) =$ _____% (growth in industrial value added); and

$S_i =$ _____ (industrial employment as fraction of total employment).

(iii) So employment growth in industry, expressed as a percentage of the initial labor force will be only:

$$\Delta E_i = \underline{\hspace{3cm}} \%.$$

This means that industrial job creation amounts to less than 1% of the labor force.

(iv) Only _____% of the *additional* workers entering the labor force in 1988 will be able to find jobs in industry. More than half of the new workers will have to find work elsewhere.

c. (i) Given S_i and η, value-added in the industrial sector would have to grow how fast to provide jobs for all 20 new members of the labor force in 1988?

$$g(V_i) = \underline{\hspace{2cm}} \%.$$

(ii) Alternatively, taking S_i and $g(V_i)$ as given, the industrial sector could provide jobs for all 20 new members of the labor force in 1988 if the employment elasticity in Kita were:

$$\eta = \underline{\hspace{3cm}}.$$

[Hint: find the value of η such that $\Delta E_i = 2\%$.]

(iii) What policies might the government of Kita use to raise the employment elasticity in order to promote more employment creation in industry?

d. The neighboring Republic of Kota is identical to Kita in all respects except that in 1987, 30% of the labor force is already employed in industry. Kota has 1,000 workers. The labor force is growing by 2% per year. Industrial value-added is expected to grow by 15% in 1988. And the industrial employment elasticity is the same as the one you calculated above for Kita.

(i) Under these conditions, calculate the employment growth in Kota's industrial sector, expressed as a percentage of the country's initial labor force.

$$\Delta E_i = \underline{\hspace{2cm}} \%.$$

(ii) Taking Kota's S_i and $g(V_i)$ as given, the industrial sector in Kota could provide jobs for all 20 new members of its labor force in 1988 if the employment elasticity were:

$$\eta = \underline{\hspace{3cm}}.$$

(iii) Why would Kota require an employment elasticity only half as large as Kita's in order for the industrial sector to create jobs for 20 new workers in 1988?

e. How would the analysis of Kita's 1988 employment problem be affected by taking into account **indirect and secondary job creation** resulting from the growth of the industrial sector?

5. In this exercise you will analyze internal migration using the Harris-Todaro model.

   a. In Samudra the urban wage is fixed by the government at 1,500 rupiah per day. Rural workers earn 1,000 rupiah per day (reflecting the opportunity cost of rural labor). The Harris-Todaro model predicts that rural to urban migration will take place as long as

   the probability of finding an urban job is at least _____.

   b. Suppose that there are 165 urban workers competing for 150 urban-sector jobs in Samudra.
      (i) Using Equation 8–3 from the textbook, the probability of finding an urban job is:

$$p = \text{_____} .$$

      (ii) The *expected* urban wage is thus

$$w_u{}^* = \text{_____} \text{ rupiah.}$$

      (iii) Assume that the response rate of potential migrants is $h = 0.01$ (review textbook equation 8–4). Given the rural wage rate and the expected urban wage, how many people will migrate to the urban area to search for jobs?

$$M = \text{_____} \text{ migrants (Round to the nearest whole person.)}$$

   c. Suppose instead that the initial 165 urban workers fall into two categories: 150 workers who already have jobs that they intend to keep, and 15 unemployed workers who are looking for jobs. In this case the probability of finding a job would be defined as:

   $p = $ (number of unemployed)/(number of new jobs opening up)

      (i) If 9 new urban jobs are opening up, then the probability of a job seeker finding a job is:

$$p = \text{_____} .$$

(ii) In this case the *expected* urban wage is

$$w_u^* = \underline{\hspace{3cm}} \text{ rupiah.}$$

(iii) What migration pattern would result?

Answers to Self-Test

Completion

1. agricultural
2. formal
3. Disguised
4. discouraged
5. capital to labor, wage to rental
6. low
7. unskilled
8. brain drain
9. decline
10. opportunity cost

True-False

1. T	6. T
2. F	7. F
3. F	8. F
4. F	9. T
5. T	10. F

Multiple Choice

1. b	5. b
2. d	6. c
3. a	7. b
4. a	8. a

CHAPTER 9   **Education**

Overview

This chapter on education and the following chapter on health examine *investment in human capital*, which is investment in people to improve workers' productivity and incomes. The relationship between economic development and investment in human capital is mutually supportive: as an economy grows, it can devote more resources to investments in human capital; it is also true that human-capital investments help to accelerate economic growth and development. Investment in education has had a very high priority in the developing countries and great progress has been made in expanding educational opportunity. But, as with any other type of investment, decisions must be made about the volume and pattern of investment in education.

The chapter explains how tools such as manpower planning and cost-benefit analysis have been used to evaluate education investments. Although neither tool can provide concrete policy guidance, the economic analysis can lead to better-informed decisions about allocating resources to education. For example, it is generally found that in low-income countries, primary education produces the highest rates of return. Economic analysis can also reveal differences between the private and social returns to education, indicating that popular demand for education is not always a sign of high social productivity. The chapter concludes with a review of a number of proposals for education reform in developing countries.

Main Learning Objectives

After studying this chapter you ought to understand and be able to explain:

1. The reasons for the importance of **investment in human capital**, and especially investment in education.

2. The broad trends and patterns that characterize education in the third world.

3. The meaning of **manpower planning**, as well as its limitations as a practical tool for determining educational requirements.

4. The application of **cost-benefit analysis** to education policy, and the limitations of this tool for analyzing education investments.

5. Why and how the **private rate of return** to education can diverge from the **social rate of return**, and the implications for education policy.

6. The different education policy views of groups categorized in the textbook as **left revisionists**, **right revisionists**, and **moderate reformers**.

Additional Key Terms, Concepts, and Institutions

Can you identify and explain each of the following?

formal vs. nonformal and informal education
"diploma disease"
educated unemployment
gross vs. net enrollment ratios (see Table 9–1 in the textbook)
educational deepening
lifetime earnings curve (age-earning profile)
explicit vs. implicit costs of education
discounted present value

Economic Tools and Techniques

From what you have learned in this chapter, can you:

1. Explain how the **Tinbergen-Parnes** methodology is used to estimate manpower requirements and education requirements?

2. Calculate the private and social rates of return to investment in education and analyze the resulting policy implications?

Self-Test

Completion

1. Organized learning programs that take place outside of schools can

   be called _____ education, whereas learning that takes place outside any organized institutional framework can

   be called _____ education.

2. As the supply of educated labor increases over time, people with more schooling gradually come to be used in jobs that were previously filled by people with less education. This process is

   termed educational _____ .

3. The chain of deduction in calculating manpower requirements is:
   GNP → industrial structure → total employment by industry →

   _____ structure of employment →

   _____ structure of employment.

4. Empirical studies show that in low-income countries the highest social rates of return are earned on _____ education.

5. The _____ enrollment ratio is defined as the percentage of the pertinent age group enrolled in a given level of schooling.

6. The "_____ revisionists" argue that choices about what kinds of education should be provided to whom should be determined primarily by the market.

7. According to the textbook, most educators believe that a child who fails to complete at least _____ years of formal education gains little from school attendance.

8. The UNESCO data reported in the text show that in the poorest countries enrollment ratios in _____ education are less than 2%.

True-False If false, you should be able to explain why.

_____ 1. Age-earnings studies generally fail to confirm the hypothesis that individual earnings are positively correlated with years of education in developing countries.

_____ 2. One important reason for high dropout rates in developing countries is that many households are too poor to bear the costs of keeping a child in school.

_____ 3. In some LDCs rapid expansion of education has led to the problem of high unemployment rates for secondary-school and university graduates.

_____ 4. Prior to the 1970s primary school enrollments did not expand rapidly in most LDCs because policymakers were not aware of the importance of human-capital investment.

_____ 5. Education specialists generally agree that manpower planning methods should be widely applied to determine education requirements in LDCs.

_____ 6. The text's case study of Indonesia illustrates that low-income countries cannot manage rapid expansion of rural primary education in a period as brief as a decade.

_____ 7. With benefits defined as the increase in earnings associated with more education, the social rate of return to education cannot exceed the private rate of return.

_____ 8. Where education costs are largely borne by the government, it is possible that investments in education yield very high private rates of return but very low social rates of return.

Multiple Choice

1. Public expenditure on education in LDCs typically accounts for

   _____% of the government budget and _____% of GNP.
   a. 15–20%; 3–6%
   b. 25–30%; 8–10%
   c. 2–4%; less than 1%
   d. 30–60%; 20–30%

2. In Figure 9–1, the axes are labeled as X and Y. The proper labels

   for this figure are $X =$ _____ and $Y =$ _____.
   a. years of schooling; age.
   b. years of schooling; earnings.
   c. earnings; age.
   d. age; earnings.

3. Ronald Dore's phrase, the "diploma disease," refers to:
   a. the difficulty that undernourished students face in completing their education.
   b. the strong tendency in LDCs to judge an individual's fitness by academic credentials.
   c. the feverish pursuit of education even at a very high cost.
   d. the high dropout rate for students from poor families.

4. Lifetime earnings curves for LDCs nearly always show all of the following except:
   a. those with more schooling achieve higher earning levels.
   b. the curve rises more steeply for those with more schooling.
   c. the curve reaches a peak at a younger age for those with more schooling.
   d. those with more schooling begin earning at a later age.

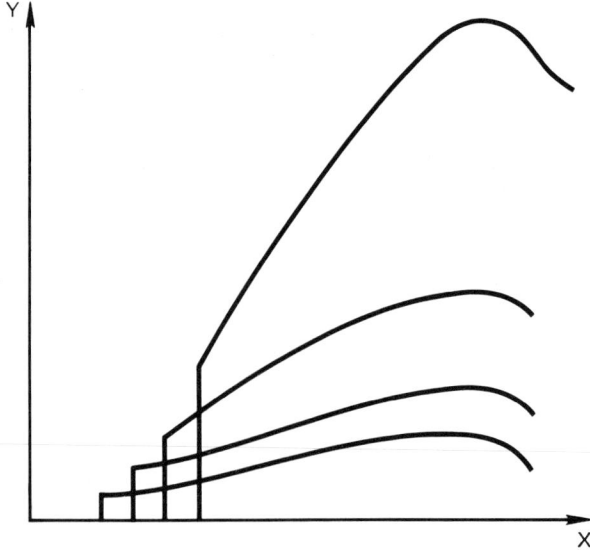

Figure 9–1

5. Which of the following is an *implicit* cost of education borne by the private household?
   a. earnings or productive household work foregone when children attend school
   b. the cost of school books
   c. transportation costs
   d. public-sector outlays not reimbursed by tuition

6. From the point of view of economic efficiency, a government should expand investment in those forms of education that:
   a. are in the greatest demand.
   b. have a low social rate of return.
   c. have a social rate of return greater than zero.
   d. have a social rate of return greater than the opportunity cost of capital.

7. Which of the following is *not* a valid criticism of the use of cost-benefit analysis to evaluate investment in education?
   a. Current data on lifetime earnings do not provide valid information on future earnings.
   b. One cannot assume that differences in earnings associated with education are the result of the education.
   c. Important personal and social benefits of education cannot be quantified.
   d. All of the above are valid criticisms.

Applications

Worked Example: Private versus Social Rates of Return

To evaluate the rate of return to education, one must calculate the discounted present value of lifetime earnings. To simplify this cumbersome task, let's assume here that people live for only two "years": youth (year 1) and adulthood (year 2). Youths either go to school and earn zero, or they work and earn $1,000, paid at the end of year 1. Everyone works as an adult. Educated adults earn $3,500 while uneducated adults earn only $2,000. Individuals thus follow one of two lifetime-earnings profiles:

	Year 1	Year 2
No school →	$1,000	$2,000
School →	$ 0	$3,500

The benefits of education are the *incremental* earnings obtained by those who have gone through school. For year 1, those who go to school actually earn less than those who don't, so the benefit is negative, −$1,000 to be precise. (This amount is the implicit opportunity cost of attending school.) For year 2, the benefit is $1,500 of extra earnings. The present discounted value of the marginal benefits is therefore:

$$V = \frac{-1,000}{1 + r} + \frac{1,500}{(1 + r)^2}$$

where r is an appropriate discount rate.

So far we have considered only the benefits. What about the costs? If the government pays all explicit costs, then V as defined above is the whole story from the point of view of the individual. The private rate of return can be calculated as the discount rate for which the discounted present value of net benefits is equal to zero—or, in other words, the effective yield earned on the investment in education. It is not hard to see that the private rate of return in this case is 50%. You "invest" $1,000 and get back $1,500 a year later. In terms of the math, $V = 0$ when $r = 0.5$.

To calculate the social rate of return, the costs must be taken into account whether paid by the individual or by the government. Suppose that the cost of education is $400 per student. Then for year 1, benefit minus cost equals −$1,400. For year 2 the net benefit remains +$1,500, showing the increased earnings or social productivity generated by the investment in education. To calculate the social rate of return, one finds the value of r such that:

$$V' = \frac{-1,400}{1 + r} + \frac{1,500}{(1 + r)^2} = 0.$$

In terms of social costs and benefits, an investment of $1,400 pays off $1,500 the following year. This represents a rate of return of 7.14%. In terms of the math, $V' = 0$ when $r = 0.0714$.

If the private rate of return is 50%, the demand for education is likely to be very high. But since the social rate of return is only 7.14%, there are probably other alternative investments that would be more productive.

Exercises

1. Now it is your turn to calculate private and social rates of return on education. In Baccalauria, primary school is compulsory but higher education is not. For simplicity, assume that people live for four "years": a year of primary-school age (age 1), a year of secondary-school age (age 2), a year of college age (age 3), and a year of adulthood (age 4). Each Baccalaurian chooses one of three alternative lifetime-earnings options, summarized in Table 9–1.

   a. In Figure 9–2 draw the three lifetime-earnings curves corresponding to the three options shown in the table. Label the three curves A, B, and C, respectively.

Table 9–1

Lifetime Earnings Options (figures in Baccalaurian dollars)

	Age 1	Age 2	Age 3	Age 4
A. Primary school only ⟶	0	1,000	1,200	1,500
B. Secondary school ⟶	0	0	1,500	2,000
C. College ⟶	0	0	0	5,000

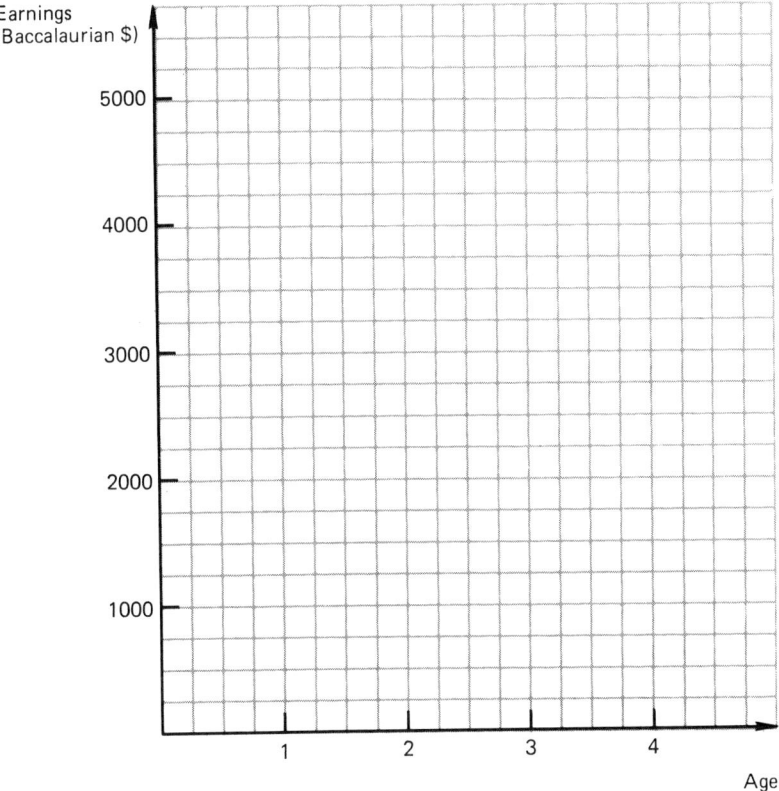

Earnings
(Baccalaurian $)

5000

4000

3000

2000

1000

1   2   3   4

Age

Figure 9–2

b. Assume that the cost of a year in college is $1,000. The student pays half of this amount, with the government picking up the tab for the other $500.

  (i) From the point of view of a student who has already completed secondary school during age 2, what is the net benefit (benefit minus cost) of a college education:

during age 3? _____ ;

during age 4? _____ .

[Hint: For age 3 the net benefit will be negative and will take into account the earnings foregone to attend college.]

  (ii) Using the numbers for net benefits for ages 3 and 4, write down the specific equation for calculating the private rate of return to investment in a college education. Use r to represent the discount rate. [Hint: For simplicity, let ages 3 and 4 correspond to years 0 and 1 in the present-value formula. Ages 1 and 2 can be disregarded completely here.]

$V =$

(iii) Calculate the private rate of return to investment in a college education. [Remember, you are looking for the value of r that sets $V = 0$. You can use trial and error, or in this simple case you might be able to deduce it directly from the data on net benefits.]

Private rate of return = _____ %.

c. Now reconsider the investment in college education from the point of view of society.

(i) Taking into account the $500 in costs paid by the government as well as the $500 paid by the individual, what is the net social benefit of a college education:

during age 3? _____ ;

during age 4? _____ .

(ii) What is the equation for calculating the *social* rate of return to investment in a college education? Again use r to represent the discount rate.

$$V' =$$

(iii) Calculate the social rate of return to investment in a college education.

Social rate of return = _____ %.

d. Suppose that the numbers in Table 9–1 are based on a study of actual earnings data for 1987. After reading about the high private rate of return to investment in higher education, a large number of 1987 high school graduates decides to attend college. One year later, the supply of college graduates in the labor market increases considerably, causing average adulthood earnings for college graduates to fall to $4,500. All the other earnings figures remain unchanged.

(i) As a result of the decline in earnings the actual net benefit of a college education for this group of graduates when they are

age 4 turns out to be only $_____ .

(ii) The rate of return on investment in college education thus turns out to be somewhat lower than expected. Specifically, it turns out that the:

private rate of return = _____ % and the

social rate of return   = _____ % .

[Hint: The social rate of return should be a very round number.]

e. A clever researcher discovers that people who attend college are more intelligent and more hardworking than those who leave school after secondary school. The researcher estimates that if college grads had gone directly into the labor market after high school, they would have earned more than the average observed for high school graduates at ages 3 and 4. Specifically, by skipping college these people could have earned $1,600 at age 3 (as opposed to $0 if in school), and $2,400 at age 4 (versus $4,500 with their degree).

(i) Assuming these estimates to be valid, what is the true net (private) benefit of a college education to an individual:

during age 3? _____ and

during age 4? _____.

(ii) What is the true net social benefit of a college education:

during age 3? _____ and

during age 4? _____.

(iii) What are the true private and social rates of return to investment in a college education?

Private rate of return = _____ %.

Social rate of return = _____ %.

2. This exercise works through a simple manpower-planning problem using the Tinbergen-Parnes methodology.

The government of Sinecure is targeting real GNP to grow by 6% per annum during the five-year planning period ending in 1992. Estimates made using input-output analysis (see Chapter 6), show that output by sector will grow as shown in Table 9–2.

a. In 1987, the labor force in Sinecure totals 1,000 workers, of whom 800 work in agriculture (A) and 200 work in manufacturing (M). Define the "labor coefficient" as the number of workers per thousand pesos output.

(i) What is the labor coefficient in A? _____

(ii) What is the labor coefficient in M? _____

(iii) In which sector is labor productivity (output per worker)

highest in 1987? Sector _____

(iv) If these labor coefficients were to remain unchanged, how many workers would be required to produce the projected output for 1991?

_____ workers in A

_____ workers in M

Table 9–2
Output by Sector (in thousands of 1986 pesos)

Sector	1987	1992	% Increase
Agriculture (A)	700	800	14.3
Manufacturing (M)	300	538	79.3
Total GNP	1,000	1,338	33.8

b. It is expected, though, that productivity gains will reduce the labor requirement per thousand pesos of output by 5% in A and by 15% in M by 1992.

   (i) This will reduce the labor coefficient in A to _____,

      and the labor coefficient in M to _____. [Hint: to reduce a number by x%, multiply it by $1 - (x/100)$.]

   (ii) Taking into account these productivity gains, agriculture in

      1992 will require _____ workers and manufacturing will

      require _____ workers.

c. Table 9–3 shows the structure of Sinecure's labor force in 1987, by sector and by occupational category.

   (i) Skilled workers represent _____% of the labor force in A,

      and _____% of the labor force in M. These figures define the **occupational structure** of the work force in each of the two sectors.

   (ii) Assuming the occupational structure in each sector to remain unchanged, how many skilled workers will be required in 1992:

in A? _____

in M? _____

d. Everyone in Sinecure completes primary school, while skilled workers must complete an additional two-year vocational program. Each year, the labor force increases by 35 workers, so the labor force in 1992 will be large enough to satisfy the total labor requirement. But only a small number of additional workers—4 per year—will be skilled workers.

   (i) After 5 years there will be a total of _____ skilled workers in the country.

   (ii) But the manpower planning projections (see c.ii above) show

      that the economy will require _____ skilled workers by 1992.

   (iii) Hence, the forecast is that the supply of skilled workers will

      fall short of requirements by _____ workers.

   (iv) Based on this calculation, what is your recommendation about investment in vocational education?

Table 9–3

Labor Force (numbers of workers)

Sector	Unskilled	Skilled	Total
A	800	0	800
M	150	50	200

e. Is this forecast accurate? Suppose that the government fails to increase the investment in vocational training, so that in fact only 4 skilled workers are added to the labor force each year.

(i) Since the supply of skilled workers would increasingly fall short of the "required" number, market forces would tend to cause real wages for skilled workers to _____ .

(ii) This change in real wages for skilled workers would provide an incentive to producers in manufacturing to alter factor proportions and the product mix so as to economize on the use of skilled labor. How large a reduction in the skilled labor requirement would be adequate to eliminate the projected shortage of skilled workers?

a reduction of _____ %

f. Section e dealt with one problem with manpower planning analysis—that labor requirements are not necessarily fixed coefficients. Identify three other distinct problems with manpower planning as a tool for determining educational investment priorities.

Answers to Self-Test

Completion

1. nonformal; informal
2. deepening
3. occupational; educational
4. primary
5. net
6. right
7. five or six
8. higher (or 3rd level)

True-False

1. F	5. F
2. T	6. F
3. T	7. T
4. F	8. T

Multiple Choice

1. a	5. a
2. d	6. d
3. b	7. d
4. c	

CHAPTER 10   Health and Nutrition

Overview

Health care is a basic human need, and also a productive investment in human capital. In LDCs poor health is responsible for generally high mortality rates, particularly for infants and children, and for life expectancies well below those observed in the developed countries. The main direct causes of premature death in low-income countries are infectious, parasitic, and respiratory diseases. In addition to the value of better health as an end in itself, investment in health can increase labor productivity while also lengthening the productive life-span of a country's population. The rate of return to such investment, however, has proved very hard to quantify.

Health status generally improves as a country's per-capita income increases. But even lower-income countries have achieved major health gains by addressing the fundamental causes of sickness and premature death: (1) environmental health hazards; (2) malnutrition; and (3) lack of adequate and appropriate medical care. Protein-calorie malnutrition among infants and children is a particularly serious problem. Policy actions that can promote better health include programs to increase food availability, nutrition improvement programs, development of clean water supplies and sanitation facilities, and improved distribution of preventive medical services.

Main Learning Objectives

After studying this chapter you ought to understand and be able to explain:

1. The empirical record on health conditions, including patterns and trends in **life expectancy**, and the main causes of death in the LDCs.

2. The effects of investment in health on economic development, in addition to the direct benefits of better health as a basic human need.

3. How **environmental sanitation** conditions—such as poor water quality, poor air quality, and inadequate waste disposal—contribute to LDC health problems.

4. The extent, the character, and the health effects of **malnutrition** in the LDCs.

5. How nutrition is related to income, food prices, and tastes, and how government **nutrition interventions** can attack the problems of malnutrition.

6. The inadequacies of the existing health-care delivery system in many LDCs and the types of reforms that can enhance the effectiveness of medical services.

Additional Key Terms, Concepts, and Institutions

Can you identify and explain each of the following?

The World Health Organization (WHO)
morbidity
parasitic conditions
protein-calorie malnutrition (PCM)
food entitlements
food supplementation (fortification)
indigenous practitioners
"barefoot doctors"
preventive vs. curative health services
oral rehydration therapy (ORT)
urban bias

Economic Tools and Techniques

From what you have learned in this chapter, can you:

1. Discuss the difficulties faced in quantifying the economic rate of return to investment in health care?

2. Explain the factors comprising a **national food-balance sheet**, and weaknesses of food-balance statistics?

3. Explain how the quantity and quality of family diets are related to incomes, prices, and tastes, including the **income and substitution effects** of a change in food prices?

4. Explain what is meant by the **cost-effectiveness** of nutrition intervention programs?

Self-Test

Completion

1. The health statistic that measures the incidence of illness is the

   _____ rate.

2. The United Nations agency responsible for health programs is

   generally referred to by the initials _____, standing for

   _____ .

3. Schistosomiasis, hookworms, and roundworms are examples of
_____ conditions that are prevalent in LDCs.

4. In China health conditions have improved dramatically, in part due
to _____ doctors working in the countryside to
provide both _____ and curative health care.

5. The most prevalent form of malnutrition in the third world is referred
to by the initials PCM, which stand for _____
_____ .

6. _____ is a simple,
effective, and inexpensive treatment that can prevent most deaths
from diarrhea, which is a major cause of death among infants and
children in LDCs.

7. According to Engel's Law, households spend a _____
proportion of their income on food as their incomes rise.

8. An increase in life expectancy should _____ the rate
of return on investment in education.

9. The term food _____ refers to a person's
ability to obtain food, whether through purchase, rationing, or other
forms of distribution.

True-False If false, you should be able to explain why.

_____ 1. To improve rural health care for the poor in many LDCs, it
is more important to train nurses and paramedics than to
train doctors.

_____ 2. Two-thirds or more of the rural population in the LDCs lack
access to safe drinking water and proper sanitation facilities.

_____ 3. Government spending on health care in low-income countries
amounted to slightly over $100 per capita in 1980.

_____ 4. The average life expectancy in most LDCs has increased only
slightly since 1960.

_____ 5. Malnutrition may continue to be a serious problem even
after a country's per-capita calorie supply has reached one-
hundred percent of requirements.

_____ 6. It is an unhappy fact that when the incomes of poor families
in LDCs rise, the nutritional content of their diet generally
declines.

_____ 7. Countries that have actively pursued basic human needs policies have achieved substantially higher life expectancies and substantially lower infant mortality rates than other countries with similar levels of income.

_____ 8. During the first ten years after Castro came to power, the ratio of doctors to population in Cuba more than doubled.

_____ 9. Health care systems in most developing countries have not been affected very much by urban bias.

Multiple Choice

1. Which of the following is the most important direct cause of death in LDCs?
   a. cancer and heart disease
   b. diseases such as malaria, cholera, and tuberculosis
   c. injury
   d. famine

2. The most important nutrition problem in LDCs is generally regarded to be:
   a. calorie deficiency.
   b. vitamin A deficiency.
   c. iron deficiency.
   d. all of the above are regarded as equally important.

3. The prevalence of malnutrition is greatest among which population group?
   a. young adults
   b. children
   c. the elderly
   d. newborn babies

4. A nation's food balance sheet provides a set of accounts showing:
   a. the nation's exports and imports of foods.
   b. the excess demand in the nation's market for food.
   c. the relationship between food production and cultivated farm area.
   d. the calorie value of actual food consumption in relation to calorie requirements of the population.

5. "Food supplementation" programs are programs to:
   a. fortify widely consumed foods with nutrients.
   b. import food to meet demand that is not satisfied by domestic production.
   c. provide extra food to target groups such as pregnant women and children.
   d. expand agricultural production.

6. Amartya Sen's study of famine episodes revealed that the main problem often was not that food supplies were inadequate, but rather that:
   a. people lacked food entitlements.
   b. too much food was exported.
   c. the food being consumed was not nutritious.
   d. food was hoarded by speculators.

7. Which of the following statements accurately applies to health conditions in Sri Lanka?
   a. At independence in 1948 health and life expectancy were unusually low even for a poor country.
   b. Malaria control explains most of the improvements.
   c. Medical care has been free to all, with the network of facilities extending to all parts of the island.
   d. The improvements occurred despite a continued high incidence of serious malnutrition.

8. The term "indigenous health practitioner" refers to:
   a. native-born doctors, nurses, and paramedics.
   b. doctors who studied medicine at local medical schools.
   c. health workers who deal with preventive rather than curative medical services.
   d. those who, like herbalists or exorcists, practice traditional healing rather than modern medicine.

Applications

Worked Example: National Food Balance Sheet

Table 10–1 shows the 1987 national food balance sheet for Tapioca, a small island country with a population of 1,000, of whom 600 live in poverty. The table shows only the foods that are important dietary items for the poor. Study the table closely. In rows 1–4 you can see that the total domestic supply of each food is equal to the amount produced plus the amount imported, less the amount exported. The balance sheet shows that Tapioca depends on imports for almost one-fourth (50/210) of its rice supplies, while over one-fifth (40/180) of its fish production is exported.

   Rows 5–9 show that not all available food supplies end up on the dinner table. For example, out of the 210,000 kg of rice, almost 5% (= 10/210) is added to the government stockpile for meeting future emergencies. And almost 24% (= 50/210) is lost to waste as a result of spoilage and rodents. Overall, only 71% (= 150/210) of the rice is consumed. Only 55% of the cassava supply gets eaten; large fractions are used for animal feed and for industrial processing.

   Rows 10–12 convert the data first into per-capita terms and then into per-capita calorie equivalent. The calculation is straightforward. For each type of food the total amount consumed is divided by the population (1,000). When the kg/year figure is multiplied by the appropriate calories/kg figure shown in row 11, the result is calories/year. Dividing by 365 gives the final figure, calories/day, as shown in row 12 for each food.

Table 10–1

National Food Balance Sheet for Tapioca, 1987

	Rice	Cassava	Fish
Sources (kg)			
1. Production	160,000	360,000	180,000
2. Imports	50,000	0	0
3. Exports	0	0	40,000
4. Total domestic supply	210,000	360,000	140,000
Uses (kg)			
5. Accumulation of stocks	10,000	0	0
6. Animal feed	0	50,000	20,000
7. Waste	50,000	10,000	20,000
8. Processed as nonfood product	0	100,000	0
9. Food consumption	150,000	200,000	100,000
10. Per-capita kg/year	150	200	100
11. Calories/kg	3,660	980	640
12. Per-capita calories/day	1,504	536	175

Total per-capita calories per day = 2,215

Source: Derived from 1976 food balance sheet for Indonesia presented ‍in C. Peter Timmer et al., *Food Policy Analysis* (Baltimore: Johns Hopkins University Press, 1983).

Together, the three foods shown in the table provide an average of 2,215 calories per person per day (= 1,504 + 536 + 175 from row 12). Given the average body size and work regimen of the population, nutritionists estimate that the average Tapiocan requires 2,100 calories per day to maintain good health. Hence the daily per-capita calorie as a percentage of requirements for Tapioca is 105% (= 2,215/2,100, times 100 to convert to a percentage).

Notice that with a few exceptions, such as the increase in government rice stock, virtually every number used above is difficult to measure with any precision. Suppose the average calorie requirement were being underestimated by 10% (so the true figure is 2,100 x 1.1 = 2,310), and that official data overestimate calorie consumption by 10% (so the true figure is 2,215/1.1 = 2,013). Then the correct figure for the daily calorie supply as a percentage of requirements would be 87% (2,013/2,310), not 105%!

Even if the numbers were all correct, the fact that calorie supplies exceed 100% of requirements does not mean that everyone is eating adequately. The national average level of rice consumption of 150 kg/year per-capita may reflect a situation in which the average poor person eats only 100 kg/year, while the average non-poor person eats 225 kg/year. [Check: 60% of the population is poor, so the overall level of consumption would be (100 × 0.6) + (225 × 0.4) = 150.] If so, the poor would be eating only 1,002 (= 100 × 3,660/365) calories of rice per day, not the 1,504 shown in the balance sheet.

Exercises

1. Now it's your turn to examine a national food balance sheet.

   a. The one million citizens of the Republic of Sucrose have a diet consisting primarily of coconut with sugar. Table 10–2 shows the 1987 food balance sheet for Sucrose, but some of the numbers are missing. Fill in the blanks in the table.

   b. Nutritionists estimate that the average Sucrosian requires 2,400 calories per day for good health.

      (i) The food balance sheet shows that the actual food supply

         provides _____ calories per capita per day.

      (ii) So the food supply equals _____% of calorie requirements.

   c. The people of Sucrose fall into two classes: 3/4 are affluent landowners and 1/4 are landless workers who live in poverty. People of both classes consume the same amount of sugar: 100 kg per year. But they differ markedly in consumption of coconuts. Each landowner, on average, consumes 450 kg/year of coconut!

      (i) If 3/4 of the population consume 450 kg/year, and the national average is 400 kg/year, then the remaining 1/4 of the population must average:

         _____ kg/year of coconuts per capita.
         [Hint: (0.75)(450) + (0.25)(X) = 400]

Table 10–2
1987 National Food Balance Sheet for Sucrose

	Coconuts	Sugar
Sources		
Production	_____	140
Imports	0	_____
Exports	150	0
Total domestic supply	500	170
Uses (million kg)		
Accumulation of stocks	_____	20
Waste	40	_____
Processed as nonfood product	40	10
Food consumption	_____	_____
Per-capita kg/year consumed	400	100
Calories/kg	1,500	_____
Per-capita calories/day	_____	962

Total per-capita calories per day = _____

Source: Derived from Timmer et al., *Food Policy Analysis* (Baltimore: Johns Hopkins University Press, 1983).

Table 10-3

Nutrition Analysis by Class, Sucrose, 1987

	Per-capita kg/year consumed (1)	Calories/ kg (2)	Per-capita calories/ day (3)
A. The Landowners			
Coconuts	_____	_____	_____
Sugar	_____	_____	_____
Per-capita cal/day			_____
B. The Landless Laborers			
Coconuts	_____	_____	_____
Sugar	_____	_____	_____
Per-capita cal/day			_____

(ii) Based on this information, fill in the first column of Table 10-3.

d. Now the rest of Table 10-3 can be completed step by step.
  (i) Fill in column 2 of Table 10-3 using figures from Table 10-2 showing the calorie/kg for each food.
  (ii) Then calculate the average daily calorie supplies and fill in column 3. (Don't forget to convert from amounts per year to amounts per day.)

e. Although the daily per-capita calorie supply in Sucrose exceeds 100% of the country's calorie requirement, has the malnutrition problem been solved? Briefly explain, referring to the data in Table 10-3.

f. Assume that there are 15 grams of *protein* per kilogram of coconut and 0 grams of *protein* per kilogram of sugar.
  (i) Then, per-capita protein consumption in Sucrose is:

_____ grams per day for the nation as a whole;

_____ grams per day for the landowners; and

_____ grams per day for the landless workers.

(ii) Nutritionists estimate that the average daily protein requirement is 40 grams per person. It seems that *everyone* in
Sucrose suffers from a protein deficiency. Is this due to an
inadequate supply of food? Explain.

2. This exercise examines the empirical relationship between per-capita
income (PCI) and infant mortality rates (IMR). The infant mortality
rate is defined as the number of infants who die before reaching age
one, per 1,000 live births. Below you will find 1983 data on PCI and
IMR for ten low-income and lower-middle-income countries (a small
sample is used to simplify the exercise).

Country	IMR	PCI (1983)
1. Bangladesh	132	130
2. Malawi	164	210
3. India	93	260
4. China	38	300
5. Sudan	117	400
6. Bolivia	123	510
7. Egypt	102	700
8. Thailand	50	820
9. Peru	98	1,040
10. Turkey	82	1,240

a. (i) Plot these ten observations on Figure 10−1 and draw an
(approximate) "best fit" straight line through the data points.
(ii) Comment on the relationship suggested by these data.

b. (i) Identify the country with the largest favorable deviation from
the apparent pattern, and the country with the largest
unfavorable deviation.

(ii) Comment on the factors that might be responsible for such
deviations.

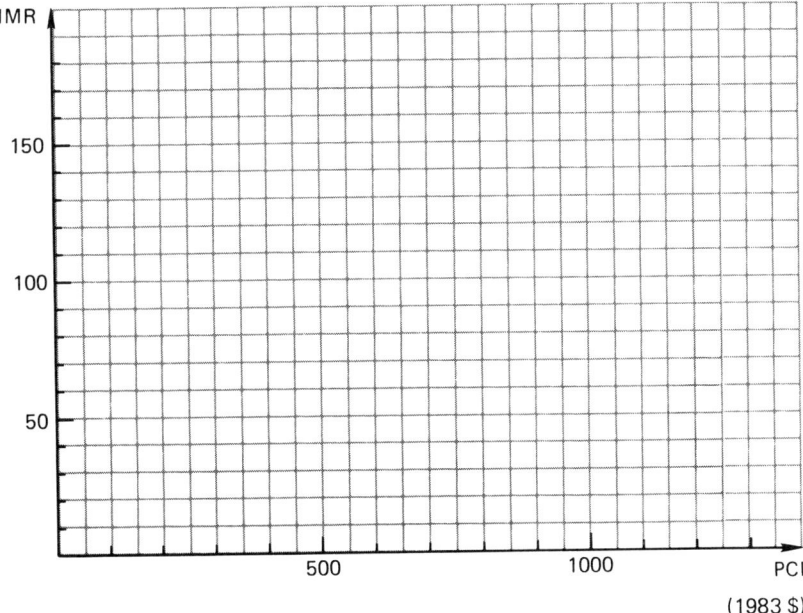

Figure 10-1

3. In this exercise you will evaluate the rate of return to an investment in better health. You may wish to refer to Chapters 6 or 9 to review the rate of return concept.

   A mosquito spraying project planned for 1988 in the province of Hinterland will cost 1,000,000 francs. Beneficial health effects in the form of a reduction in malaria are expected to last for two years. In economic terms, these benefits consist of three elements:

   —greater productivity for some existing workers;
   —an increase in the number of workers in the labor force; and
   —the direct value of better health, as a benefit in itself.

   a. Table 10–4 summarizes estimates that have been made of the value of each category of benefit. Some government planners consider the estimate of the direct health benefit to be far too subjective to include in the analysis.
      (i) Looking only at the production benefits (column 5 in Table 10–4), what is the net present value (NPV) of the project, using a discount rate of 15%?

      NPV = _____ thousand francs.

   (ii) What is the NPV using a discount rate of 10%?

      NPV = _____ thousand francs.

Table 10–4

Costs and Benefits of Health Project in Hinterland (thousands of francs)

Year	Cost (1)	Benefits			Production Benefits = (2) + (3) (5)	Total Economic Benefits = (2) + (3) + (4) (6)
		Productivity gains (2)	Output from increased labor force (3)	Value of health (4)		
1988	1,000	0	0	0	0	0
1989	0	100	500	200	600	800
1990	0	100	500	200	600	800

(iii) What is the internal rate of return on the project? Recall that the IRR is the discount rate for which NPV = 0.

$$IRR = \underline{\hspace{2cm}}\%.$$

[Hint: the above calculations guarantee that the IRR lies between 10% and 15%.]

b. Ministry of health officials, however, consider provision of basic human needs to be an important policy objective in its own right. Thus they prefer to include an estimate of direct health benefits in their appraisal of the project.
  (i) Using column 6 in Table 10–4, as the measure of benefits, what is the NPV using a discount rate of 15%?

$$NPV = \underline{\hspace{2cm}} \text{ thousand francs.}$$

  (ii) What is the NPV using a discount rate of 10%?

$$NPV = \underline{\hspace{2cm}} \text{ thousand francs.}$$

  You need not bother to calculate the IRR. In this case it is 38%.

c. The text claims that the rate of return on investments in health is very hard to quantify. Explain this contention in the context of the anti-malaria project in Hinterland.

4. This exercise illustrates the concept of cost-effectiveness.

   In the small African nation of Maskini, people eat only maize. The minimum consumption requirement for good health is 20 kilograms of maize per month per person. Figure 10–2 is a graph of the market for maize. It is more complicated than the usual supply-and-demand diagram, so study it carefully. Line S is the supply curve; it is horizontal to the right of point A because maize supplies beyond this point are imported at a fixed world price. Line D is the demand curve; its strange shape is explained below. The free market price is $P^0 = 15$ shillings per kilogram. At this price the minimum consumption requirement per person (20 kg) costs 300 shillings per month.

   a. Altogether 200 people live in Maskini. Half are poor. The poor earn only 150 shillings per month, and always spend 100% of their income on maize. Line D_p shows the quantity of maize demanded by the poor at various possible prices.

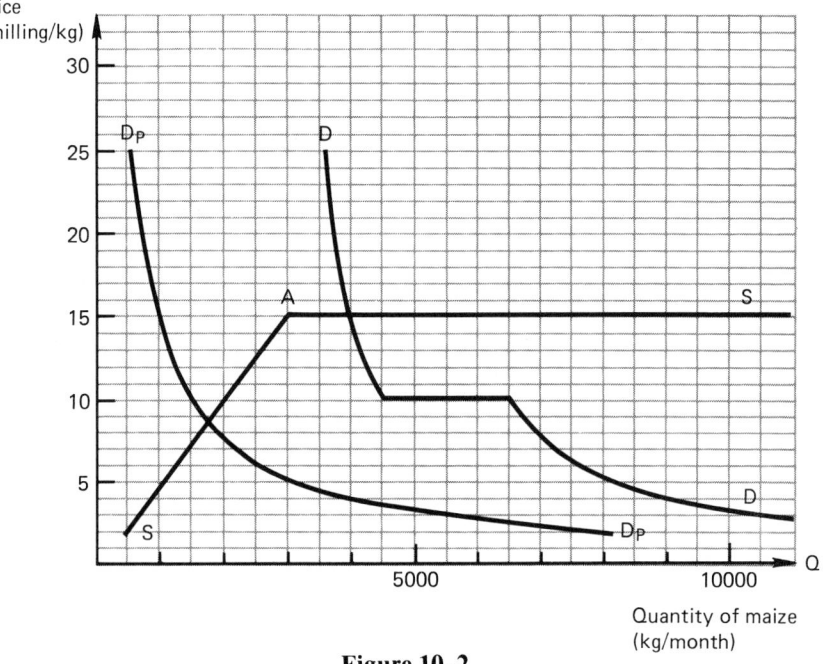

Figure 10-2

(i) At a price of:

15 sh per kg, the poor (all 100 of them) buy a total of

_____ kg per month;

10 sh per kg, the poor would demand _____
kg per month;

5 sh per kg, the poor would demand _____
kg per month.

(ii) Given their income level, the poor would be able to afford a nutritionally adequate amount of maize (20 kg per month per person) if the price fell to:

$$P^* = \text{_____} \ sh/kg.$$

b. For any possible price, the horizontal gap between line D_p and line D reflects the demand for maize by the 100 richer citizens of Maskini. These people have incomes high enough that they always eat their fill—exactly 30 kg per month each. So at the initial equilibrium price:

the 100 rich people are buying _____ kg per month;

the 100 poor people are buying _____ kg per month; and

total demand is _____ kg per month,

of which _____ kg per month are imported.

What about the kink in line D in Figure 10–2? This occurs because if the maize price were to drop to 10 shillings or less, the

-152-

rich people would buy an *extra* 2,000 kg per month as feed for their chickens, mules, dogs, and fish.

c. Now you are in a position to consider two alternative policies to provide adequate nutrition for Maskini's poor. The first (Policy 1), is for the government to assume control of maize marketing and sell maize at a price low enough so that the poor can afford a nutritious diet.

   (i) As seen in part a, the poor can afford to consume an adequate amount of maize only if the price were:

$$P* = \underline{\hspace{2cm}} \text{ sh/kg.}$$

   (ii) At this price:

   the poor (in aggregate) would buy \underline{\hspace{3cm}}
   kg per month;

   the rich would buy \underline{\hspace{3cm}} kg per month; and

   total demand would be \underline{\hspace{3cm}} kg per month.

   (iii) Total consumer expenditure ($P* \times Q$) on maize would be:

   \underline{\hspace{3cm}} shillings.

   (iv) Label the corresponding point on the demand curve D as *point X*.

   (v) To procure enough maize to satisfy this market demand, the government would pay a price of:

   \underline{\hspace{3cm}} shillings per kg.

   (vi) Label the corresponding point on the supply curve (S) as *point Y*.

   (vii) The government's total expenditure on maize is

   \underline{\hspace{3cm}} shillings,

   whereas the government's total revenue from selling the maize to consumers (you calculated this above) is:

   \underline{\hspace{3cm}} shillings.

   (viii) So the program would involve a net cost to the government of:

   \underline{\hspace{3cm}} shillings per month.

d. The second policy alternative (Policy 2) is to let the free market function while giving the poor food-stamp entitlements to extra maize imported and paid for by the government.

   (i) In part a you calculated that in the absence of such food stamps each poor person can afford to purchase only:

   \underline{\hspace{3cm}} kg per month of maize at the free-market price.

   (ii) So in order to raise the poor's maize consumption to the minimum nutrition standard, the government must provide each poor person with food-stamp entitlements good for an extra:

   \underline{\hspace{3cm}} kg per month of maize.

-153-

(iii) Considering that there are a total of 100 poor people in Maskini, the government must procure enough maize to augment the market supply by:

_____ kg per month

at a cost of _____ shillings per kg.

[Hint: Examine the supply curve.]

(iv) So Policy 2 would cost the government:

_____ shillings per month.

e. (i) To summarize the calculations, adequate nutrition for the poor can be provided at a cost to the government of:

_____ shillings per month under Policy 1 and

_____ shillings per month under Policy 2.

(ii) The required volume of extra maize imports would be:

_____ kg per month under Policy 1 and

_____ kg per month under Policy 2.

(iii) Discuss the cost-effectiveness of the two policy options.

5. *Optional* This exercise analyzes in more depth the demand for maize in Maskini as described in exercise 4.

a. (i) First consider only the poor. Exercise 4 provides enough information for you to calculate the income elasticity of demand for maize on the part of the poor. The value of this elasticity is:

_____.

(ii) Still considering only consumers who are poor, explain the income and substitution effects of a decline in maize price from $P = 15$ to $P = 5$.

b. (i) Now consider only the rich. What is the income elasticity of demand for maize on the part of this group?

elasticity = _____

(ii) Still considering only the rich, explain the income and substitution effects of a decline in the price of maize from 15 shillings to 5 shillings.

Answers to Self-Test

Completion

1. morbidity
2. WHO, World Health Organization
3. parasitic
4. barefoot, preventive
5. protein-calorie malnutrition
6. Oral rehydration therapy (ORT)
7. declining
8. increase
9. entitlement

True-False

1.	T	6.	F
2.	T	7.	T
3.	F	8.	F
4.	F	9.	F
5.	T		

Multiple Choice

1.	b	5.	a
2.	a	6.	a
3.	b	7.	c
4.	d	8.	d

CHAPTER 11   Capital and Saving

Overview

Although capital accumulation is no longer viewed as the central problem in economic development, saving and investment are indeed vital determinants of economic growth. Just as important as the level of investment is the efficiency of investment. Where capital is used less efficiently, a greater share of GDP must be saved in order to achieve any given growth rate. For most LDCs, investment's share of GDP has increased substantially over the past few decades. Most developing countries have made a significant effort to mobilize domestic savings. In addition, foreign saving has been an important source of investment finance. The record, however, varies greatly from country to country.

Domestic savings can be divided into two components: government savings and private savings. Development specialists once believed that increased domestic savings depended primarily on the government budget, implying a need to increase the ratio of taxes to GDP. But experience shows that government current expenditures have grown much more quickly than government revenues in most countries. Consequently, government savings have not contributed greatly to increased domestic savings rates. The available evidence indicates that the most important source of private domestic saving has been household saving, including saving out of income from unincorporated businesses. For this reason, the text examines household savings behavior in some detail.

Main Learning Objectives

After studying this chapter you ought to understand and be able to explain:

1. The relationship between the **investment ratio**, the efficiency of investment, and economic growth.

2. The empirical record of saving and investment in the developing countries.

3. The decomposition of total savings into **domestic savings** plus **foreign savings**, and the disaggregation into seven components as identified in text Equation 11−2.

4. The relation between tax revenues, **public sector consumption** expenditures, government **budgetary savings**, and total domestic savings.

5. The observed patterns of household savings behavior, and the economic theories of household savings that explain these patterns.

6. The importance of international capital mobility and especially how **capital flight** can be a major drain on domestic savings when policies discourage domestic investment.

Additional Key Terms, Concepts, and Institutions

Can you identify and explain each of the following?

capital fundamentalism
incremental capital-output ratio (ICOR)
tax ratio
foreign direct investment
marginal propensity to consume (MPC)
"Please effect"
permanent and transitory income

Economic Tools and Techniques

From what you have learned in this chapter, can you:

1. Apply the Harrod-Domar model (from Chapter 3) to analyze the relationship between GDP growth, investment ratios, and ICOR values, as in Table 11−2 of the textbook?

2. Calculate government savings from data on tax revenues and government expenditures?

3. Use text Equations 11−3 through 11−6 to explain how the Keynesian **absolute-income hypothesis**, the **relative-income hypothesis**, the **permanent-income hypothesis**, and the **class-savings hypothesis** relate to the observed patterns of household savings behavior?

Self-Test

Completion

1. To achieve sustained output growth of 6% per year with an ICOR equal to 5.0 requires an investment ratio of _____ %.

2. The view that the develpment problem is essentially one of securing resources for investment is called capital _____.

3. The "tax ratio" is the ratio of _____ to

_____ .

4. In 1983, both low- and middle-income countries, on average, had investment ratios that were _____ than the average for the industrial-market economies.

5. Private domestic savings arises from two sources: _____ savings and _____ savings.

6. The Please effect occurs when an increase in _____ leads to a lower level of total domestic savings.

7. According to the Keynesian absolute-income hypothesis, household savings are a simple function of current _____.

8. According to the permanent-income hypothesis, people save a higher proportion of _____ income as opposed to _____ income.

9. There is a strong tendency for rural households to save a _____ fraction of their income than urban households at comparable income levels.

10. Foreign private savings in the form of equity finance is called foreign _____ investment.

True-False If false, you should be able to explain why.

_____ 1. Sources-of-growth studies find that physical capital accumulation accounts for no more than half of the economic growth in the LDCs.

_____ 2. In most LDCs for which data are available, the value of the ICOR exceeds 5.0.

_____ 3. Two countries having the same investment ratio and the same ICOR must have the same rate of growth of per-capita income.

_____ 4. The group of low-income countries excluding China and India had lower domestic savings rates in 1983 than in 1960.

_____ 5. "Capital flight" refers to the movement of international capital into those LDCs whose policies favor investment and growth.

_____ 6. If the government's marginal propensity to consume (MPC) out of tax revenues exceeds the private sector's MPC out of income used to pay taxes, then higher taxes will lower total domestic savings.

_____ 7. Increased government budgetary savings have been a major source of growth in total domestic savings in most LDCs.

_____ 8. ICORs tend to be higher with capital-intensive investments than with labor-intensive investments.

_____ 9. Countries A and B are similar in all respects except that income is more stable in A. The permanent-income hypothesis suggests that savings rates should be higher on average in country A.

_____ 10. In LDCs the primary source of domestic savings is corporate savings.

Multiple Choice

1. If an LDC with a population growth rate of 2.4% seeks to increase real per-capita income by 3% per annum, then real GNP must grow by:
   a. 5.4% per annum.
   b. 3% per annum.
   c. 0.6% per annum.
   d. 7.2% per annum.

2. Text Table 11–3 shows that low-income countries other than India and China had a "resource gap" in 1983 equal to 11% of GDP. This figure refers to:
   a. the excess of government expenditures over revenues.
   b. the extent to which GDP fell short of the target.
   c. the excess of domestic investment over domestic savings.
   d. the extent to which domestic investment fell short of the target.

3. Which of the following items would not be included in the category of government consumption expenditure?
   a. Government spending on military hardware.
   b. Government expenditure on an irrigation project.
   c. Payment of teachers' salaries.
   d. None of the above is a government consumption expenditure.

4. A few countries actually had negative levels of domestic savings in 1983. This means that:
   a. GDP must have been declining.
   b. gross domestic investment must have been negative.
   c. aggregate consumption expenditures exceeded GDP.
   d. all of the above

5. Which of the following is one of the three observed patterns of household savings behavior discussed in the text?
   a. Within a country, higher-income households save a smaller fraction of their income than lower-income households.
   b. Within a country over time, household savings ratios tend to be roughly constant.
   c. Across countries, household savings ratios rise systematically with income.
   d. All of the above

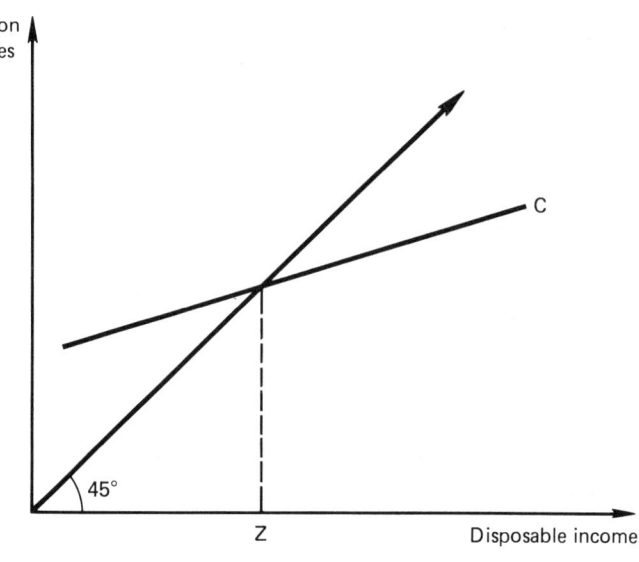

Figure 11-1

6. Figure 11-1 shows a Keynesian consumption function. When income rises above level Z:
   a. household savings become greater than consumption.
   b. household savings become positive.
   c. household consumption begins to exceed subsistence levels.
   d. total domestic savings become positive.

7. One model of household savings holds that workers save a much lower fraction of their income than do those who receive income primarily from property. This is:
   a. the class-savings model.
   b. the relative-income model.
   c. the permanent-income model.
   d. the Harrod-Domar model.

8. In the equation: $S = a + b_1 Y_p + b_2 Y_t$, expressing the permanent-income hypothesis, the term Y_t stands for _____ and the coefficient b_2 is _____ b_1.
   a. income at time t; less than
   b. income at time t; greater than
   c. transitory income; less than
   d. transitory income; greater than

Applications

Worked Example: Investment and Growth

Textbook Table 11-2 shows the interaction between investment (I), the ICOR, and growth. Here we will look behind the scenes to see where some of the numbers come from. Countries A and B both start in 1980 with GDP = Y = 1,000 and I = 150. The text example assumes that the growth rate of investment, $g(I)$, is constant. Two alternative values for $g(I)$ are explored. For present purposes, the "low rate," $g(I) = 5.0\%$ per annum, will be used. On this assumption investment grows from $I = 150$ in 1980 to:

$$I = 150(1.05) = 157.5 \text{ in } 1981;$$
$$I = 150(1.05)^2 = 165.4 \text{ in } 1982;$$
$$I = 150(1.05)^3 = 173.6 \text{ in } 1983;$$

and so on. At this growth rate, investment in 1990 would be $I = 150(1.05)^{10} = 244.3$.

The Harrod-Domar model studied in Chapter 3 can be written in the form $Y_{t+1} = Y_t + (I_t / \text{ICOR})$. If we know the values of Y, I, and the ICOR for any one year, we can compute the value of GDP for the subsequent year, and so on for each succeeding year. At the moment we know I_t for each year. Following the textbook we will let ICOR = 4 for country A and ICOR = 3 for country B. We also know $Y(1980)$ for each country. So we can compute $Y(1981)$:

$$\text{for A, } Y(1981) = 1{,}000 + (150/4) = 1{,}037.5 \text{ and}$$
$$\text{for B, } Y(1981) = 1{,}000 + (150/3) = 1{,}050.0.$$

And knowing $Y(1981)$, we can calculate $Y(1982)$:

$$\text{for A, } Y(1982) = 1{,}037.5 + (157.5/4) = 1{,}076.9 \text{ and}$$
$$\text{for B, } Y(1982) = 1{,}050 + (157.5/3) = 1{,}102.5.$$

And so on, generating the values shown in the text table, or beyond. For example, Table 11−1 shows the results for country A to 1990.

Over the period 1980 to 1990, GDP increases by just under 50% in country A. Similar calculations for country B (see exercise 1) show that with ICOR = 3 and identical investment levels, GDP would increase by over 60% during the decade.

Suppose the population in each country grows by 3% per year, or 34% for the decade $[(1.03)^{10} = 1.34]$. What is the increase in per-capita income for the decade? In country A, GDP increases by a factor of 1.47, while population increases by a factor of 1.34. Hence, per-capita GDP (= GDP/POP) will increase by a factor of $1.47/1.34 = 1.10$, or 10%. In exercise 1 you will compute the corresponding figure for country B, and

Table 11−1
GDP and Investment Projections to 1990, Country A

	1985	1986	1987	1988	1989	1990
Y_t	1,207.3	1,255.2	1,305.4	1,358.2	1,413.6	1,471.7
I	191.4	201.0	211.0	221.6	232.6	244.3
ICOR	4.0	4.0	4.0	4.0	4.0	4.0
Y_{t+1}	1,255.2	1,305.4	1,358.2	1,413.6	1,471.7	—

see that per-capita income in B increases more than twice as much as in A. This difference is wholly due to the difference in ICORs. If, more realistically, investment grows more quickly in B due to its higher income, then the disparity would be even more dramatic.

Exercises

1. Now its your turn to investigate the relationship between investment and growth.

    a. Table 11–2 below is set up for you to project country B's economic growth over the period 1985–1990. Country B's ICOR equals 3.0; its investment growth rate (5.0% per year) is identical to that of country A in the Worked Example. Country B's GDP for 1985 is taken from the example in the textbook. Complete Table 11–2 by finding GDP for the years 1986–1990.
    b. (i) In 1980, country B had a level of GDP = 1,000. So over the decade 1980–1990, the country's GDP grows by a factor of

    _____ .

    (ii) Suppose that the population grows by 3% per annum. This means that the population would increase by a factor of

    _____ over the decade.
    (iii) Per-capita income (GDP/POP) in B will rise by _____ %. In country A per-capita income rises by only 10%. What explains the difference?

    c. As the level of income (and income per-capita) in country B steadily increases relative to country A, one may assume that country B could afford more rapid investment growth. Let $g(I) =$ 10% after 1985 in country B. In Table 11–3 fill in the row showing the level of I for 1986 to 1989. Then complete the table by finding GDP for the years 1986 through 1990.

Table 11–2

GDP and Investment Projections to 1990, Country B

	1985	1986	1987	1988	1989	1990
Y_t	1,276.3	____	____	____	____	____
I	191.4	201.0	211.0	221.6	232.6	244.3
ICOR	3.0	3.0	3.0	3.0	3.0	3.0
Y_{t+1}	____	____	____	____	____	

Table 11-3

GDP and Investment Projections to 1990, Country B

	1985	1986	1987	1988	1989	1990
Y_t	1,276.3	———	———	1,487.5	———	———
I	191.4	———	———	———	———	308.3
ICOR	3.0	3.0	3.0	3.0	3.0	3.0
Y_{t+1}	———	———	———	———	———	

d. (i) Assuming $g(I) = 10\%$ per year after 1985, GDP in country B increases by a factor of _____ over the decade 1980–1990 (starting from GDP = 1,000 in 1980).

(ii) Still assuming 3% per year population growth, per-capita GDP will increase by _____ % for the decade.

e. (i) Beginning in 1985 with $Y = 1,207.3$, what annual rate of GDP growth would country A require over the ensuing five years to match the 1990 level of GDP achieved by country B in Table 11–3?

$$g(Y) = \text{_____} \% \text{ per year.}$$

[Hint: Work backwards from the 1990 target level of GDP to find $g(Y)$.]

(ii) With ICOR = 4, find the investment ratio that country A would require to achieve the growth rate that you just calculated. [Remember that $s = I/Y$ in the Harrod-Domar model.]

$$I/Y = \text{_____} \%.$$

(iii) In Table 11–3, country B achieves this level of income with an investment ratio in 1990 of:

$$I/Y = \text{_____} \%.$$

2. This exercise investigates some saving facts. Table 11–4 provides data on the 1983 level of per-capita income (PCI) and the 1973–1983 annual rate of growth (G) of real GDP for sixteen LDCs. You will find data on the savings ratios (S/Y) and investment ratios (I/Y) for these countries in Table 11–4 of the textbook. (Only those countries with PCI < $1,000 are used here to simplify the exercise.)

a. In Figure 11–2, PCI is measured on the horizontal axis and S/Y on the vertical axis. Plot the sixteen points representing the country data on PCI and S/Y. Draw in the approximate "best-fit" line showing the empirical relationship between P ̃I and S/Y.

Table 11–4

Per-Capita Income and GDP Growth Rates, Selected Countries

Country	Per-capita income (1983 U.S. $)	GDP growth 1973–1983 (% per annum)
Low-income countries		
Ethiopia	120	2.3
Bangladesh	130	5.2
Mali	160	4.1
Tanzania	240	3.6
India	260	4.0
China	300	6.0
Ghana	310	−1.3
Sri Lanka	330	5.2
Kenya	340	4.6
Pakistan	390	5.6
Middle-income countries		
Senegal	440	2.6
Bolivia	510	1.5
Indonesia	560	7.0
Egypt	700	8.8
Philippines	760	5.4
Nigeria	770	1.2

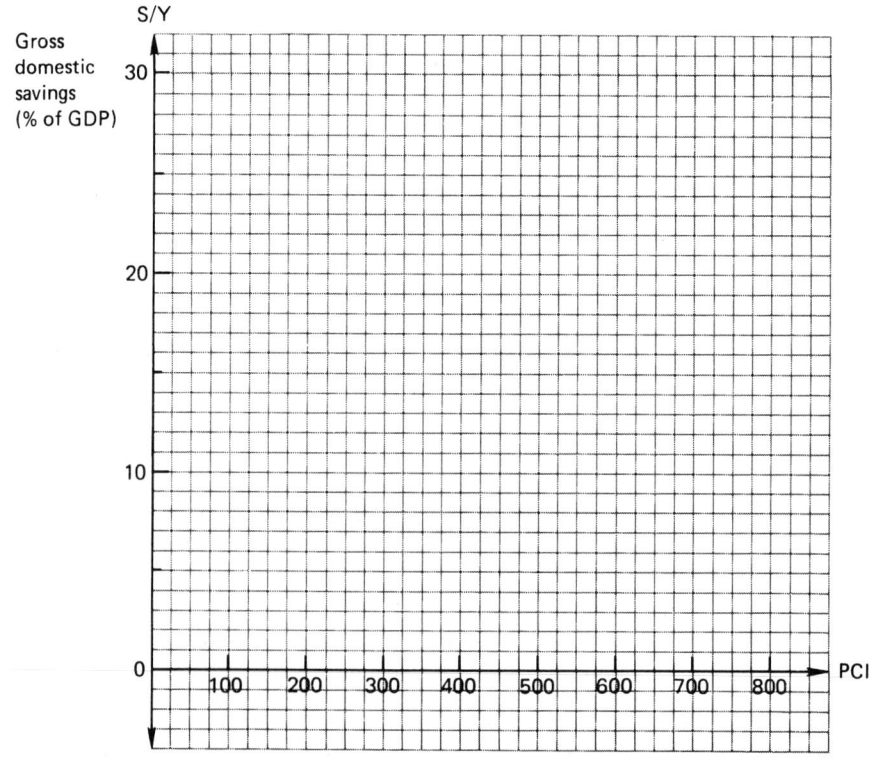

Source: *World Development Report 1985.*

Per capita income (1983 $)

Figure 11–2

-164-

b. Comment briefly on the results found in part a.

c. In Figure 11–3, I/Y is measured on the horizontal axis and G is measured on the vertical axis. Plot the sixteen points representing the country data on I/Y and G. Draw an approximate "best-fit" line showing the empirical relationship between I/Y and G.

d. Comment briefly on the results found in part c.

3. This exercise examines the relationship between domestic savings and investment.

a. Table 11–5 shows data relating to savings and investment in Thailand for the years 1975 and 1980.
    (i) Using these data, calculate government savings (S_g) as government revenue less current expenditures, and fill in the first line of Table 11–6.

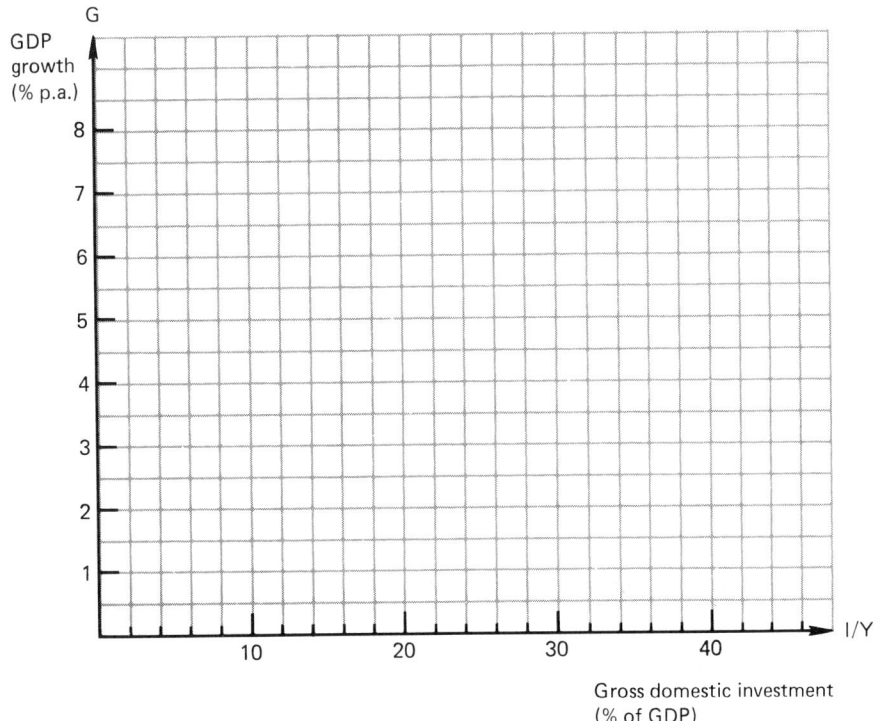

Figure 11–3

Table 11-5

Savings and Investment Data for Thailand, 1975 and 1980[a]

	1975	1980
Government budget		
Revenue	38.0	57.8
Current expenditure	34.9	59.2
Capital expenditure	9.3	18.0
Gross domestic product	298.8	429.9
Gross domestic savings	61.8	85.9
Gross domestic investment	75.8	116.9

Source: World Bank, *World Tables 1983.*
[a]All figures in billions of constant 1975 baht.

Table 11-6

	1975	1980
Government Savings (S_g)	_____	_____
Private Savings (S_p)	_____	_____
Private sector income (Y_p)	_____	_____

(ii) Calculate private savings (S_p) as the difference between gross domestic savings and government savings, and fill in the second line of Table 11-6.

(iii) Finally, calculate private-sector income (Y_p) as the difference between GDP and government tax revenue, then fill in the third line of Table 11-6.

b. The marginal propensity to save is calculated as:

$$MPS = (\text{change in savings})/(\text{change in income}).$$

(i) Over the period 1975–1980, the marginal propensity to save was:

MPS_g = _____ for the government sector, and

MPS_p = _____ for the domestic private sector.

(ii) Given these MPS figures, a transfer of 10 billion baht from the private sector to the government sector would cause total

domestic savings to _____ by _____ billion baht.

c. Define the "tax ratio" as the ratio of government revenue to GDP.

(i) Thailand's tax ratio went from _____ % in 1975 to _____ % in 1980.

(ii) Was the "Please effect" in operation here? Explain.

(iii) Would your answer change if you knew that in both 1980 and 1975 approximately one-third of government current expenditures went to health and education? Explain.

d. (i) Observe in Table 11−5 that gross domestic investment exceeded government savings. How can a government finance How can a country finance investment in excess of domestic savings?

(ii) Observe in Table 11−5 that government capital expenditures exceeded government savings. How can a government finance capital expenditures in excess of government savings?

4. In this exercise you will work with some of the models of household savings behavior discussed in the textbook.

a. According to the Keynesian absolute-income hypothesis, savings is a simple function of disposable income. Assume here that the savings function is:

$$S = -100 + 0.5Y^d.$$

(i) Calculate savings (S) and the savings ratio (S/Y^d) when:

		S	S/Y^d
$Y^d =$	200	_____	_____
	300	_____	_____
	400	_____	_____

(ii) In what way is this simple savings function inconsistent with the observed tendency of the household savings ratio to be roughly constant over time within a particular country?

b. According to Duesenberry's relative-income hypothesis, current consumption depends on past consumption habits as well as current disposable income. To illustrate this hypothesis, let the consumption function be:

$$C = -25 + 0.5 Y^d + 0.5 C_H.$$

(i) Suppose that the previous high level of consumption had been $C_H = 250$. Calculate C, S ($= Y^d - C$) and S/Y^d when:

		C	S	S/Y^d
$Y^d =$	200	_____	_____	_____
	300	_____	_____	_____
	400	_____	_____	_____

The savings behavior should look familiar.

(ii) In the long run, consumption habits change as income rises. Suppose, for example, that household consumption habits have adjusted to $Y^d = 400$ in such a way that $C_H = 310$. With these adjusted consumption habits, at $Y^d = 400$, we find that

$C =$ _____ and $S =$ _____.

(iii) In the short run (before C_H changed), $Y^d = 400$ produced

$S/Y^d =$ _____. But in the long run (after the adjustment

in C_H), $Y^d = 400$ produces $S/Y^d =$ _____. In the long run,

the savings ratio fluctuates much _____ than in the short run.

c. According to the permanent-income hypothesis, current consumption depends primarily on "permanent" income, and a large fraction of transitory income is saved. To illustrate this hypothesis, let the savings function be:

$$S = 0.167 Y_p + 0.5 Y_t,$$

where Y_t is the transitory component of current disposable income. Over time the transitory component averages out to zero.

(i) Suppose that households consider permanent income to be $Y_p = 300$. Calculate S and S/Y^d when:

		S	S/Y^d
$Y^d =$	200	_____	_____
	300	_____	_____
	400	_____	_____

The savings behavior should again look familiar.

(ii) In the long run, perceived permanent income rises as actual incomes rise. Suppose, for example, that households adjust to a level of permanent income of $Y_p = 400$. With this adjusted level of permanent income, when actual disposable income is

$Y_d = 400$, we find that $S =$ _____.

(iii) Using this model of savings behavior, in the short run (before Y_p adjusts), $Y^d = 400$ produces $S/Y^d =$ _____. But in the long run (after Y_p adjusts), $Y^d = 400$ produces $S/Y^d =$ _____.

d. Briefly explain how Kaldor's class theory reconciles short-run savings patterns with the tendency for savings to be a roughly constant fraction of disposable income in the long run.

Answers to Self-Test

Completion

1. 30%
2. fundamentalism
3. tax collections; GNP (or GDP)
4. higher
5. corporate; household
6. taxes
7. disposable income
8. transitory; permanent
9. higher
10. direct

True-False

1. T	6. T
2. F	7. F
3. F	8. T
4. T	9. F
5. F	10. F

Multiple Choice

1. a	5. b
2. c	6. b
3. b	7. a
4. c	8. d

CHAPTER 12   Fiscal Policy

Overview

As defined in the text, fiscal policy refers to government tax policy and decisions concerning government consumption expenditures. The primary focus of this chapter is on the relationship between fiscal policy and mobilization of domestic savings. Increasing government budget savings requires raising taxes relative to government consumption—a difficult task for developing countries. LDC governments face a double bind: The constraints on increasing tax revenues share an uneasy alliance with the pressing need for public services, which make it difficult to curb the growth of recurrent expenditures. Notwithstanding these difficulties, it is important for LDCs to establish an effective revenue system and prudent controls over the expansion of recurrent expenditures.

Mobilization of savings through the government budget is only part of the story. Government tax and spending policies also have a major influence on private sector savings and investment incentives, as well as on macroeconomic stability. Consequently, fiscal policy can have far reaching effects on capital formation and on the economic efficiency of resource allocation. Also discussed are the important income distribution effects of fiscal policy. Administrative and economic realities limit the extent to which tax policy can serve redistributive goals. Expenditure policy, however, can be an effective instrument for transferring resources to the poor.

Main Learning Objectives

After studying this chapter you ought to understand and be able to explain:

1. The main determinants of a country's **taxable capacity**, and the links between taxable capacity and **government savings**.

2. The potential for increasing tax revenues through higher **tax rates**, introduction of new types of taxes, improvements in **tax administration**, and **fundamental tax reform**.

3. The often limited scope for increasing government savings through curbing the growth of **recurrent expenditures**.

4. The effects of the tax structure on private domestic savings and on domestic investment incentives.

5. The uses and the practical limitations of tax and expenditure policies as instruments for redistributing income.

6. The importance of **ex-ante revenue elasticity** in the tax system to avoid growing **budget deficits** that can worsen inflation and **macroeconomic instability**.

7. How various taxes create **economic inefficiency**, and the desirability of **neutrality** in taxation.

Additional Key Terms, Concepts, and Institutions

Can you identify and explain each of the following?

fiscal policy vs. development policy
import tariffs or duties
sales and excise taxes
tax avoidance vs. tax evasion
Wagner's Law
provident fund
tax haven
tax holidays and tax credits
progressive vs. regressive taxes and expenditures
tax base

Economic Tools and Techniques

From what you have learned in this chapter, can you:

1. Explain the relationship between taxable capacity, **tax effort**, and **tax ratios**?

2. Explain how an increase in an import duty may fail to increase revenues because of the price elasticity of demand and the domestic supply response to "accidental" protection?

3. Explain the determinants of the **incidence** of a corporate profits tax or a property tax, in the short run and in the long run?

4. Calculate the revenue elasticity of a tax system, and show the relationship between ex-ante revenue elasticity and the income elasticity of the tax base?

5. Use the text's simple macroeconomic model to determine what government budget surplus (or deficit) is consistent with macroeconomic stability?

6. Analyze the **excess burden** of a commodity tax, and show why a neutral tax is not necessarily either an **efficient tax** or an **optimal tax**?

Self-Test

1. _____ taxes are taxes levied on consumption of specifically enumerated goods such as tobacco or fuel.

2. In the text, fiscal policy refers to Ministry of _____

   policies concerning taxes and government _____ expenditures.

3. A tax on an imported good is usually called an import

   _____ .

4. Tax avoidance involves taking advantage of legal arrangements to

   reduce tax payments, whereas tax _____ involves illegal maneuvers to reduce tax payments.

5. On balance, _____-based taxes are likely to be more favorable to growth of private savings than are income-based taxes.

6. Recognizing the international _____ of capital, many developing countries have fairly moderate tax rates on income from capital.

7. One type of investment incentive is a tax _____, wherein approved investments are exempted from income tax for a specified number of years.

8. _____ taxes are those that bear more heavily on citizens with greater ability to pay.

9. Tax _____ refers to the issue of whose income is ultimately affected by a tax, as distinct from who initially pays the tax to the government.

10. Tax _____ means that the same tax rate is applied to all elements of the tax base.

True-False If false, you should be able to explain why.

_____ 1. Import duties account for more than 50% of total tax revenues in a number of low-income countries.

_____ 2. In most LDCs the personal income tax provides only a minor share, generally under 20%, of total tax revenues.

_____ 3. Government budgetary savings equals the difference between total government revenues and total government expenditures.

_____ 4. In most LDCs, governments could easily increase revenues by improving tax administration to cut down on tax evasion.

_____ 5. Public-sector capital stock often deteriorates quickly due to underfinancing of recurrent maintenance costs in many LDCs.

_____ 6. For most LDCs the cost of government subsidy payments represents less than 2% of total government expenditures.

_____ 7. In most LDCs income tax revenues come almost entirely from taxpayers in the top 20% of the income distribution.

_____ 8. For all practical purposes corporate profit taxes are unambiguously progressive taxes.

_____ 9. Measures that enhance the revenue elasticity of the tax system generally make the tax system more progressive as well.

_____ 10. In theory, a higher tax rate might reduce tax revenues, but in practice, higher tax rates will always increase tax revenues in the context of developing countries.

Multiple Choice

1. Empirical studies consistently find that taxable capacity is most strongly related to a country's:
   a. total GNP.
   b. fuel and mineral production.
   c. openness.
   d. literacy rate.

2. If the price and income elasticities of demand for alcohol are low, then an increase in the excise tax rate on alcohol:
   a. will be regressive.
   b. will cause tax revenues to decline.
   c. will cause a large "excess burden."
   d. all of the above are correct.

3. Wagner's Law states that the _____ size of the public sector tends to _____ as per-capita income increases.
   a. relative, increase
   b. absolute, increase
   c. relative, decrease
   d. absolute, decrease

4. A provident fund is a fund that serves the purpose of:
   a. stabilizing foreign exchange reserves.
   b. cushioning the government budget from cyclical declines in tax revenues.
   c. financing social security programs.
   d. financing disaster- and famine-relief programs.

5. The term "tax haven" refers to:
   a. a country with a high tax effort.
   b. a high-priority industry that is granted a tax holiday.
   c. an industry such as minerals or fuels that provides a major source of tax revenue.
   d. a country that attracts substantial capital inflows as a result of very low tax rates on capital income.

6. Recent studies of irrigation projects in Southeast Asia concluded that:
   a. benefits accrued primarily to wealthy large farmers.
   b. large farmers gained at the expense of small farmers.
   c. small farmers and landless laborers experienced significant gains in income.
   d. small farmers benefited but incomes for landless laborers declined.

7. Which of the following taxes generally does not have an income-elastic tax base in LDCs?
   a. a personal income tax
   b. an excise tax on tobacco
   c. an excise tax on luxury consumption items
   d. a sales tax that exempts sales of food

8. As a general principle, an effective tax system in a developing country should *not*:
   a. have a revenue elasticity less than one.
   b. be progressive.
   c. include taxes on wealth or property.
   d. all of the above.

Applications

Worked Example: Tax Rates and Tax Revenues

A wave of purchases by the teenagers of Buibui have made Spider-comrade T-shirts the country's major import. These T-shirts are imported at a cost of $5, or Sh50 (50 shillings) each. The demand curve for T-shirts, curve DD in Figure 12–1, is drawn so that the price elasticity at any point is equal to -3.0. Initially the T-shirts are imported duty free, so the domestic price is equal to the world price of $P_0 = $ Sh50. At this price, $Q_0 = 1,000$ T-shirts per day are bought. The government then decides to levy an import duty of $t = $ Sh20 per Spidercomrade T-shirt. As a result, the domestic price rises to $P_1 = $ Sh70 ($=$ the world price plus the tariff). Consequently, the quantity demanded drops to $Q_1 = 364$ (see Figure 12–1). The government's tariff revenue equals $R_1 = $ Sh7,280 ($= 364 \times 20$).

In an effort to collect even more revenue, the government decides to double the tariff to $t = $ Sh40 per T-shirt. The new tariff causes the domestic price to rise to $P_2 = $ Sh90. At this new price the demand curve shows that consumers will buy only $Q_2 = 171$. So government revenue from the duty totals only $R_2 = $ Sh6,840 ($= 171 \times 40$). The tax officials are chagrined to find that tariff revenues have actually dropped as a result of this higher duty.

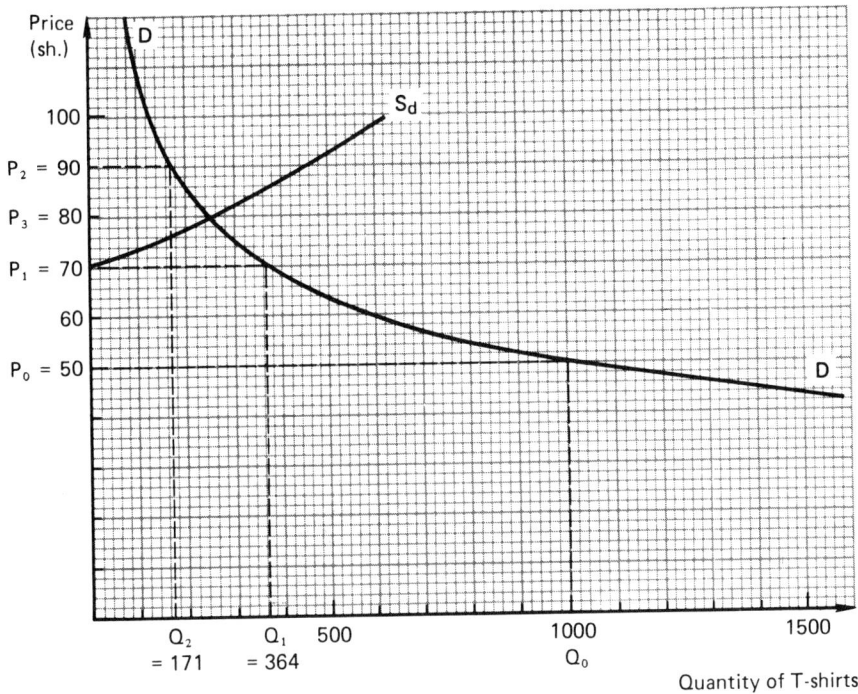

Figure 12-1

They are even more chagrined to find that the high duty-ridden price
of imports soon sprouts a new domestic industry. Businessmen begin to
import blank T-shirts at $5 per shirt, silk-screen the Spidercomrade logo,
and sell their product for $P_3 = $ Sh80. In Figure 12-1 curve S_d shows the
domestic supply curve for the T-shirts. You can see that domestic production becomes profitable when the domestic price of imported shirts
rises above Sh70. As a result of this domestic supply response to what
the textbook calls **accidental protection**, imports of Spidercomrade
T-shirts drop to zero. And so do import duties. The increased tax **rates**
have led to a precipitous drop in tax **revenues**. An attempt to levy a
tariff on blank T-shirts fails due to lobbying by the new domestic Spidercomrade T-shirt industry.

Had the tariff remained at Sh20 per shirt, tax revenues would have
grown over time at a rate that depends on the **income** elasticity of
demand. On the graph the demand curve would shift outward as domestic
incomes increase. If the income elasticity of demand equals 1.5, then a
10% increase in incomes would increase the quantity of T-shirts demanded
by 15%: from 364 to 419 (= 364 × 1.15). This 15% increase in the tax
base would cause tax **revenues** to rise by the same percentage, leading to
an increase in the tax ratio. With an income-elastic tax base, the tax
system has **built-in (ex-ante)** revenue elasticity. Together with prudent
controls on the growth of public consumption expenditures, such revenue
elasticity facilitates public-sector investment and contributes to macroeconomic stability.

1. This exercise gives you a turn to investigate the relationship between tax rates and tax revenues in Buibui, as discussed in the Worked Example.

    a. Some of the price-quantity combinations from the demand curve DD in Figure 12−1 are listed in Table 12−1. The three completed rows (for prices of Sh50, Sh70, and Sh90) were discussed in the Worked Example. Note that the domestic supply response is being ignored temporarily.

        (i) Given the world price of Sh50 per Spidercomrade T-shirt, the domestic price depends on the tariff rate (so many shillings per shirt). Fill in column 3 of Table 12−1 with the tariff rate corresponding to each price.

        (ii) Then fill in column 4 of Table 12−1 with the amount of revenue the government would collect with each tariff rate. [Hint: Revenue = $t \times Q$.]

    b. (i) From among the various tariff rates shown in Table 12−1, government tariff revenues will be maximized when the tariff is:

    $t^* = $ Sh _____ per T-shirt,

    and the domestic price is:

    $P^* = $ Sh _____ per T-shirt.

Table 12–1
Tariff Revenues in Buibui

Price (shillings) (1)	Quantity (2)	Tariff (Sh per T-shirt) (3)	Tariff revenue* (4)
50	1,000	0	0
55	751	_____	_____
60	579	_____	_____
65	455	_____	_____
70	364	20	7,280
75	296	_____	_____
80	244	_____	_____
85	204	_____	_____
90	171	40	6,840

(ii) Briefly explain why tax collections would decline if the tariff rate is increased beyond t^*.

c. Now let's stop ignoring the domestic supply response.

(i) Look at the domestic supply curve S_d in Figure 12–1. What quantity of Spidercomrade T-shirts will be produced domestically when the tariff rate is t^* and the price is P^* (from part b)?

$Q_s =$ _____ T-shirts.

(ii) Given the quantity demanded and the quantity supplied domestically at price P^*, what quantity will be imported at this price?

$Q_m =$ _____ T-shirts.

(iii) So what will be the actual amount of government tariff revenue when the tariff level is t^*?

Revenue $=$ Sh _____ .

(iv) Briefly explain why government revenues from a tariff of t^* fall so far short of the amount you calculated when completing Table 12–1.

(v) Taking into account the domestic supply response, the government would actually maximize revenues with a tariff rate of:

$t' =$ Sh _____ per T-shirt.

[Note: limit your attention to those tariff rates shown in Table 12–1.]

d. Suppose that the government had adopted an excise tax on Spidercomrade T-shirts, instead of an import duty. The excise tax is levied on domestically produced units as well as imports.

(i) With the excise tax, what revenue would the government collect at a tax rate of Sh25 per shirt?

Revenue $=$ Sh _____ .

(ii) What revenue would the government collect with a tax of Sh40 per shirt?

Revenue = Sh _____ .

e. (i) Which type of tax—the excise tax or the import duty—is superior in terms of neutrality? Explain.

(ii) With the excise tax, would a tax rate higher than Sh20 per shirt stimulate domestic production in place of imports? Explain.

(iii) Considering that production of Spidercomrade T-shirts is a very low priority use of domestic resources in the development plan for Buibui, which tax is superior in terms of resource-allocation efficiency? Explain.

(iv) Which type of tax is likely to have lower tax administration costs? Explain.

2. This exercise examines the relationship between a country's taxable capacity, its tax effort, its tax ratio, and its domestic savings.
   Suppose that statistical analysis has found that taxable capacity (call it TC) is related to a country's level of per-capita income (PCI) and to natural resource exports (NRE) as a percentage of GDP. Let Equation 12–1 summarize the average statistical relationship:

$$TC = 10 + 0.005 \text{ PCI} + 0.9 \text{ NRE,} \qquad [12-1]$$

where TC is measured as a percentage of GDP.

a. (i) In 1982–83 Pakistan had a per-capita income level of $390 and NRE equal to 1% of GDP. Plug these figures into Equation 12–1 to calculate the estimated value of Pakistan's taxable capacity:

$$TC(Pak) = \underline{\hspace{1cm}}\%.$$

(ii) In 1982–83 Peru had a per-capita income level of $1,040 and NRE equal to 14% of GDP. Plug these figures into Equation 12–1 to calculate the estimated value of Peru's taxable capacity:

$$TC(Per) = \underline{\hspace{1cm}}\%.$$

(iii) Of these two countries, _____ had the higher taxable capacity. Briefly explain why the taxable capacity was higher in this country.

b. The actual tax ratio in 1982–83 was 17% for Peru and 15% for Pakistan. Recall that tax effort is the extent to which a country uses its taxable capacity to increase its tax ratio.

(i) Peru has a higher tax ratio and a higher taxable capacity. Does Peru also have a higher tax effort? Explain briefly.

(ii) Even though Pakistan has a lower tax ratio, it has a higher level of government budgetary savings—4% of GDP versus 2% for Peru. How can a country with less tax revenue have more government budgetary savings? Be specific.

c. Suppose the government of Peru were to increase its tax ratio up to the level of its estimated tax capacity.
   (i) Would government budgetary savings necessarily increase as a result of the improved tax effort? Explain briefly.

   (ii) Would total domestic savings necessarily increase as a result of the improved tax effort? Explain briefly.

3. This exercise presents a revenue elasticity problem.

   a. The government of Bazooka relies for its revenues on an income tax. The tax code is very simple: there is a flat-rate tax of 30% on income above the subsistence level of $100 per person.
      (i) Initially, each person earns $Y_0 = \$140$ per year. The amount of tax revenue collected by the government is then:

   $$T_0 = \$\text{_____} \text{ per person.}$$

      (ii) A decade later, the same tax code is in place but everyone earns $200 per year. The amount of tax revenue collected by the government is then:

   $$T_1 = \$\text{_____} \text{ per person.}$$

   b. (i) Over the decade, incomes rise by:

   $$\text{_____} \%.$$

      [Note: Here, use the formula from Footnote 25 in the textbook. This formula calculates $\Delta Y/Y$ using as the denominator the mid-point value of Y between Y_0 and Y_1. And the same for $\Delta T/T$, below.]
      (ii) Over the decade, tax revenues rise by:

   $$\text{_____} \%.$$

      (iii) What is the numerical value of the built-in, or ex-ante revenue elasticity of Bazooka's tax structure?

   $$\epsilon_R = \text{_____} .$$

   c. Suppose that during the decade, the government increased the tax rate from 30% to 50%, while continuing to apply the tax only to income in excess of $100.
      (i) Assume that incomes increase, as above, to $200 per person. The amount of tax revenue collected by the government at the end of the decade would then be:

   $$T_1' = \$\text{_____} \text{ per person.}$$

(ii) In this case, tax revenues over the decade would have risen by:

_____ %.

(iii) What is the numerical value of the ex-post revenue elasticity, taking into account both the built-in change in tax revenue and the legislated increase in the tax rates?

$\epsilon_R =$ _____ ex post

vs. _____ ex ante

d. (i) Is it plausible to assume that incomes increase by the same amount whether the tax rate is 30% or 50%? Explain briefly.

(ii) A second assumption is hidden in the above calculation: that the government of Bazooka succeeds in collecting 50% of incomes above subsistence as mandated by the new tax law. Explain why this assumption is very likely to be unrealistic, especially for a low-income country like Bazooka.

4. This exercise applies the textbook's macroeconomic stabilization model to determine the desirable size of the government surplus or deficit. To simplify the model, the exercise follows the text in assuming that net exports equal zero.

a. (i) The basic condition for macroeconomic stability is that total

planned _____ must equal total planned savings.
(ii) This condition can be expressed algebraically by the equation (fill in the blanks):

$$\text{_____} + I_p = \text{_____} + S_p \qquad [12\text{--}2]$$

b. Suppose that private-sector planned savings is $S_p = 15\%$ of GDP. But many private-sector savers place their funds into foreign bank accounts, either legally or illegally, so that private-sector planned investment is $I_p = 9\%$ of GDP.
(i) Given this disparity between S_p and I_p, macroeconomic stability

requires that government _____ exceed govern-

ment _____ by _____% of GDP. [Hint: Check your answer by plugging the numbers into equation 12–2.]
(ii) If government investment is $I_g = 8\%$ of GDP, government savings should be:

$$S_g = \text{_____} \% \text{ of GDP.}$$

c. Let's see what these numbers imply about the government budget balance. Recall that government savings is defined as the excess of total tax revenues (T) over and above government consumption expenditures (G). In symbols, $S_g = T - G$.

(i) Continuing the numerical example, if $I_g = 8\%$ of GDP, then macroeconomic stability requires that:

$$T - G = \underline{\hspace{1cm}}\% \text{ of GDP.}$$

(ii) In other words, $I_g - (T - G) = \underline{\hspace{1cm}}\%$ of GDP.

(iii) Consequently, $(I_g + G) - T = \underline{\hspace{1cm}}\%$ of GDP.

(iv) And therefore, macroeconomic stability requires a government

budget \underline{\hspace{2cm}} (surplus or deficit?) equal to

\underline{\hspace{1cm}}\% of GDP. [Note: The required government budget condition is independent of the value used for I_g. Do you see why?]

d. Still assuming that $I_p = 9\%$ and $S_p = 15\%$, suppose that the government were to run a balanced budget. This means that total government expenditures are exactly equal to tax revenues, or:

$$I_g + G = T.$$

(i) In this case, what is the relationship between I_g and S_g? Be precise.

(ii) With a balanced government budget, the macroeconomic stability condition expressed in Equation 12–2 is no longer

satisfied. In particular, total planned \underline{\hspace{2cm}} now

exceeds total planned \underline{\hspace{2cm}} for the economy.

(iii) Why does this imbalance between total planned savings and investment mean that there will not be macroeconomic stability? Is the result a macroeconomic contraction, or an inflationary expansion? Explain briefly.

e. In the textbook discussion of this model, a government budget surplus is required for macroeconomic stability. You should have found that a deficit is required in the present exercise. What accounts for the difference?

5. The textbook discusses in some detail the incidence of the corporate profits tax. In this exercise you will analyze the incidence of excise taxes.

   a. Figure 12–2 shows the supply and demand for turbans in Hatistan. Note that demand is fairly inelastic, whereas supply is quite elastic. The initial equilibrium market price is $P_0 = $ Rs10 (10 rupees). The equilibrium quantity is Q_0. Now let the government impose an excise tax of Rs5 per turban.
      (i) The supply curve will shift position to reflect the tax. For example, output Q_0 would now be supplied at a market price of Rs10 *plus* the tax, or Rs15. Each point on the supply curve similarly shifts upward by the amount of the tax. Carefully draw in the new market supply curve; label it $S'S'$.
      (ii) The new equilibrium price in the turban market will be:

$$P_1 = \text{Rs}\underline{\hspace{1cm}} \text{ (to the nearest integer).}$$

      (iii) Why does the equilibrium price rise by less than the amount of the tax? Explain briefly.

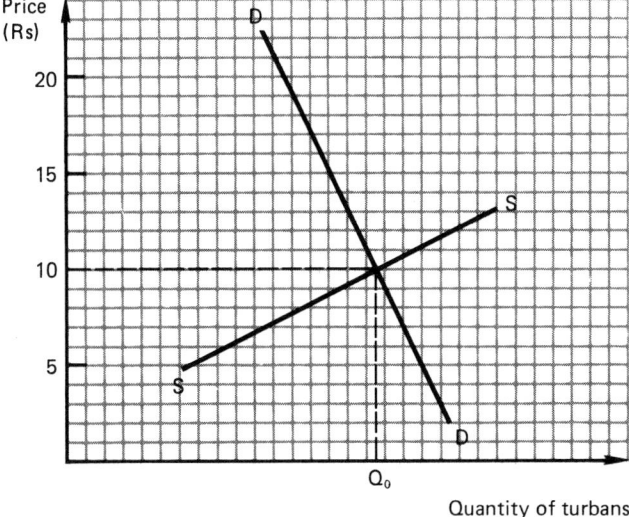

Figure 12–2

-183-

b. (i) At the new equilibrium price the turban sellers are actually

   receiving a net revenue of Rs_____ per hat, after taking out
   the Rs5 that goes to the government.

   (ii) Compared to the pre-tax market equilibrium, consumers now

   pay Rs_____ per hat more than before, while sellers receive

   (net) Rs_____ per hat less than before. [Hint: these two
   answers sum to Rs5, the amount collected by the government
   on each hat.]

   (iii) In this simple example, the incidence of the tax is:

   consumers bear _____% of the tax burden and

   sellers bear _____% of the tax burden.

c. Figure 12−3 shows the supply and demand for mangoes in
   Hatistan. Note that demand for mangoes is fairly elastic, whereas
   supply is quite inelastic—just the opposite of the turban market.
   The initial equilibrium market price is P_0 = Rs10 (10 rupees) per
   bag. The equilibrium quantity is Q_0. Now suppose that the
   government imposes an excise tax of Rs5 per bag of mangoes.

   (i) Carefully draw in the new market supply curve; label it $S'S'$.

   (ii) The new equilibrium price in the mango market will be:

   $$P_1 = Rs\text{_____} \text{ per bag.}$$

d. (i) At the new equilibrium price, the mango sellers actually

   receive a net revenue of Rs_____ per bag, after taking out
   the Rs5 that goes to the government.

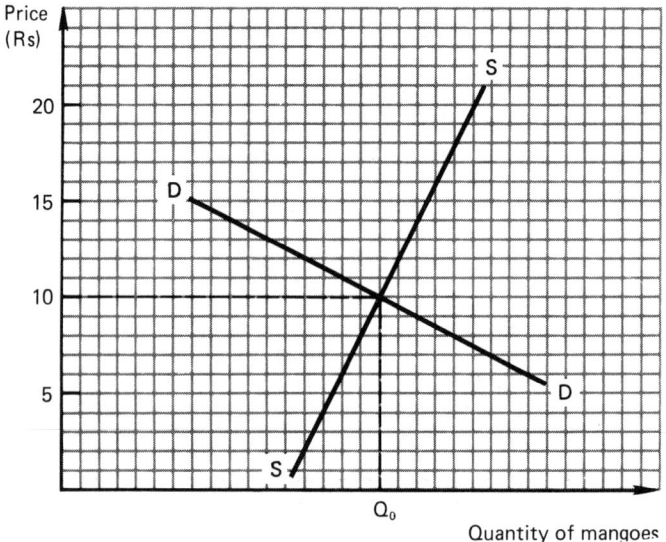

Figure 12–3

(ii) Compared to the pre-tax market equilibrium, consumers are

now paying Rs_____ per bag more than before, while sellers

are receiving (net) Rs_____ per bag less than before.
(iii) In this example, the incidence of the tax is:

consumers bear _____ % of the tax burden and

sellers bear _____% of the tax burden.

e. Consider the longer-run effects in the mango market.
(i) Following imposition of the excise tax on mangoes the profit-

ability of growing mangoes will _____.
(ii) In the short run, producers will not chop down mango trees
and put up banana trees. But in the long run the tax-induced
change in the profit rate will cause mango capacity to

_____.

(iii) In the mango market the long-run change in the stock of

mango trees will cause the _____ curve to shift

to the _____.
(iv) In the long run, the equilibrium price of mangoes will there-

fore be _____ than P_1.
(v) Therefore, in the long run consumers will bear a

_____ share of the tax burden than in the short

run.

6. *Optional* The graphs from exercise 5 are used here to study the
excess burden of the excise taxes on turbans and mangoes. Unlike
Figure 12−1 of the textbook, the supply curves here are not assumed
to be horizontal. Because of this, a brief explanation is required.

With competitive markets the height of the (pre-tax) supply curve
at each point represents the social opportunity cost of producing the
marginal unit of output. The height of the demand curve corresponds
to the social value of that same unit of output when consumed. The
vertical gap between the two curves at any value of Q thus shows the
gain in total welfare achieved from having the marginal unit of output
produced and consumed. Hence, the area enclosed by the supply and
demand curves over any interval along the horizontal axis represents
the welfare gain when the units of output in that interval are produced and consumed. Or, this area represents the welfare loss when
those units of output don't get produced and consumed.

a. In Figure 12−2 shade in the triangle corresponding to the welfare
loss caused by the drop in turban production and consumption
due to the excise tax.

b. In Figure 12–3 shade in the triangle corresponding to the welfare loss caused by the short-run drop in mango production and consumption due to the excise tax.

c. Review the textbook's Figure 12–1 so you understand the rectangle showing the amount of tax revenue collected by the government. You should be able to visualize how such rectangles can be drawn in Figures 12–2 and 12–3 here. Briefly explain why these rectangles are not added onto the welfare loss triangles in order to measure the excess burden of a tax. After all, they do represent a loss to consumers and producers.

d. In Figures 12–2 and 12–3 here, equal tax rates are imposed on turbans and mangoes. Prove that the resulting excess burdens are *not* equal. [Hint: for a triangle, area = 1/2 base × height.]

Answers to Self-Test

Completion

1. Excise
2. Finance; consumption (or recurrent)
3. duty (or tariff)
4. evasion
5. consumption
6. mobility
7. holiday
8. Progressive
9. incidence
10. neutrality

True-False

1. T		6. F	
2. T		7. T	
3. F		8. F	
4. F		9. T	
5. T		10. F	

Multiple Choice

1. b		5. d	
2. a		6. c	
3. a		7. b	
4. c		8. a	

CHAPTER 13   Financial Policy

Overview

In developing countries financial policy encompasses a broad range of measures to influence the operation and development of the financial system, as well as monetary tools for macroeconomic stabilization. The financial system, in turn, serves functions that are essential to development and growth, including the vital role of financial intermediation in mobilizing and allocating private domestic savings.

After surveying these fundamentals, Chapter 13 turns to an assessment of inflationary financial policies in developing countries. The text contends that the disadvantages of inflation far outweigh any potential positive effects on savings, investment, and efficiency. The adverse impact of inflation on real interest rates is emphasized, because real interest rates strongly affect the mobilization of savings through the financial system. Sharply negative real interest rates cause the financial system to grow slowly or even to shrink (shallow finance). Avoidance of such negative real interest rates is a key to promoting the growth of financial intermediation (deep finance).

Finally, the chapter discusses how monetary policy affects a country's inflation rate. The factors that determine the growth rate of the money supply are explained, together with monetary policy instruments commonly employed in developing countries. A major conclusion is that fiscal policy deficits and changes in international reserves often constrain the ability of monetary authorities to control the growth of the money supply.

Main Learning Objectives

After studying this chapter you ought to understand and be able to explain:

1. The role of **financial policy** and the functions of the **financial system** —especially the role of **financial intermediation** in mobilizing and allocating savings.

2. The meaning and significance of fundamental terms such as **central bank, commercial bank, narrow money** (M_1), and **broad money** (M_2).

3. The diversity of inflation experience among developing countries since 1950, and the pros and cons of inflation as a device to mobilize domestic savings.

4. The effect of inflation on **real interest rates** and on the demand for **liquid financial assets**.

5. The characteristics and the economic consequences of **deep finance** in contrast to **shallow finance**.

6. The causes and the consequences of excessive money-supply growth.

7. The monetary policy instruments used to control inflation in developing countries.

Additional Key Terms, Concepts, and Institutions

Can you identify and explain each of the following?

monetization ratio
checking deposits and time deposits
chronic, acute, and runaway inflation
life-cycle hypothesis, and permanent-income hypothesis
informal credit market
fixed vs. floating exchange rate
managed float, crawling peg and adjustable peg
credit ceilings

Economic Tools and Techniques

From what you have learned in this chapter, can you:

1. Calculate the implicit tax rate on holdings of money at a given rate of inflation?

2. Calculate the real interest rate, given the **nominal interest rate**, the inflation rate, and the tax rate on interest income?

3. Explain how changes in **international reserves** under a fixed-exchange rate system limit the ability of the central bank to control the money supply?

4. Work through a numerical example of how government budget deficits relate to **domestic credit creation**, expansion of the money supply, and inflation?

Self-Test

Completion

1. A low-income country in which a sizable fraction of economic activity is transacted without the use of formal money is said to have a low _____ ratio.

2. The textbook uses the term _____ inflation to describe inflation in excess of 50% for more than three years.

3. Inflation acts as a tax on holdings of _____ balances.

4. Rapid inflation inhibits private-sector long-term investments because it increases the degree of _____ in investment decisions.

5. When real interest rates on deposits become _____, savers strongly tend to increase their holdings of liquid financial assets.

6. A deep-finance policy _____ the economy's capacity for financial intermediation.

7. The essence of a deep-finance policy is the avoidance of sharply negative _____.

8. As the formal financial system expands and develops, the informal credit market tends to _____ in size and coverage.

9. Changes in the domestic money supply can be broken down into two components: expansion of _____, and changes in international reserves.

10. Under a _____-exchange rate system, a country's central bank has very limited control over the international component of changes in the domestic money supply.

True-False If false, you should be able to explain why.

_____ 1. A commercial bank that is located in the capital city is called a central bank.

_____ 2. The ratio of liquid financial assets to GDP is often used as an approximate measure of the extent of financial intermediation in developing countries.

_____ 3. Most LDCs have suffered chronic inflation, as defined in the text, for most of the period since 1950.

_____ 4. If nominal interest rates are held constant, then real interest rates will drop as the inflation rate increases.

_____ 5. If the income elasticity of demand for liquid assets is above unity, then price stability is not necessarily threatened when the broad money supply grows more quickly than income.

_____ 6. Shallow finance tends to lower the efficiency of investment and increase the capital-output ratio for the economy.

_____ 7. Markets for stocks and bonds evolve most rapidly in countries where the commercial banking system is poorly developed due to shallow financial policies.

_____ 8. In the LDCs, as in the developed countries, open market operations are the most widely used monetary policy instrument.

_____ 9. The government budget deficit in most LDCs is financed primarily by borrowing from the country's central bank, a process that causes an increase in the money supply.

_____ 10. If monetary authorities combat inflation by restricting domestic credit creation, then a large government budget deficit means that little bank credit can be extended to the private sector.

Multiple Choice

1. Which of the following assets is included in the broad money supply (M_2), but not in the narrow money supply (M_1)?
   a. checking deposits
   b. time deposits
   c. both a and b
   d. None of the above; in LDCs, M_1 and M_2 are identical.

2. Which of the following statements about inflation in the LDCs has proved generally to be valid?
   a. Even moderate growth of per-capita income cannot be sustained in a country with double-digit inflation.
   b. The efficiency losses from an inflation tax are small relative to those from a conventional tax.
   c. Government's marginal propensity to invest out of inflation taxes is unity or greater.
   d. None of the above.

3. In most developing countries the ratio of liquid assets to GDP is in the range of:
   a. 1–10%.
   b. 10–50%.
   c. 50–100%.
   d. 100–300%.

4. According to the life-cycle hypothesis, the effect of real interest rates on domestic savings is _____; according to the permanent-income hypothesis the effect is _____.
   a. zero; also zero.
   b. positive; also positive.
   c. positive; negative.
   d. positive; zero.

5. Which of the following is characteristic of shallow finance?
   a. The ratio of liquid assets to GDP grows slowly or even declines.
   b. Sharply negative real interest rates.
   c. Pervasive nonprice rationing of credit.
   d. All of the above.

6. In Peru from 1974 to 1982, nominal interest rates rose from 5% to 55% but real interest rates fell from −19% to −43%. From these observations one can infer that:
   a. inflation grew much worse.
   b. there was rapid financial deepening.
   c. the banking system was a monopoly.
   d. there was a large government budget surplus.

7. Where authorities intervene in the foreign exchange market at their discretion without being committed to defending a particular exchange rate, the exchange rate regime is called:
   a. a managed float.
   b. a crawling peg.
   c. an adjustable peg.
   d. any of the above; they are synonymous.

8. The textbook's boxed example on the austral plan in Argentina shows:
   a. the importance of controlling government budget deficits in order to control inflation.
   b. the importance of controlling the growth of the money supply in order to control inflation.
   c. that runaway inflation can be brought under control quickly with an appropriate set of policies.
   d. all of the above.

9. Which of the following instruments of monetary control is widely used in LDCs, but only infrequently used in developed countries?
   a. changes in reserve requirements
   b. credit ceilings imposed by the central bank
   c. changes in the rediscount rate
   d. moral suasion

10. In LDCs, sharply negative real interest rates are generally:
    a. an explicit policy objective of the monetary authorities.
    b. encouraged because they induce savers to invest directly rather than hold liquid financial assets.
    c. a result of inflexibly controlled nominal interest rates during a period of increasing inflation.
    d. a major instrument for combating inflation.

Applications

Worked Example: Inflation and Real Returns on Financial Assets

In an inflationary environment nominal interest rates overstate the real cost of borrowing as well as the real return to lending or holding financial assets. Suppose that the (nominal) interest rate on a one-year loan is 15% (so $i = 0.15$). A bank that lends $1,000 at this rate will be repaid an amount of $1,000(1 + i) = \$1,150$ one year later. If the inflation rate during this time period is 10% (so $p = 0.10$), then the **real** value of the $1,150 repayment is $\$1,150/(1 + p) = \$1,045.45$. After controlling for inflation, the lender earns $45.45 on a loan of $1,000. The real interest rate is therefore just over 4.5%. Algebraically, $\$1,000(1 + r) = \$1,045.45$, so $r = 0.0454$.

If the inflation rate were 25% ($p = 0.25$), then the repayment of principle plus interest on the same loan would have a real value of $1,150/(1 + p) = 920. In this case the lender earns $-$80 on the loan after controlling for inflation. So the real interest rate is -8%. More formally, $1,000(1 + r) = 920, so $r = -0.08$. Borrowing under these conditions is an obvious bargain, but lending is a losing proposition. As a result, savings in the form of financial assets would decline; available savings would flow toward assets such as jewelry or gold that offer a hedge against inflation. Financial intermediation would be repressed. This is an example of shallow financial policy.

In the numerical examples above, the real interest rate is found by applying Equation 13-4 from the textbook:

$$r = [(1 + i)/(1 + p)] - 1.$$

In the present case the relationship between r and p can be expressed as:

$$\$1,000(1 + r) = \$1,000(1.15)/(1 + p).$$

The simpler and more familiar relationship, $r = i - p$, is actually an approximation to the correct formula. The approximation is satisfactory when p is fairly small, but less accurate for larger values of p. In the examples above, with 10% inflation the approximation gives a real interest rate of $15 - 10 = 5\%$, compared to the true value 4.5%. With 25% inflation, the approximation gives a real interest rate of $15 - 25 = -10\%$, compared to the true value of -8%.

Money is a special case of the same relationship. Some money balances are held in the form of interest-bearing deposits, but in most countries cash and checking deposits earn zero nominal interest. In the latter case, $i = 0$. So with 10% inflation, the real return to such money balances will be $r = [1.00/(1 + p)] - 1 = -0.09$, or -9%. With 25% inflation, the real real return is -20%. The decline in the purchasing power of money represents a loss of command over real resources on the part of the money holders. These resources can then be utilized by the government. Hence, this effect is called the **inflation tax**. If the tax becomes too onerous due to runaway inflation, the private sector will avoid holding money balances. Monetization, with all of its efficiency advantages, then suffers.

Exercises

1. Now it is your turn to calculate the real interest rate and the inflation tax.

   a. Table 13-1 shows the nominal interest rate and inflation rates for five countries in 1981.
      (i) Calculate the real interest rate for each of the five countries and put your answer in column 3.
      (ii) For comparison, also calculate the approximation to the real interest rate, using the simple formula $r = i - p$; put your answers in column 4.

Table 13-1
Real versus Nominal Interest Rates, 1981[a]

Country	Nominal interest rate (1)	Inflation rate (2)	Real interest rate (3)	Approximation of real interest rate (4)	Inflation tax rate (5)
Malaysia	11.3	8.8	_____	_____	_____
Korea	19.3	12.6	_____	_____	_____
Turkey	49.1	30.3	_____	_____	_____
Ghana	13.8	100.2	_____	_____	_____
Argentina	158.7	131.3	_____	_____	_____

Source: IMF, "Interest Rate Policies in Developing Countries" (Occasional Paper No. 22, 1983).

*All figures are percentages.

     (iii) Finally, calculate the rate of the inflation tax on money balances, and put your answer in column 5. [Hint: If the real return on money balances is $-X\%$, then the inflation tax rate is $X\%$.]

b. Who will benefit when the inflation rate exceeds the nominal interest rate on a financial asset: borrowers (issuers of financial assets) or lenders (holders of the financial assets)? Briefly explain.

c. (i) When the inflation rate is 20%, the rate of inflation tax on money balances is _____%.

    (ii) Suppose that money balances equal 30% of GDP. Then with 20% inflation the aggregate amount of inflation tax is equal to _____% of GDP.

d. Consider again the Korean data on nominal interest rates and inflation shown in Table 13–1.

    (i) Suppose that lenders pay 10% of their nominal interest income in taxes. Then the nominal interest rate of 19.3% would represent a nominal yield to lenders **after taxes** equal to _____%. [Hint: If $X\%$ is paid in taxes, then $(100 - X)\%$ is retained after taxes.]

    (ii) The corresponding after-tax real interest rate earned by lenders is _____%.

    (iii) Suppose that the borrowers are corporations facing a 40% tax rate on income. Since interest costs are deductible from taxable income, 40% of nominal interest costs are effectively offset by reduced tax payments. When these corporations pay a nominal interest rate of 19.3% on borrowed funds, the net-of-tax nominal interest rate is _____%.

    (iv) The corresponding after-tax real interest rate paid by borrowers is _____%.

2. This exercise analyzes the efficiency gains from financial intermediation and the efficiency costs of shallow finance.

    Each family in Kapital saves $100 per year. Initially there are no banks or other financial intermediaries, so household savings are either invested directly in hens (productive capital) or held in the form of jewelry (unproductive assets).

a. The top panel of Figure 13–1 refers to family A. The curve R_A shows the relationship between this family's investment in hens (at $1 each) and the rate of return earned on the marginal hen. Curve R_B in the bottom panel of Figure 13–1 shows the same relationship for family B. The rate of return on jewelry is always zero.

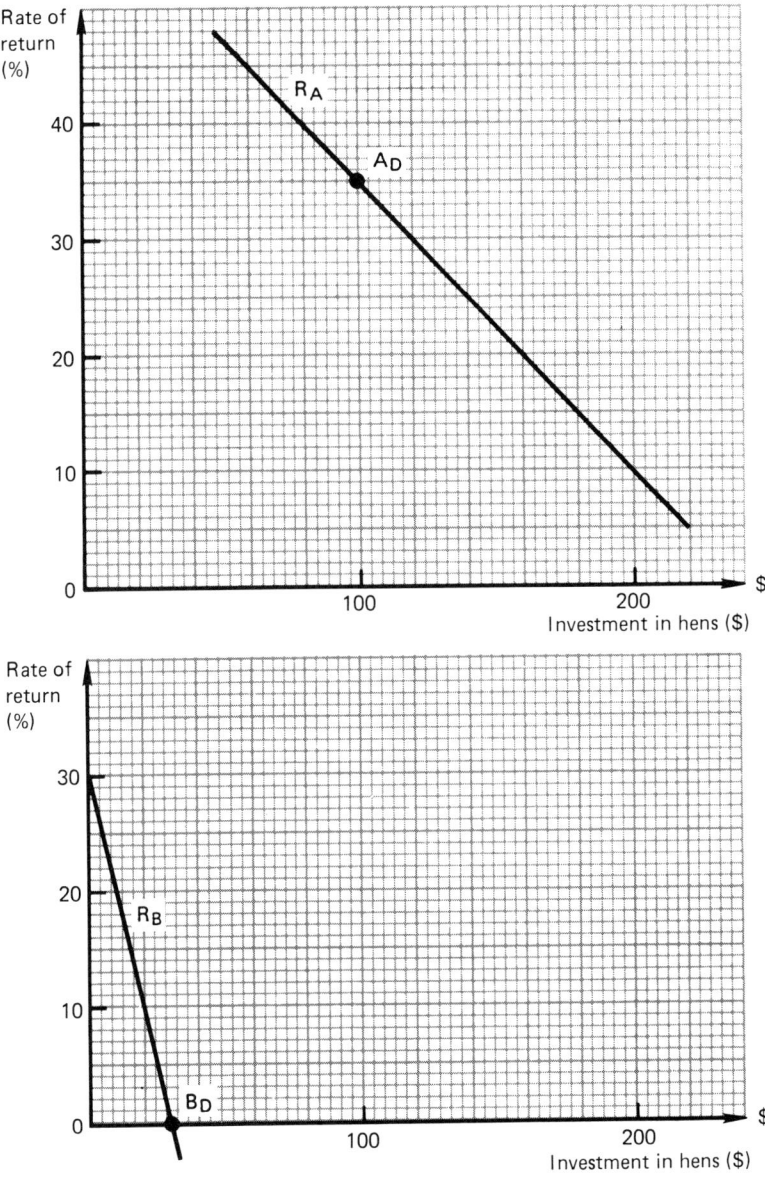

Figure 13-1

(i) Members of family A are terrific hen farmers. They invest all $100 of their savings and still earn a rate of return on the

marginal hen equal to _____% (see point A_0). Only the lack of finance prevents them from investing productively in more hens.

(ii) Members of family B are terrible hen farmers. If they have

more than _____ hens, the marginal rate of return actually becomes negative (see point B_0).

(iii) So at $1 per hen, they will invest only $_____ in pro-

ductive assets; the remaining $_____ of savings will be held in the form of jewelry.

b. In aggregate, the two families are saving $200. Are the savings being allocated to investment as efficiently as possible? Explain.

c. Banks now appear. In addition to hens and jewelry, savings can now be held in the form of deposits that pay 10% interest. Also, loans are now available at an interest rate of 15%.
   (i) Curve R_B shows that family B earns a rate of return in excess of the deposit rate (10%) on hen investments of up to

   $_____ of their own savings.
   (ii) The rest of family B's $100 in savings now earns the highest

   return when held in the form of _____ .

(iii) So banks receive deposit funds of $_____ from family B.
(iv) Examine curve R_A. Explain why it would not pay for family A to hold any of its $100 savings in bank deposits rather than hens.

   (v) Explain why family A will be interested in obtaining a bank loan at 15% interest to supplement its $100 of self-finance.

(vi) How much money will family A wish to borrow? [Hint: Borrowing is profitable as long as the marginal rate of return on hens exceeds 15%.]

d. In aggregate, the two families are still saving $200. In what respects has financial intermediation increased efficiency in the allocation of savings to investment in Kapital?

e. Suppose that the *nominal* interest rates on bank loans and deposits remain unchanged, but the inflation rate in Kapital rises to 100% per year.

(i) How will this inflation affect family B's willingness to hold savings in the form of bank deposits?

(ii) How will this inflation affect the volume of funds flowing through the financial intermediaries?

(iii) Why will it now be profitable for people to seek bank loans for unproductive investment in jewelry?

(iv) How will this inflation affect the efficiency of the allocation of savings to investment in Kapital? Be sure to take into consideration the productivity of investments financed by bank loans, as well as the volume of intermediation.

3. This exercise explores the relationship between money-supply growth and inflation.

a. (i) In Harganya the 1987 level of GDP is $Y = \$1,000$. The money supply is $M = \$300$, so the ratio of money to GDP is $M/Y =$ _____.

(ii) Real GDP is expected to grow by 6% during the following year. Based on past experience, the income elasticity of the demand for money is $E = 1.5$. So if real GDP grows by $g_Y = 6\%$, the money supply can expand by $g_M =$ _____% without causing inflationary pressure. [Hint: $g_Y \times E$. Do you see why?]

(iii) As GDP grows 6%, from $1,000 to $1,060, an increase in the money supply to $_____ would maintain price stability.

(iv) The money supply can grow more rapidly than GDP without stimulating inflation because E (the income elasticity of demand for money) exceeds unity. Why would the value of E in LDCs be likely to exceed unity?

b. Suppose that the government of Harganya is quite content to hold the inflation rate to 10%.
   (i) Simplifying a bit, assume that prices rise by 1% for every 1% that g_M exceeds the noninflationary value found above. Then 10% inflation is compatible with g_M = _____%.
   (ii) So the policymakers can permit M to increase from $300 to $_____ without the inflation rate exceeding 10%.
   (iii) In fact, if the money supply were to grow by g_M = 22%, then inflation would spurt to a rate of _____%, other things being unchanged.

4. The example from exercise 3 is continued here, with a focus on the relationship between the government deficits and the growth of the money supply.

   Expansion of the money supply is equal to the net inflow of international reserves (since this creates new deposits in local banks) plus the expansion of domestic credit to either the government or the private sector. Repeating Equation 13–12 from the textbook:

$$\Delta M = \Delta DC + \Delta IR.$$

a. Recall the 1987 conditions in Harganya: Y = $1,000, M = $300, and E = 1.5.
   (i) In exercise 3 you calculated that a 10% inflation rate would result if the money supply increased to M = $_____. Call this the money supply "target."
   (ii) Assume that the change in international reserves equals zero. In this case the money supply target can be achieved by permitting domestic credit to expand by ΔDC = $_____.
   (iii) This amount of domestic credit creation may consist of the government borrowing $50 and the private sector borrowing $_____.
   (iv) Or it may consist of the government borrowing $20 and the private sector borrowing $_____.
   (v) Or any other combination of government plus private-sector borrowing adding up to $_____.

-198-

b. Government revenues in Harganya are expected to fall short of
   expenditures by an amount equal to 5% of GDP during 1987.
   (i) In absolute terms this means that the budget deficit is pro-

   jected to be $BD = \$$_____.
   (ii) This deficit is financed by borrowing from the central bank—
   i.e., by domestic credit creation of an amount equal to BD.
   Given the credit creation needed to finance the government
   deficit, the money-supply target can be achieved only if credit

   expansion for the private sector is limited to $_____.
   (iii) Assume that outstanding bank credit to the private sector had
   previously totaled $250. Now it can increase to no more than

   $_____.
   (iv) In percentage terms, credit to the private sector can expand by

   only _____%.
   (v) With an inflation rate of 10%, this means that *real* bank

   credit to the private sector will _____ by _____%.
   (vi) Is this consistent with the projected 6% growth rate of real
   GDP? Explain briefly.

c. (i) To avoid a real decline, credit to the private sector must expand

   in nominal value by no less than _____%, or $_____.
   (ii) If this increase in nominal credit to the private sector were to
   occur, then the money-supply target can be achieved only by
   holding the government budget deficit to no more than

   $_____, or _____% of GDP.

d. Suppose that excellent policy administration achieves an appropriate expansion of domestic credit: ΔDC has exactly the value
   required to hit the money-supply target. Unhappily, though, an
   unexpected influx of international reserves occurs, with the result
   that $\Delta IR = \$25$. (Recall that $\Delta IR = 0$ had been anticipated.)
   How will this unexpected event affect ΔM and the inflation rate?
   Be specific.

5. This exercise investigates some empirical savings facts.

   a. Table 13–2 shows 1982 data on real interest rates (r) and domestic
      savings rates (S_d/Y) for eight of the countries listed in textbook
      Table 13–4. The other countries listed therein are excluded here
      because of missing data or because their numbers don't fit on the
      graph to be used.
      (i) In Figure 13–2, plot the eight points showing the values for r
          and S_d/Y for each country.
      (ii) Do the plotted data reveal any evident relationship between
           real interest rates and savings rates? Briefly explain.

Table 13–2

Country	Real interest rate (%)	Domestic savings rate (%)
Korea	4.3	24
Malaysia	−0.6	25
Bangladesh	−2.3	−3
Thailand	3.1	21
Pakistan	0.4	5
Brazil	−25.0	19
Chile	30.0	8
Uruguay	−24.9	12

Source: Textbook Table 13–4 and World Bank, *World Development Report 1984.*

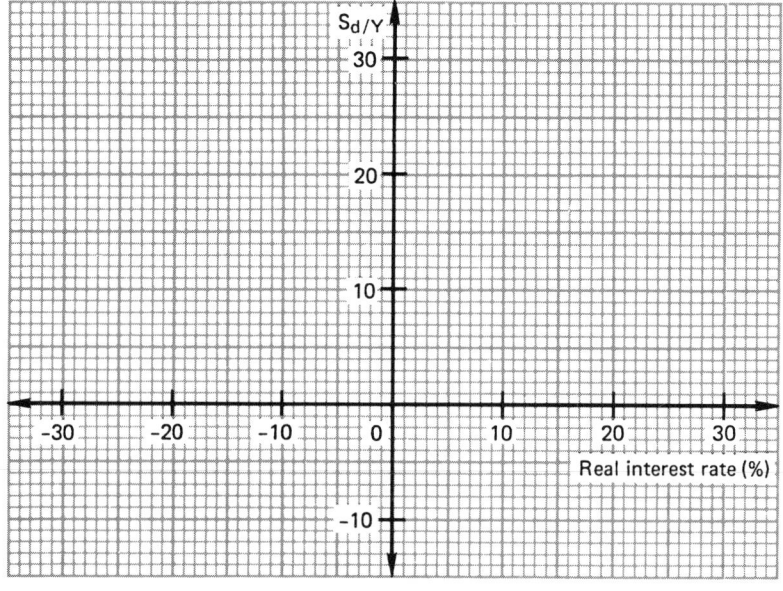

Figure 13–2

b. From Figure 13−2 it is apparent that factors other than the real interest rate must have a major influence on savings rates.
   (i) What other factors are major determinants of *private* savings rates in LDCs? [Hint: Review the life-cycle hypothesis and the permanent-income hypothesis.]

   (ii) What other factors are major determinants of *total* domestic savings rates?

c. Table 13−3 shows data on real interest rates (*r*) and growth of the ratio of the broad money supply to GNP ($g_{M2/Y}$) in Indonesia over the period 1970 to 1979. As the textbook explains, the ratio *M2/Y* can be considered as an indicator of financial deepening.
   (i) In Figure 13−3, plot the ten points showing each year's *r* and $g_{M2/Y}$.
   (ii) Do these data reveal any evident relationship between the real interest rate and financial deepening in Indonesia during this period? Briefly explain.

Table 13–3
Financial Data for Indonesia, 1970–1979

Year	Real interest rate (%)	Growth rate of *M2/Y* (%)
1970	13.8	15.1
1971	20.4	29.3
1972	−6.3	18.8
1973	−9.4	−3.9
1974	−2.3	−6.8
1975	4.0	14.7
1976	8.8	8.9
1977	5.4	−3.5
1978	7.5	3.7
1979	−5.7	−1.8

Source: Calculated from data reported in Bank Indonesia annual and weekly reports.

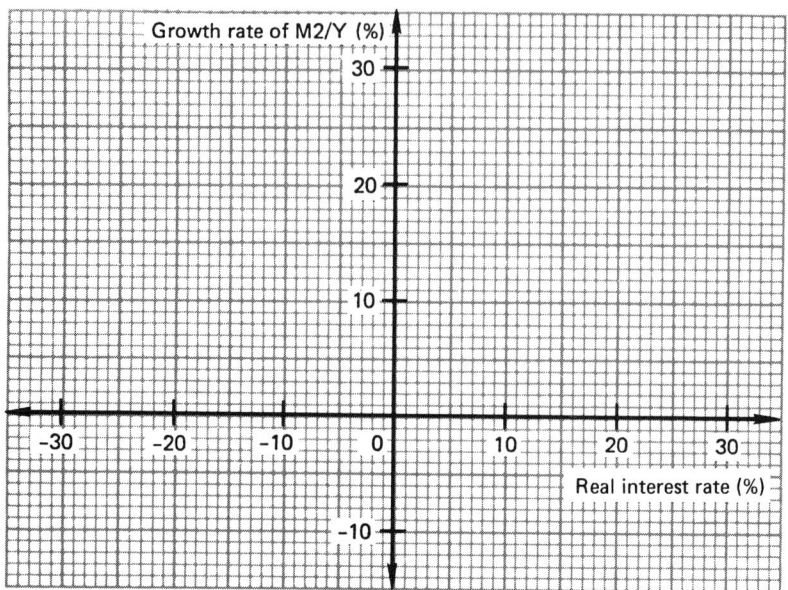

Figure 13-3

6. *Optional* This exercise shows how changes in international reserves lead to changes in the money supply under a fixed-exchange rate system.

Consider Sombrero, a country in which the peso is the domestic currency. For simplicity assume that the dollar is the only foreign exchange unit. The government is committed to maintaining a fixed-exchange rate of 20 pesos per dollar. Think of this as the "price of the dollar" in terms of the Sombrero peso.

a. Suppose that Sombrero's international transactions generate a supply of dollars (e.g., from exports) in excess of the demand for dollars (e.g., for imports) by an amount of $100 million.
(i) With supply in excess of demand, free-market forces would

cause the price of the dollar to _____. [Hint: think supply and demand.]
(ii) The government can prevent this change in the exchange rate by eliminating the excess supply of dollars. This can be

accomplished by purchasing $_____ million in the foreign-exchange market, to add to Sombrero's stock of international reserves.

(iii) The government pays for the dollars with _____.
(iv) As a result of the government's action to maintain the fixed-exchange rate, the supply of domestic money in circulation

increases by _____ million pesos.

b. Now suppose that international transactions create a demand for dollars in excess of the supply of dollars by an amount equal to $50 million.

(i) With demand in excess of supply, free-market forces would

cause the price of the dollar to _____ .

(ii) The government can prevent this change in the exchange rate

by _____ $50 million in the foreign-exchange
market.

(iii) As a result of the government's action to maintain the fixed-
exchange rate, Sombrero's stock of international reserves will

_____ by $50 million.

(iv) And the supply of domestic money in circulation will

_____ by _____ million pesos.

c. Finally, suppose that the foreign-exchange market is in equilibrium
at the exchange rate of 50 pesos per dollar. But the domestic inflation rate is zero, whereas the foreign inflation rate averages 15%.

(i) As prices in foreign markets rise, dollar earnings from

Sombrero's exports will _____ .

(ii) Because foreign goods become increasingly expensive, the

people of Sombrero will _____ their purchases
of imports.

(iii) Consequently, in Sombrero's foreign-exchange market the

supply of dollars will increasingly _____ the
demand for dollars.

(iv) To prevent market forces from causing a change in the exchange

rate, the government of Sombrero must _____
dollars in the foreign-exchange market.

(v) This government action will cause Sombrero's stock of inter-

national reserves to _____ .

(vi) And it will cause the domestic money supply to _____ .

(vii) This change in the domestic money supply will tend to cause

Sombrero's inflation rate to _____ .

Answers to Self-Test

Completion

1. monetization
2. acute
3. money
4. uncertainty
5. positive
6. expands
7. real interest rates
8. shrink
9. domestic credit
10. fixed

True-False

1. F	6. T
2. T	7. F
3. F	8. F
4. T	9. T
5. T	10. T

Multiple Choice

1. b	6. a
2. d	7. a
3. b	8. d
4. b	9. b
5. d	10. c

CHAPTER 14   Foreign Savings: Aid and Investment

Overview

This chapter concludes the coverage of capital resources with a broad discussion of foreign savings, including both official and private flows of international capital. The major components of foreign savings are defined, and broad trends are reviewed. Then the text examines the empirical, institutional and economic dimensions of foreign aid, direct foreign investment by multinational corporations, and commercial borrowing by the LDCs.

Foreign aid provides foreign savings on very favorable financial terms, though often with strings attached. In economic terms aid can promote growth by supplementing the savings, foreign exchange, and technical resources available to an LDC. However, it can also end up substituting for domestic savings and exports, thereby increasing consumption and dependency rather than growth. Similarly, the effects of direct foreign investment can be either positive or negative. Multinational corporations provide resource bundles that can include capital, technology, management, and market access. But the benefits accruing to the host country—such as employment, technology transfer, and foreign exchange—will depend on economic conditions and host-country policies. Commercial borrowing, the third major type of foreign savings, can benefit a debtor country when used to finance efficient investments. But debt can also become an onerous burden. This has been amply demonstrated by the recent debt crisis, which was precipitated by a combination of heavy borrowing, unprecedented external shocks, and economic mismanagement.

Main Learning Objectives

After studying this chapter you ought to understand and be able to explain:

1. The terminology used to distinguish various forms of foreign savings, such as: **official vs. private** foreign savings; **concessional vs. non-concessional** official savings; **foreign direct investment**; and **portfolio investment**.

2. The broad empirical record of foreign savings and its major components.

3. The institutional characteristics of **foreign aid**, including the forms in which aid can be packaged, the major aid agencies, and the evolution of aid allocation patterns.

4. The economic impact of foreign aid, including **substitution** effects and **policy leverage** effects of aid.

5. The characteristics of **multinational corporation** (MNC) investments in LDCs.

6. The debate about the benefits for host countries from foreign direct investment, and the policies used by LDCs to deal with MNC investments.

7. The institutional mechanisms for **commercial borrowing** by LDCs, and the advantages and disadvantages of such borrowing.

8. The external and internal factors that transformed LDC **debt service** into a **debt crisis** in the early 1980s.

Additional Key Terms, Concepts, and Institutions

Can you identify and explain each of the following?

"soft" loan
bilateral vs. multilateral aid
World Bank (IBRD)
International Development Association (IDA)
International Monetary Fund (IMF)
regional development banks
United Nations Development Programme (UNDP)
saturation laws
transfer pricing
Eurocurrency market
sovereign debt
"scissors" effect

Economic Tools and Techniques

From what you have learned in this chapter, can you:

1. Explain the **substitution** effect of aid using a graph of indifference curves and a production possibilities frontier?

2. Calculate the **grant equivalent** of an aid flow, given the terms of the aid and the appropriate commercial interest rate?

3. Demonstrate how an **income tax holiday** for multinational corporations can result in what the textbook calls "reverse foreign aid"?

4. Explain how a multinational can use transfer pricing to understate a subsidiary's reported income—and how abuse of transfer prices may be related to host-country policies?

Self-Test

Completion

1. Foreign savings is the difference between gross domestic investment and gross domestic _____.

2. The purchase of host country bonds or stocks by foreigners, without managerial control, is called _____ investment.

3. A _____ loan is one bearing lower interest rates and longer repayment periods than would be available on the commercial capital markets.

4. The _____ is the World Bank affiliate that channels contributions from the richer member countries to the poorer LDCs on very soft terms.

5. _____ laws require multinational corporations to sell a specified percent of the equity in an overseas affiliate to host-country nationals.

6. LDCs often impose _____ requirements on MNCs, such as mandating that parts must be procured from local suppliers, or that jobs must be filled by local workers.

7. The objectives of multinational enterprise investments in LDCs can be summarized in two words: profits and _____.

8. _____ incentives are the most widely used inducements offered to multinationals to invest in developing countries.

9. Most commercial borrowing by LDCs takes place through syndicates of banks in the _____ market.

10. _____ debt is backed by the full faith and credit of the borrowing national government, though collection is not enforceable by law.

True-False If false, you should be able to explain why.

_____ 1. In 1983 the ratio of foreign savings to GDP no longer exceeded 5% in any developing country.

_____ 2. The net flow of official development assistance increased nearly six-fold in real value from 1960 to 1983.

_____ 3. Most World Bank loans are nonconcessional flows consisting of funds borrowed by the World Bank at prevailing interest rates, and re-lent to the LDCs at slightly higher rates.

_____ 4. During the late 1960s and the 1970s, aid programs were reoriented to incorporate concerns such as education, health, poverty alleviation, and rural development.

_____ 5. Multinational corporations have employed more than 1% of the labor force in only a very few LDCs.

_____ 6. Though in theory foreign direct investment can produce a technology transfer, in practice LDCs obtain no technology benefits from MNCs.

_____ 7. After 1979–1980, not a single LDC with a large debt burden managed to service its debt on schedule while controlling inflation and maintaining economic growth.

_____ 8. A country benefits from external debt when the funds are used to finance projects with rates of return higher than the interest rate on the debt.

_____ 9. The "scissors" effect discussed in the text refers to the combination of escalating debt-service costs together with a decline in the availability of new loans for the LDCs.

_____ 10. The textbook concludes that the LDC debt crisis resulted from a combination of external shocks and domestic policy mismanagement in the LDCs themselves.

Multiple Choice

1. Which of the following would not be considered a form of foreign aid, or official development assistance (ODA)?
   a. multilateral aid
   b. food aid
   c. technical assistance
   d. loans on commercial terms from official agencies

2. Four statements about foreign aid are listed below. Only one is factual. Which one is it?
   a. The ratio of aid to GDP is generally higher for low-income countries than for middle-income countries.
   b. Small LDCs tend to receive less aid than large LDCs relative to GDP or to population.
   c. The United States has provided an increasingly large share of total foreign aid.
   d. Most capital assistance is in the form of program aid rather than project aid.

3. Which of the following institutions provides the largest amount of concessional assistance to developing countries?
   a. IMF
   b. OPEC
   c. UNDP
   d. the regional development banks

4. Which of the following institutions provides loans for balance-of-payments support, under conditionality that often requires devaluation and reductions in the government budget deficit?
   a. IMF
   b. IBRD
   c. UNDP
   d. IDA

5. Four statements about multinational corporations (MNCs) are listed below. Only one of them is factual. Which one is it?
   a. International investments by MNCs are located primarily in developing countries.
   b. Most MNC investment in the LDCs is for manufacturing activity that takes advantage of cheap labor.
   c. MNCs use far more capital-intensive production methods than domestic firms in the same industry.
   d. Increasingly, LDCs have been able to renegotiate contracts with MNCs to obtain more favorable terms.

6. In addition to capital, the special "package" provided by multinational investments typically includes all of the following except:
   a. access to natural resources.
   b. technology.
   c. managerial resources.
   d. access to world markets.

7. Transfer pricing is used by multinationals to:
   a. shift reported income to lower tax jurisdictions.
   b. evade host-country foreign-exchange controls.
   c. circumvent host-country restrictions on profit remittances.
   d. all of the above.

8. Which of the following is not an advantage of commercial borrowing over foreign aid?
   a. much shorter delays in receiving funds
   b. more favorable financial terms
   c. fewer political strings tied to the funds
   d. much more flexibility in the use of funds

9. Which of the following was a significant factor contributing to the LDC debt crisis in the early 1980s?
   a. A sharp increase in real interest rates.
   b. A decline in LDC export earnings due to the deep recession in the industrial economies.
   c. A large accumulation of debt during the preceding years.
   d. All of the above.

10. According to the textbook, some countries such as South Korea and Turkey were able to avoid a debt "crisis" because:
    a. they did not have a large debt burden in the first place.
    b. they adopted successful adjustment policies to cope with the external shocks.
    c. they allowed domestic income to decline in order to meet their debt obligations.
    d. they received massive amounts of foreign aid that allowed them to pay their debt service.

Applications

Worked Example: Sources of the Debt Crisis

Morocco and Thailand are similar in many respects, including per-capita income, dependence on primary-product exports, and experience with inflation. Both countries have maintained fairly rapid GDP growth rates over the past two decades. But Morocco was forced to reschedule its foreign debts in 1983 and 1984, whereas Thailand has had no serious problems managing its external debt. Some pertinent data on the two countries are provided in Table 14–1. This Worked Example will examine the origins of the debt crisis in Morocco. Then in exercise 1 you will analyze the differences that helped Thailand to escape the debt crisis.

What led to Morocco's debt crisis? The major elements were the extent of debt accumulation during the 1970s; the external shock encountered during the early 1980s; and the country's domestic policies. Table 14–1 shows clearly that Morocco borrowed heavily during the 1970s. The debt/GNP ratio rose from 18% to 70% (item 1). This alone would have generated an increasing debt service burden. But in addition, Morocco faced an external shock estimated in magnitude to equal 10% of GNP (item 2). For Morocco the shock did not include a major drop in export volume (item 3), but the country's terms of trade (i.e., the unit value of exports relative to the unit price of imports) did decline (item 4). This was due primarily to higher oil prices (item 5). Much of the shock can be

Table 14–1
The Debt Burden in Morocco and Thailand

Item	Years	Morocco	Thailand
1. External debt/GNP	1970	18%	8%
	1983	70%	38%
2. External shock/GNP	1981–82	10%	10%
3. Index of dollar export earnings (1979 = 100)	1983	106	122
4. Terms of trade (1979 = 100)	1983	91	86
5. Energy imports/total exports	1983	57%	39%
6. U.S. real interest rate, long-term bonds	1975	−1%	−1%
	1983	7%	7%
7. Debt service/exports	1970	8%	3%
	1983	38%	11%
8. Growth of exports	1973–83	0.5%	9%
9. Growth of agricultural production	1973–83	0.7%	3.8%
10. Government deficit/GNP	1972	−4%	−4%
	1982	−12%	−6%
11. Gross domestic savings/GDP	1965–72 av.	12%	21%
	1979–83 av.	12%	21%
12. Foreign savings/GDP	1983	9%	5%
13. Domestic credit/foreign debt	1982	41%	144%
14. Gross domestic investment/GDP	1970–81 av.	24%	26%
15. GDP growth rate	1973–83	4.7%	6.9%
16. ICOR	1970–81 av.	4.6	3.6

Source: World Development Report 1985 and *World Tables 1983*; various tables. Some figures derived by author from data reported in these sources.

attributed to the increase in real interest rates (item 6)—and in turn, the size of the debt itself. Debt service, which had been quite manageable in 1970, now rose to a burdensome 38% of export earnings (item 7).

Apart from the heavy borrowing, how did domestic policy influence the debt burden? The data provide many clues. The volume of exports grew very little during the decade of heavy borrowing (item 8), while stagnant agricultural production (item 9) put pressure on import costs. Fiscal policy generated a large government deficit (item 10), which helps to explain the country's failure to mobilize domestic savings (item 11) and the increasing reliance on foreign savings (item 12). In addition, the relatively small volume of domestic credit (item 13) suggests that financial deepening was not being stressed. Although the investment ratio (item 14) and GDP growth (item 15) were fairly high, the incremental capital-output ratio (ICOR) was also fairly high (item 16). This indicates that investment, on average, was not highly efficient. All of these policy-influenced factors contributed to the severity of the debt crisis.

In short, Morocco borrowed to grow, with weak performance of exports, agricultural production, and domestic savings, and relatively inefficient use of capital. Under these conditions, the large external shock led to a debt crisis.

Exercises

1. In this exercise you will see how Thailand's external debt situation differed from that in Morocco. Be sure that you have read the Worked Example carefully. Your answers should rely on the data from Table 14—1.

   a. Consider first the extent of debt accumulation.
      (i) Did Thailand use foreign savings, and foreign borrowing in particular, to finance investment? Explain.

      (ii) Briefly explain how Thailand's accumulation of foreign debt differed from that of Morocco.

   b. How did the size of the external shock encountered by Thailand in 1980—1981 compare to that of Morocco?

c. Consider now the *components* of the external shock faced by Thailand during the period leading up to the LDC debt crisis.
  (i) How did the change in terms of trade for Thailand compare to that for Morocco? [Note: A decline in the terms of trade means that the average unit price of exports has dropped relative to the average unit price paid for imports.]

  (ii) Thailand faced an increase in real interest rates similar to that of Morocco. Yet Thailand's debt service burden increased far less (item 7 in the Table). Why?

  (iii) Thailand had to deal with the same oil-price increases as did Morocco. Neither country was a major energy producer, and per-capita energy consumption was virtually the same in both. Yet Table 14−1 shows that the burden of energy import costs relative to export earnings increased much less in Thailand than in Morocco. How can you account for this?

d. Finally, consider the domestic policy positions of the two countries:
  (i) Compare Thailand with Morocco in terms of mobilization of domestic savings, citing at least two pieces of evidence from Table 14−1.

  (ii) Compare Thailand with Morocco in terms of export promotion, citing two pieces of evidence from the table.

  (iii) Compare Thailand with Morocco in terms of agricultural development.

(iv) Compare Thailand with Morocco in terms of the investment efficiency, citing at least two pieces of evidence from the table.

(v) How was Thailand's ability to avoid the debt crisis that befell Morocco related to its performance with regard to:
—domestic savings?

—exports?

—agriculture?

—investment efficiency?

e. (i) Considering the facts shown in Table 14—1, do you think that Thailand would have been wise to avoid foreign borrowing altogether? Explain your position.

(ii) Considering the facts shown in Table 14—1, do you think that Morocco would have been wise to avoid foreign borrowing altogether? Explain your position.

2. This exercise analyzes the economic impact of foreign aid.

  a. Begin with the simple Harrod-Domar growth equation: $g = s/k$.
     The Republic of Xanadu has a domestic savings ratio of $s = 12\%$,
     and an ICOR of $k = 4.6$.

     (i) If Xanadu relied only on domestic savings, what growth rate
        would be achieved, according to the Harrod-Domar model?

$$g = \underline{\hspace{1cm}} \% \text{ per annum.}$$

     (ii) Now suppose that Xanadu receives foreign aid equal to 10%
         of GDP. If the domestic savings rate and the ICOR remain
         unchanged, then the ratio of total savings to GDP will rise to:

$$s = \underline{\hspace{1cm}} \%.$$

     According to the Harrod-Domar model, Xanadu would then
     achieve a growth rate of:

$$g = \underline{\hspace{1cm}} \% \text{ per annum.}$$

  b. But will total savings increase by the full amount of the aid?
     Figure 14–1 shows Xanadu's production possibilities frontier
     (PPF). For simplicity, the PPF is a straight line, indicating that
     any combination of investment goods (I) plus consumption goods
     (C) totaling $100 (the level of GDP) is feasible. The figure also
     contains representative indifference curves. The initial optimum
     point along the PPF is at point X, where $C = \$88$ and $I = \$12$ (so
     $s = 12\%$).

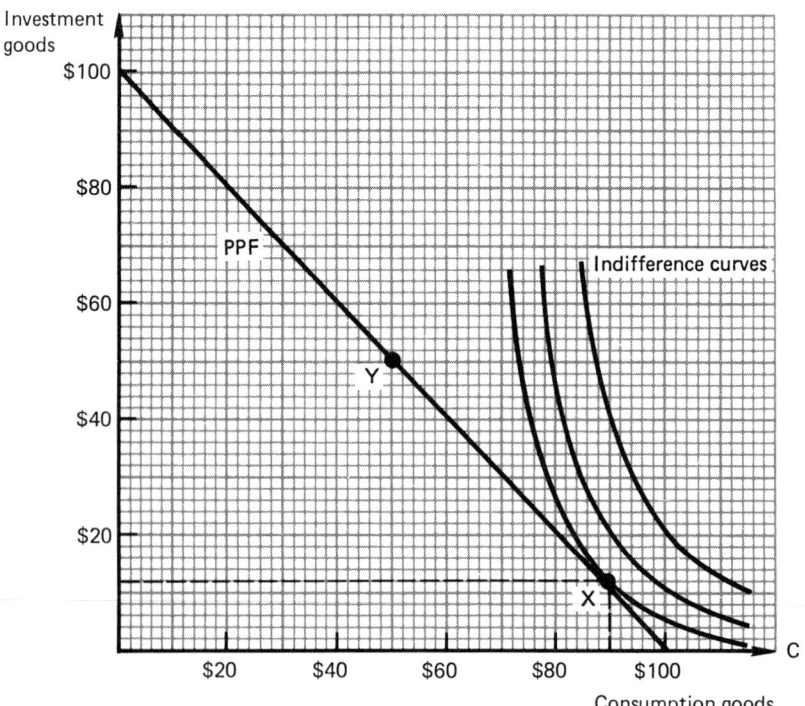

Figure 14–1

Consider now the impact of foreign aid in the form of $10 worth of investment goods (= to 10% of GDP). Identify the point in Figure 14−1 that would be attained if I increased by the full $10 of aid, as assumed in part a. Label this as *point X'*.

c. Point X' is indeed one possible outcome following the receipt of the aid. But Xanadu could choose to use the aid for investment while shifting its *domestic* resources to some point such as Y, where $C = \$50$ and $I = \$50$.

  (i) Carefully find and label as Y' the point showing the combination of C and I that Xanadu would attain if domestic resources were reallocated to point Y when the country receives $10 worth of investment aid.

  (ii) A similar post-aid outcome can be identified for every possible reallocation of domestic resources—in other words, for every point on Xanadu's PPF. Carefully draw in the line showing all of these potential post-aid outcomes. Label it *line AA*.

  (iii) Given the indifference curves in Figure 14−1, find Xanadu's optimal point along line AA. Label it as *point E*.

  (iv) At point E, Xanadu will have:

$$C = \$\underline{\hspace{2cm}}, \text{ and}$$

$$I = \$\underline{\hspace{2cm}}.$$

d. Therefore, following receipt of the aid, total savings (and investment) in Xanadu will not increase by the full $10.

  (i) Total savings (domestic plus foreign) would now equal:

$$\$\underline{\hspace{2cm}}.$$

  (ii) The aid causes the ratio of total savings to GDP (still $100) to increase to:

$$s = \underline{\hspace{1.5cm}}\%$$

[Notice that investment still exceeds domestic savings by $10, the amount of the foreign savings.]

  (iii) Applying the Harrod-Domar equation, the rate of growth therefore increases to:

$$g = \underline{\hspace{1.5cm}}\% \text{ per annum.}$$

  (iv) How has the substitution effect altered the analysis of the economic effect of foreign aid?

e. Aid may also affect Xanadu's ICOR. For example, suppose that the policy advice accompanying the aid enables Xanadu to reduce its ICOR to $k = 3.6$.

-215-

(i) Then, using the value for s found in part d, the country would achieve a growth rate of:

$$g = \underline{\qquad}\% \text{ per annum.}$$

(ii) Is it possible for aid to cause Xanadu's ICOR to rise rather than fall? Briefly explain.

f. The foreign aid supplements Xanadu's domestic savings rate, albeit with some substitution effects. In terms of the Harrod-Domar model, how would the impact of foreign direct investment and commercial borrowing differ from the impact of aid:
   (i) in the year received?

   (ii) in future years?

3. This exercise involves calculating the grant equivalent of concessional aid. Recall the definition: the grant equivalent (GE) is the difference between the face value (F) of aid funds received and the present discounted value of required repayments (call this PVR). In symbols, $GE = F - PVR$. You may wish to review the present-value concept from Chapter 6 or Chapter 9. Throughout this exercise assume that the discount rate for calculating present value is 10% ($r = 0.10$).

a. First take the case of $1 million worth of aid in the form of an interest-free loan that must be repaid in a lump sum after five years.
   (i) What is the face value of the aid funds received?

   $$F = \$\underline{\qquad}$$

   (ii) What is the present discounted value of the required repayments? [Hint: There is a single repayment due that must be discounted for five years using a discount rate of $r = 0.10$.]

   $$PVR = \$\underline{\qquad}$$

(iii) What is the grant equivalent of this soft loan?

$$GE = \$\underline{\hspace{2cm}} \text{ , or}$$

$$\underline{\hspace{2cm}}\% \text{ of the face value of the aid.}$$

b. Now take the case of $1 million worth of aid in the form of an interest-free loan that must be repaid in a lump sum after ten years.

(i) What is the face value of the aid funds received?

$$F = \$\underline{\hspace{2cm}}$$

(ii) What is the discounted present value of the required repayments?

$$PVR = \$\underline{\hspace{2cm}}$$

(iii) What is the grant equivalent of this soft loan?

$$GE = \$\underline{\hspace{2cm}} \text{ , or}$$

$$\underline{\hspace{2cm}}\% \text{ of the face value of the aid.}$$

c. Finally, take the case of $1 million worth of aid in the form of a loan that must be repaid in a lump sum after ten years. No interest is charged during the first five years, but 2% interest is due each year during years six through ten.

(i) What is the face value of the aid funds received?

$$F = \$\underline{\hspace{2cm}}$$

(ii) What is the discounted present value of the required repayments? [Hint: There are now five separate repayments due; each must be discounted an appropriate number of years.]

$$PVR = \$\underline{\hspace{2cm}}$$

(iii) What is the grant equivalent of this soft loan?

$$GE = \$\underline{\hspace{2cm}} \text{ , or}$$

$$\underline{\hspace{2cm}}\% \text{ of the face value of the aid.}$$

d. Based on your calculations above, briefly explain how the grant equivalent of a soft loan varies according to:

(i) the maturity period;

(ii) the interest rate charged;

(iii) the grace period (i.e., the number of years before repayments must begin).

4. This exercise probes the relationship between multinationals and host LDCs. A subsidiary of Colossus Enterprises produces gadgets in Dirigiste, a developing country that imposes a 40% tax rate on corporate income. Dirigiste also limits annual profit remittances to a maximum of 10 million francs. Colossus would prefer to remit all but F2 million of its after-tax profits.

   a. Column 1 in Table 14-2 shows the subsidiary's reported income statement for 1987. The technology and all imported components are obtained from divisions of Colossus located in the United States. Hence, neither the import expense nor the technology license fee is an "arm's-length" transaction for which an objective market price can be established.

      (i) In its reported accounts Colossus has used transfer prices for the items on lines 4 and 6 that are exactly twice the "proper" values. Complete column 2 of Table 14-2 to show how the income statement would look if the proper values had been used for these two transfer price items. [Remember that the tax rate is 40%.]

      (ii) Comparing columns 1 and 2, you can see that the use of artificially high transfer prices caused net income before taxes to be understated by:

      F_____ million.

      As a result, income tax payments to the government of Dirigiste were reduced by:

      F_____ million.

      (iii) In column 2 you should find that with proper accounting the *desired* profit remittance would exceed F10 million. Due to the legal ceiling, no more than F10 million would be permitted. But through manipulation of transfer prices (column 1) Colossus has managed to remit the legal F10 million *plus*:

      F_____ million,

      hidden in the form of artificially inflated expenses for imports and technology. The total effective remittance with false transfer pricing is therefore:

      F_____ million.

   b. The inflated transfer prices will raise Colossus's taxable earnings in the United States. Suppose Dirigiste reforms its policies by reducing the tax rate on corporate income to 30% and removing remittance restrictions. Colossus no longer has an incentive to use inflated transfer prices.

      (i) Fill in column 3 of Table 14-2 to show the accounts that would be reported under the reformed policies. [Hint: Lines 1-8 will be the same as in column 2.]

      (ii) Compare the pre- and post-reform reported accounts (columns 1 and 3, respectively). The reforms will cause the actual amount of tax paid in Dirigiste to:

      _____ by F_____ million.

Table 14-2
1987 Income Statement (all figures in millions of francs)

	Reported accounts (1)	Proper accounts (2)	With policy reforms (3)	With incentive policies (4)
1. Revenue from gadget sales	F66	F66	F66	F80
2. *Less expenses*				
3. Locally purchased components	F12	F12	F12	F12
4. Imported components	20	10	10	10
5. Labor	10	——	——	——
6. Technology license fee	4	——	——	——
7. *Total expense*	46	——	——	——
8. Net income before tax	20	——	——	——
9. Income tax	8	——	——	——
10. Net income after tax	12	——	——	——
11. Desired retained earnings	2	2	2	2
12. Residual to remit to Colossus	10	——	——	——

(iii) And the total effective remittance of profits will:

_____ by F_____ million.

c. Finally, suppose that Dirigiste goes one step further and introduces incentive policies. A tax holiday is granted, relieving the subsidiary of all tax obligations for six years. Also, the Colossus subsidiary is granted monopoly rights in the domestic gadget market.

(i) With the grant of monopoly rights the subsidiary can maximize

profits by _____ output (and costs) while

_____ prices.

(ii) For simplicity, assume that the company's revenues increase to F80 million, with expenses staying the same as those shown in column 3. Fill in column 4 to show how the accounts would appear under the incentive policy.

(iii) The textbook refers to such incentives as "reverse foreign aid." Comparing columns 3 and 4, you can see that the incentive policies result in a transfer to Colossus of:

F_____ million

from gadget consumers in Dirigiste, plus:

F_____ million

in the form of lower tax revenues.

(iv) In the process, Dirigiste loses the equivalent of:

F_____ million

worth of foreign exchange from the increased profit remittances.

(v) Is it likely in this instance that the costs incurred by Dirigiste under the incentive policy are more than offset by benefits to the country? Briefly explain.

Answers to Self-Test

Completion

1. savings
2. portfolio
3. soft
4. International Development Association (IDA)
5. Saturation
6. performance
7. stability
8. Tax
9. Eurocurrency
10. Sovereign

True-False

1. F	6. F
2. F	7. F
3. T	8. T
4. T	9. T
5. T	10. T

Multiple Choice

1. d	6. a
2. a	7. d
3. c	8. b
4. a	9. d
5. d	10. b

CHAPTER 15 Primary-Export-Led Growth

Overview

This chapter begins by introducing the fundamentals of international trade: balance of payments accounts and the theory of comparative advantage, which states that any country can gain from trade. Next, empirical patterns of trade are reviewed. Smaller countries tend to be more dependent on trade than larger countries, which have broader domestic markets. And as per-capita incomes rise, the share of exports in GDP tends to increase.

Many LDCs rely heavily on exports of primary products to earn the foreign exchange needed for importing consumer goods, capital goods, and raw materials for domestic industry. According to conventional wisdom, primary-product exporters are at a disadvantage in world trade due to sluggish growth of world demand, declining terms of trade, unstable export earnings, and weak linkage effects. The text examines the merits and weaknesses of each of these claims, concluding that exports of primary products can indeed serve as an engine of growth. A number of proposed policies to improve world-market conditions for primary-product exporters are analyzed, including major elements of the call for a New International Economic Order. Primary product cartels are also examined and shown to be generally unworkable.

Main Learning Objectives

After studying this chapter you ought to understand and be able to explain:

1. The structure of **balance of payments accounts**, including the **current account**, the **capital account**, and the **basic balance.**

2. The meaning of **comparative advantage** and the major implications of this theory.

3. The broad characteristics of LDC trade patterns.

4. How **primary-product exports** can improve resource utilization, expand factor endowments, and generate **linkage effects** (including backward, forward, fiscal, and consumption linkages).

5. The pros and cons of arguments about barriers to growth through the export of primary products, specifically: sluggish demand growth, declining **terms of trade**, earnings instability, and weak linkage effects.

6. The institutional and economic characteristics of primary product **cartels**, and of proposals for international **commodity agreements** and **buffer stocks**.

Additional Key Terms, Concepts, and Institutions

Can you identify and explain each of the following?

foreign exchange, or foreign reserves
the trade triangle
enclave export
autarky
vent for surplus
Engel's law
permanent-income hypothesis
New International Economic Order (NIEO)
U.N. Conference on Trade and Development (UNCTAD)
Integrated Programme for Commodities
Compensatory Finance Facility, and Stabex
overvalued exchange rate

Economic Tools and Techniques

From what you have learned in this chapter, can you:

1. Demonstrate the theory of comparative advantage using the production possibilities curve and community indifference curves?

2. Differentiate between the **net barter terms of trade**, the **income terms of trade**, and the **single factoral terms of trade**, and calculate each from appropriate data?

3. Analyze the supply and demand for foreign exchange to show how earnings from traditional exports can impede the development of nontraditional exports?

4. Apply supply-and-demand analysis to explain sources of export instability, the functioning of a cartel, or the operation of a buffer stock?

Self-Test

Completion

1. A nation's record of annual receipts and payments of foreign currency is called the _____ accounts.

2. The average price of a country's exports relative to the average price of its imports is called the _____.

3. Given two countries, even if one can produce all goods more efficiently, trade can benefit both. This is a major implication of the theory of _____.

4. The condition of self-sufficiency without trade is called _____.

5. Government revenues derived from exports of primary products such as petroleum can be called a _____ linkage.

6. For the industrial countries, the income elasticity of demand for staple foods and beverages is probably less than 0.5. This is consistent with _____ Law.

7. Export volumes and export prices are negatively correlated when instability of export earnings is caused by shifts in _____.

8. Applied to export instability, the _____ hypothesis implies that less stable export earnings are associated with a higher rate of savings, *ceteris paribus*.

9. Export industries such as mining and petroleum generally remain remote from other centers of production, generating few domestic linkage effects. In short, they are _____.

10. A country's currency is *overvalued* when the price of the dollar in terms of the local currency is too _____.

True-False If false, you should be able to explain why.

_____ 1. The *basic balance* refers specifically to payments associated with exports and imports of physical merchandise, excluding services or flows of finance.

_____ 2. A country's foreign exchange reserves can rise even if its current account balance is negative.

_____ 3. The case study of Ghana is an illustration of successful development relying on primary products as an engine of growth.

_____ 4. In most LDCs one or two primary products account for over 90% of the country's exports.

_____ 5. During the period 1960–1973, the volume of world trade in nonfuel primary products declined steadily.

_____ 6. A country's earnings from the export of primary products do not necessarily decline when there is a decline in the country's terms of trade.

_____ 7. Evidence suggests that there is little or no association between export instability and the fraction of exports that are primary products.

_____ 8. The Compensatory Finance Facility of the IMF and The Stabex scheme operated by the European Economic Community are buffer stocks used to stabilize world prices for primary products.

_____ 9. Restricting the supply of a primary product will improve earnings for exporters only if world demand is inelastic.

_____ 10. A buffer stock operates by intervening in a commodity market to buy when the price is falling and to sell when the price is rising.

Multiple Choice

1. Which of the following would enter the balance of payments as a credit in the capital account?
   a. Export sale of machinery and equipment.
   b. Import purchase of machinery and equipment.
   c. Repayment of a loan from a foreign bank.
   d. Receipt of loan funds from a foreign bank.

2. In Mexico a unit of furniture (F) requires 9 labor days; a unit of corn (C) requires 3 labor days. In the United States a unit of F requires 4 labor days; a unit of C requires 2 labor days.
   a. The United States should export C and import F.
   b. The United States should export F and import C.
   c. The United States should not trade with Mexico because it can produce both products at a lower cost.

3. On average, the ratio of exports to GDP _____ as a country develops; on average, this ratio is _____ for a small country than for a large country.
   a. rises, lower
   b. rises, higher
   c. declines, lower
   d. declines, higher

4. A tea plantation in country X will generate large consumption linkage effects when:
   a. lots of tea is consumed in country X.
   b. the tea plantation uses domestically produced implements.
   c. tea exporters spend their foreign exchange earnings on imports of consumer goods.
   d. plantation workers are paid more than what they would earn elsewhere, expanding the demand for domestic consumer goods.

5. When growth of one industry such as textiles stimulates domestic production of an input, this is called:
   a. vent for surplus.
   b. a forward linkage effect.
   c. a backward linkage effect.
   d. comparative advantage.

6. The income terms of trade is determined by:
   a. export earnings relative to import prices.
   b. export earnings relative to expenditures on imports.
   c. export prices relative to import prices.
   d. export earnings relative to export quantities.

7. Empirical studies of export instability indicate that export instability:
   a. seriously impairs LDC investment and economic growth.
   b. is more severe where exports are not well diversified.
   c. both of the above.
   d. neither of the above.

8. UNCTAD's proposal for an Integrated Programme for Commodities would establish:
   a. a buffer stock fund to stabilize commodity prices.
   b. third-world solidarity in support of commodity cartels.
   c. compensatory payments to countries faced with major declines in export earnings.
   d. a fund to assist countries to diversify their exports.

9. An economic reality underlying political opposition in LDCs to trade liberalization policies is that:
   a. only the industrial countries actually gain from trade.
   b. workers in industries facing import competition can be hurt by trade liberalization.
   c. LDCs cannot compete successfully in world markets.
   d. all of the above.

10. Which term refers to the mobilization of underutilized domestic resources as a consequence of international trade opportunities?
    a. terms of trade
    b. buffer stock
    c. permanent-income hypothesis
    d. vent for surplus

Applications

Worked Example: Comparative Advantage and Gains from Trade

Figure 15–1 shows the production possibilities curve (PPC) for Imara, a country that produces food (F) and clothing (C). In the absence of international trade, point *A* represents the combination of F and C that maximizes welfare, achieving the highest attainable social indifference curve (II). The slope of the PPC at point *A* (equal to −1/4) indicates the opportunity costs of the two goods: 1 more ton of F could be produced at the cost of giving up 4 bales of C, or 1 additional bale of C could be

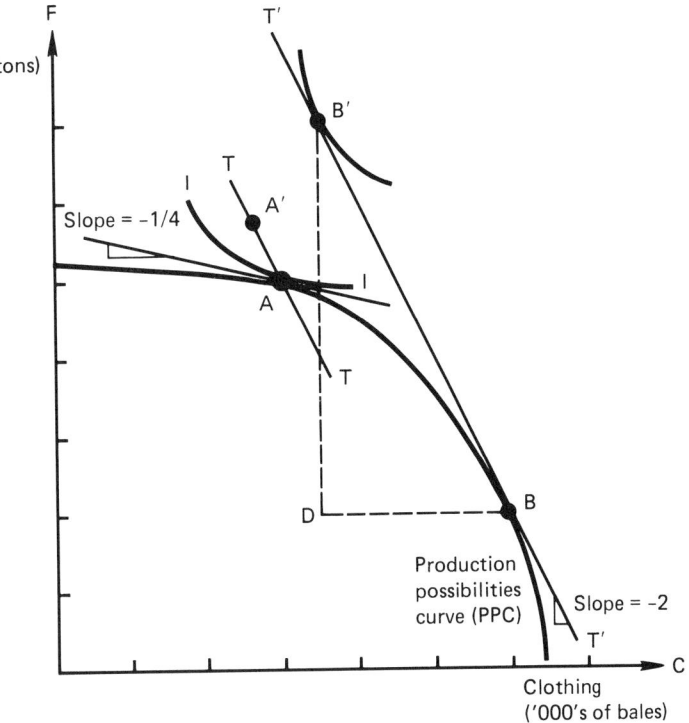

Figure 15–1

produced by foregoing 1/4 ton of F. In a market economy the slope at *A* would also equal the ratio of the prices of the two goods, since relative prices would reflect the relative costs.

Suppose now that on the world market the price of food is $1,000 per ton and the price of clothing is $2,000 per bale. One can trade 2 F for 1 C, or vice versa. If Imara continues to produce at point *A*, any point along line *TT* is attainable through trade. Line *TT* shows the trade opportunities; its slope (−2) is equal to the ratio of the price of clothing to the price of food on the world market. Some of the points on *TT* (such as point *A′*) clearly lie above indifference curve II, which had been the best attainable welfare level in the absence of trade.

But Imara can do even better. For each 1-ton reduction in F production, 4 extra bales of C can be produced. In the world market 4 extra bales of C can be sold for $8,000, with which 8 F can be purchased. Giving up 1 F to get 8 is a good deal! In short, F can be "produced" more efficiently by shifting resources to C and trading. Imara has a **comparative advantage** in clothing production.

As Imara moves down along its PPC the opportunity cost of C increases. At point *B* the slope of the PPC equals −2. To this point, but no farther, specialization and trade continue to be a good deal. With production at *B*, trade opportunities are given by line *T′T′*. Since *T′T′* is tangent to the PPC at *B*, you can see that there is no further reallocation of domestic resources that would provide more favorable trade opportunities. At *B*, Imara's domestic price ratio reflects relative prices on the world market.

Compared to the pre-trade best outcome at A, Imara can obtain more C, more F, or more of both goods through specializing in F and trading along line $T'T'$. The highest possible social indifference curve is reached by producing at B and consuming at B'. The corresponding "trade triangle" involves exporting BD of clothing in exchange for DB' of imported food. Or for other goods it could not produce on its own.

Exercises

1. It is your turn to analyze a country's comparative advantage and gains from trade, along with some related issues.

   a. El Desoto is a small agrarian country with land well suited to grow maize (M) and bananas (B). Most people prefer maize as the main item of their diet. Figure 15–2 show El Desoto's production possibilities curve (PPC).

   (i) In the absence of trade, assume that maximum social welfare is achieved by producing and consuming at point A, where:

   $$M = \text{_____} \text{ thousand tons and}$$

   $$B = \text{_____} \text{ thousand tons.}$$

   (ii) The slope of the PPC at point A is:

   $$\text{slope} = \text{_____} .$$
   [Hint: the slope is an integer.]

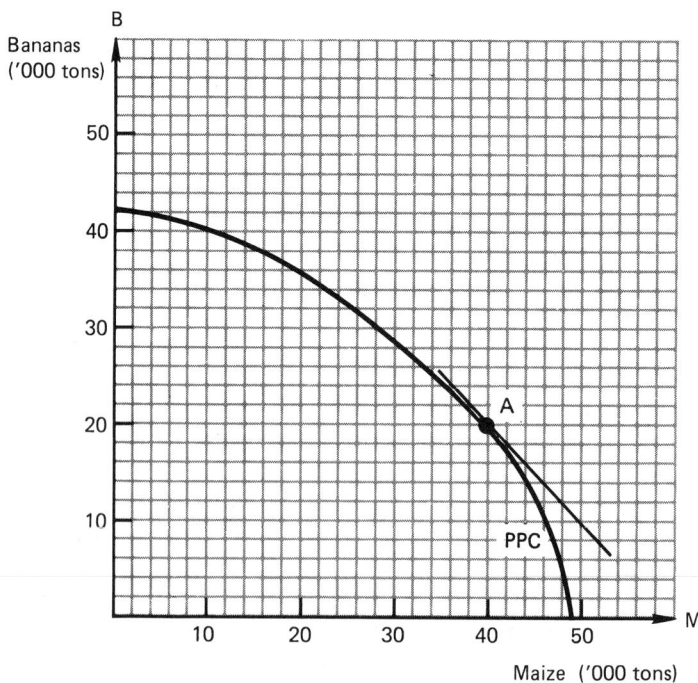

Figure 15–2

(iii) Starting from point A, producing an extra ton of bananas would involve an opportunity cost of:

_____ of maize.

Alternatively, an extra ton of maize would have an opportunity cost of:

_____ of bananas.

(iv) In the domestic market 1 ton of M trades for:

_____ ton of B.

thus the relative price ratio is:

P_M/P_B = _____ .

b. On the world market a ton of maize goes for $2,000 per ton, while bananas sell for $6,000 per ton.
  (i) Hence, on the world market one can trade a ton of M for:

_____ tons of B.

or one can trade a ton of B for:

_____ tons of M.

(ii) Draw a line through point A showing the trade opportunities open to El Desoto when it produces at point A. Label this line TT.
(iii) The slope of TT is:

slope = _____ .

(iv) El Desoto could benefit from trade by reallocating resources and trading. Specifically, it could give up domestic production of 1 ton of:

_____

in order to produce:

_____ extra ton of _____ .

(v) This additional production of:

_____

could then be sold on the world market for:

$_____ ,

which could then be used to buy:

_____ tons of the other good.

(vi) In short, by reducing domestic production of _____ by 1 ton, El Desoto can obtain _____ tons indirectly through trade. El Desoto has a comparative advantage in the production of:

_____ .

c. As resources are reallocated to production of the export good, successive increments of that good have increasingly high opportunity costs. At some point X on the PPC, further specialization no longer produces additional gains from trade.
(i) Carefully identify point X in Figure 15–2, and draw a line T'T' showing the trade opportunities open to El Desoto if it were to produce at point X. [Hint: point X involves nice round production numbers.]
(ii) At point X, El Desoto produces:

M = _____ thousand tons and

B = _____ thousand tons.

(iii) By producing at X and trading, El Desoto can attain exactly the same level of M consumption that it had originally (at point A), while enjoying an extra:

_____ thousand tons of B.

Or it can attain exactly the same level of B consumption that it had originally, while enjoying an extra:

_____ thousand tons of M.

(iv) Or it can have more of both goods. Draw a point showing the latter outcome and label it point X'.
(v) Draw the "trade triangle" associated with points X and X' and identify clearly the corresponding volume of exports and imports.

d. The country as a whole can unambiguously gain from trade. Is it possible that some groups in the country are hurt as a result of this trade? Explain.

e. (i) A decline in El Desoto's terms of trade would occur if the world price of:

_____ dropped relative to the price of _____.

    (ii) How would a decline in the terms of trade alter the position of the optimal production point (identified as X' above) and the optimal trade triangle?

2. This exercise deals with balance-of-payments accounts.

    a. Table 15-1 shows the 1983 balance-of-payments accounts for Colombia, using a format identical to that found in the textbook. The answer to each of the following questions can be found in Table 15-1, or calculated using data from the table.

Table 15-1

1983 Balance of Payments for Colombia
(All figures in millions of SDRs)[a]

	Receipts (+)	Payments (−)
A. Current account		
Merchandise exports	2,808	—
Merchandise imports	—	4,450
Transport and travel	748	997
Investment income	173	—
Profits remitted/reinvested	14	83
Debt service (interest)	—	889
Other services and transfers	401	286
Total current receipts/payments	4,144	6,705
Balance on current account:		
B. Long-term capital		
Direct investment	365	98
Private loans	1,271	416
Official loans	309	186
Total long-term capital	1,945	700
Basic balance:		
C. Short-term capital (net)	—	470
Total receipt/payments	6.089	7,875
Balance of payments:		

Source: IMF, *Balance of Payments Yearbook 1984*; see explanatory notes in textbook. Table 15-2.
[a]1 SDR = 84.31 Colombian pesos.

(i) Fill in the missing values in Table 15-1 for:

—the balance on current account,
—the basic balance, and
—the overall balance of payments.

[Be sure to put each answer in the correct column.]
(ii) Merchandise imports exceeded merchandise exports by

_____ million SDR.

[The SDR is an international unit that was worth about 1.25 U.S. dollars in early 1987.]
(iii) How did Colombia pay for this large merchandise trade deficit?

(iv) These balance of payments data show that the country's reserves of foreign exchange:

_____ by _____ million SDR during 1983.

(v) Gross debt service (interest payments plus repayments of principle on both private and official loans) totaled:

_____ million SDR, equal to

_____ % of the country's merchandise exports.

b. Identify each of the following transactions as a debit (D) or a credit (C) item in the balance-of-payments accounts for Kenya. Also identify the account in which it would be entered: the current account = C; the long-term capital account = LT; or the short-term capital account = ST.

	D/C	C/LT/ST
(i) An American pays for a hotel in Kenya:	_____	_____
(ii) A Kenyan buys an English sweater:	_____	_____
(iii) A Kenyan business repays a long-term loan from a German bank:	_____	_____
(iv) A Kenyan trucking firm is hired by a Ugandan company to transport goods:	_____	_____
(v) An American business puts dollars into its checking account at a Kenyan bank:	_____	_____
(vi) An Indian company invests in a new textile factory in Kenya:	_____	_____

(vii) A German business remits profits earned
in Kenya to Germany: _____ _____

(viii) A Kenyan working in England sends
some of his income to his family back
home: _____ _____

3. This exercise applies the formulas for the various terms-of-trade
concepts. You may wish to review these formulas in the textbook.
Table 15-2 shows data on trade, factor productivity, and economic
growth in Colombia and Malawi for 1970 and 1980. Each figure is
an index number defined as being equal to 100 for 1970. Each 1980
figure represents the value for that year *relative to* the value for
1970. Notice that GDP growth was identical in the two countries.

a. With 1970 = 100, what is the net barter terms-of-trade index for
1980?

—for Colombia: T_n = _____ and

—for Malawi: $T_n/$ = _____ .

b. (i) With 1970 = 100, calculate the *income* terms-of-trade index
for 1980

—for Colombia: T_i = _____ and

—for Malawi: T_i = _____ .

(ii) Why is the income terms-of-trade index higher than the net
barter terms-of-trade index for both countries?

Tables 15-2

Trade, Factor Productivity, and Growth Indexes
for Colombia and Malawi, 1970 and 1980

	Colombia		Malawi	
	1970	1980	1970	1980
1. Average price of exports (P_x)	100	391	100	253
2. Volume of exports (Q_x)	100	133	100	198
3. Average price of imports (P_m)	100	320	100	351
4. Volume of imports (Q_m)	100	172	100	117
5. Labor productivity[a] (Z_x)	100	123	100	129
6. GDP	100	172	100	172

Source: Derived from data in World Bank, *World Tables 1983* and *World Development Report 1984.*

[a]Defined as GDP ÷ labor force. Z_x ought to measure factor productivity in the export
industry, but the present data will suffice for the purpose of this exercise.

(iii) How can T_i for Malawi exceed 100 when T_n is less than 100?

c. (i) Calculate the single factoral terms-of-trade index for 1980 (with 1970 = 100)

—for Colombia: T_s = _____ and

—for Malawi: T_s = _____ .

(ii) Briefly interpret the differences between the single factoral terms of trade and the income terms of trade.

4. This exercise uses a simple supply-and-demand diagram to analyze export instability, buffer stock operations, and cartel behavior. Figure 15–3 shows conditions in the world market for copper. As drawn, the supply curve (S) is price-inelastic and the demand curve (D) exhibits a price elasticity equal to unity. The initial equilibrium price and quantity are $P(0)$ and $Q(0)$.

a. Compared to the initial situation, how will the world-market price of copper (P) and the revenues earned by copper exporters ($P \times Q$) change as a result of:

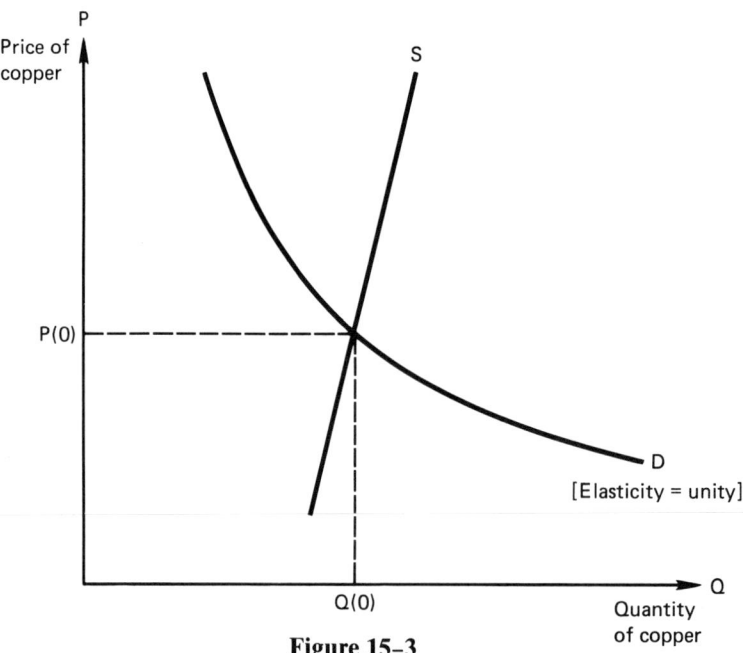

Figure 15–3

-234-

(i) a 20% increase in demand? [I.e., a shift in the D curve.]

—the price will _____;

—export earnings will _____ .

(ii) a 20% increase in supply? [I.e., a shift in the S curve.]

—the price will _____;

—export earnings will _____ .

(Hint: don't forget that the price elasticity of demand here is unity!)

b. Now think about the effects of different sources of *instability* in the export markets. The price elasticity of demand is still assumed to be unitary.

(i) How is the *stability* of the copper *price* affected by:

—fluctuations in world demand?

—fluctuations in world supply?

(ii) How is the *stability* of *export earnings* for copper producers affected by:

—fluctuations in world demand?

—fluctuations in world supply?

(iii) How would the above answers be changed if demand were inelastic? Be specific.

c. An international fund is created to finance a buffer stock for stabilizing copper prices at $P(0)$. The fund has $5 billion to be used to build up an initial stock of copper.

(i) Thereafter, whenever the market price falls below $P(0)$ the fund would:

_____ copper.

And whenever the price rises above $P(0)$, the fund would:

_____ copper.

(ii) Starting with the initial conditions shown in Figure 15–3, suppose that demand increases by 20%. Draw the new demand curve (approximately). Label it D' (precision is not essential here) and show the quantity of copper that the fund must purchase or sell to stabilize the price at $P(0)$.

(iii) Starting again with the initial conditions, suppose that demand declines by 20%. Draw the new demand curve (approximately). Label it D'', and show the quantity of copper that the fund must purchase or sell to stabilize the price at $P(0)$.

(iv) Figure 15–4 is just a fresh diagram of the conditions shown in Figure 15–3. Suppose now that supply increases by 20%. Draw the new supply curve (approximately) in Figure 15–4. Label it S', and show the quantity of copper that the fund must purchase or sell to stabilize the price at $P(0)$.

(v) Starting again with the initial conditions, suppose that supply drops by 20%. Draw the new supply curve (approximately) in

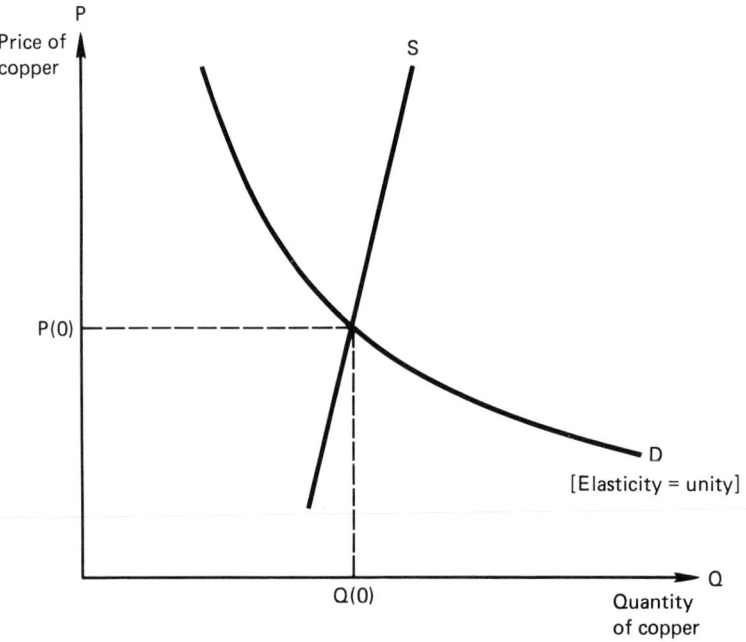

Figure 15–4

-236-

Figure 15–4. Label it S'', and show the quantity of copper that the fund must purchase or sell to stabilize the price at $P(0)$.

d. These buffer stock operations will succeed in stabilizing the price of copper. But will they succeed in stabilizing the export *earnings* of the copper producers?
   (i) Will earnings be stabilized by the fund operations when the supply curve is shifting? Explain.

   (ii) Will earnings be stabilized by the fund operations when the demand curve is shifting? Explain.

e. Figure 15–5 is a fresh drawing of the initial conditions. Suppose that the buffer stock is in operation, following the operating rules established in part c. Let's examine the effects of *permanent shifts* in S and D as opposed to temporary fluctuations.

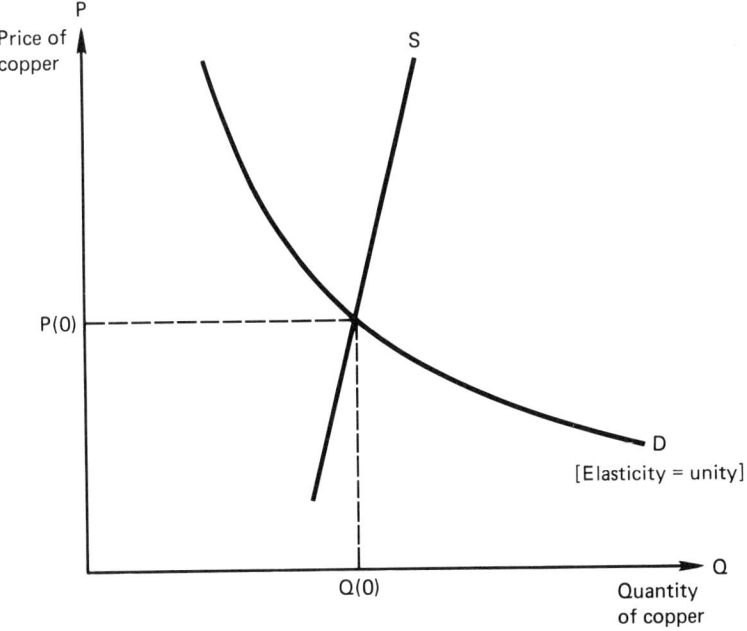

Figure 15–5

(i) Let *D* permanently shift out by 20% while *S* permanently shifts out by 40%. Draw the new curves in Figure 15–5 (approximately). Label them *D′* and *S′*, respectively.

(ii) What will be the fund's fate if it continues to defend *P*(0) under these conditions?

(iii) Suppose instead that *D* shifts permanently by 40% and *S* shifts permanently by 20%. If the fund continues to defend *P*(0) under these conditions, what will be its fate?

f. Start again from initial conditions in the copper market, redrawn one last time in Figure 15–6. Suppose that exporters band together to form a cartel. They agree to coordinate production cutbacks that reduce the supply of copper to 75% of its original volume.

(i) In Figure 15–6, draw a vertical line showing the new fixed volume of copper that is being supplied to the market. Label it as *line C*.

(ii) Given this quantity restriction, show the price *P*(C) that the cartel can charge. [Hint: It charges what the market will bear.]

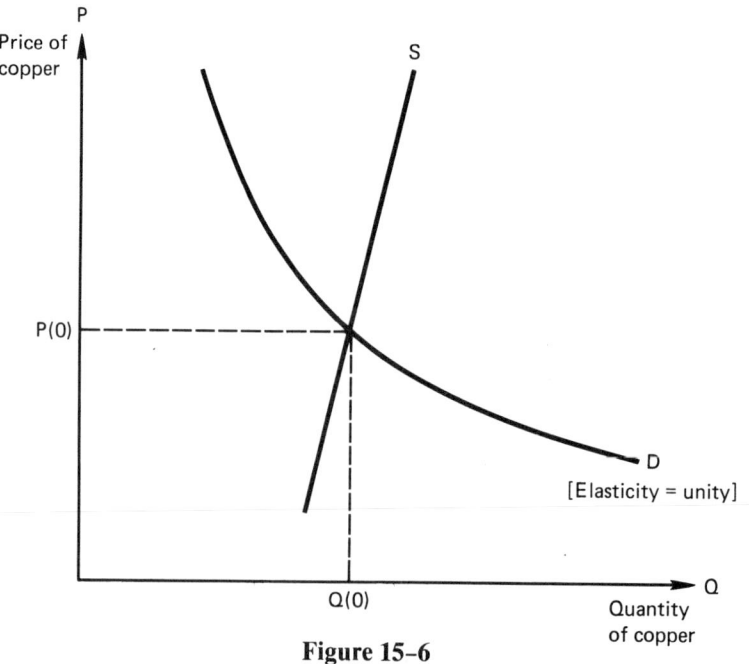

Figure 15–6

-238-

(iii) Taken as a whole, have the copper exporters increased their revenues by the action of the cartel? Explain briefly. [Note: Don't forget that the demand elasticity is unity.]

(iv) In the cartel situation depicted in Figure 15–6, why would each individual exporting country have a strong incentive to "cheat" on the cartel?

(v) If the cartel manages to maintain price $P(C)$, the high price will attract new producers who would not otherwise find copper mining profitable. Also, consumers will have a strong incentive to find substitutes or new ways to conserve their use of copper. Explain, in terms of the supply-and-demand curves, how these long-run forces will erode the cartel's strength.

5. This exercise uses supply and demand to study a case of the curse of resource riches. Figure 15–7 shows the market for foreign exchange in Bounty, a country on the verge of riches. The vertical axis shows the price of foreign exchange (PFX, in shillings per dollar). The quantity of dollars is indicated on the horizontal axis.

a. A devaluation of the Bountian shilling is equivalent to a _____ in the price of foreign exchange.

b. Bounty exports gold and radios. The supply of dollars earned from exporting gold (S_G) is perfectly inelastic, whereas the supply of dollars earned from exporting radios (S_R) is a positive function of PFX. [Why? The world price of radios may be a fixed dollar amount, but for domestic producers profitability depends on how many shillings are received per dollar earned.] For any given PFX the line HIJ shows the "total supply" of foreign exchange Bounty would earn from its exports. Bounty's demand for dollars is shown by line D.

   (i) Identify the equilibrium price of foreign exchange and label it *PFX(0)*.

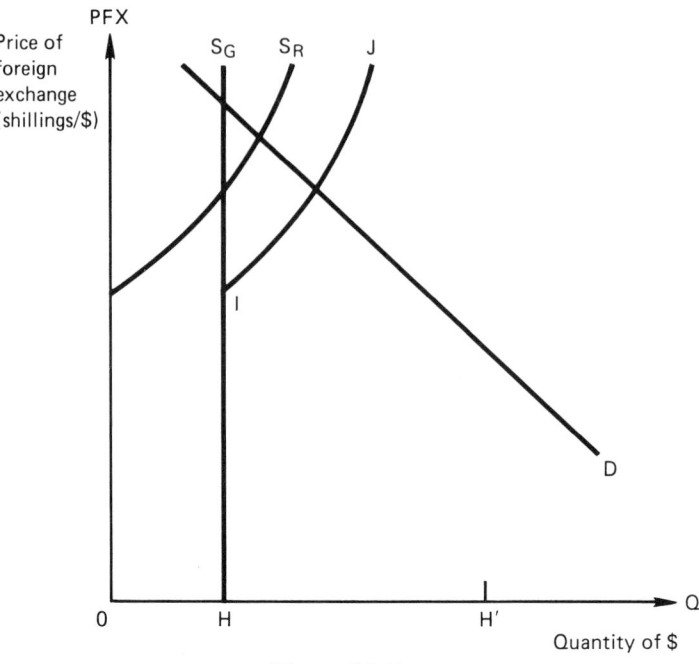

Figure 15-7

(ii) Show the quantity of dollars earned by exporting radios at this initial equilibrium. Label it *QR(0)*.

c. A major new gold field is discovered. The supply of dollars from gold exports expands from *OH* to *OH'*.
    (i) Draw in the new *total* supply curve and label it *H'I'J'*.
    (ii) Identify the new equilibrium price of foreign exchange and label it *PFX(1)*.
    (iii) Explain what happens to exports of radios following the massive expansion in gold exports.

d. Suppose that gold production is highly capital intensive and radio production is very labor intensive.
    (i) What will happen to employment and real wages in Bounty as a result of the gold bonanza? Briefly explain.

(ii) Suggest three possible policies to cope with these new problems.

Answers to Self-Test

Completion

1. balance of payments
2. terms-of-trade; (more precisely, net barter terms-of-trade)
3. comparative advantage
4. autarky
5. fiscal
6. Engel's
7. supply
8. permanent income
9. enclaves
10. low

True-False

1. F	6. T
2. T	7. T
3. F	8. F
4. F	9. T
5. F	10. T

Multiple Choice

1. d	6. a
2. b	7. b
3. b	8. a
4. d	9. b
5. c	10. d

CHAPTER 16   Import Substitution

Overview

Most LDCs have pursued industrialization through a strategy of import substitution. The basic elements of this strategy are: (1) to identify large domestic markets being supplied by imports; (2) to select from among these markets the products that could be produced at home; and (3) to foster domestic production of these products by protecting domestic industry from import competition. The primary tools used for this purpose are protective tariffs, import quotas, and an overvalued exchange rate.

In principle, these protective policies should be applied temporarily as infant industries overcome initially high costs and emerge as efficient producers able to compete successfully against imports. But most often the infant industries fail to grow up and remain high-cost inefficient producers. Indeed, protection tends to breed such inefficiency. The policy tools used to implement import substitution breed other distortions as well. The policies inhibit development of exports and agriculture, weaken potential backward linkages, and foster dependence on imported intermediate goods and capital goods. These policies also tend to encourage excess capital intensity, thereby reducing employment creation and intensifying income inequality.

Main Learning Objectives

After studying this chapter you ought to understand and be able to explain:

1. The basic objectives and policy instruments of an **import substitution** strategy of industrialization.

2. The economic effects of **tariffs** and **quotas**.

3. The distinction between **nominal protection, the effective rate of protection** (ERP), and the **domestic resource cost** (DRC).

4. How an **overvalued exchange rate** is used to promote import substitution.

5. Empirical trends in trade associated with import-substitution industrialization.

6. Why import substitution strategies typically have reinforced **import dependence** and retarded self-sustaining development.

Additional Key Terms, Concepts, and Institutions

Can you identify and explain each of the following?

infant industries
ad valorem tariff
prohibitive tariff
value-added at domestic prices and at world prices
quota premium
composition of imports

Economic Tools and Techniques

From what you have learned in this chapter, can you:

1. Use supply-and-demand analysis to evaluate the effects of a tariff? Specifically, can you identify: the **protective effect, producer surplus, consumer surplus, resource cost**, and **deadweight loss**, as well as the government's tariff revenue?

2. Calculate an industry's effective rate of protection and domestic resource cost, given appropriate data?

3. Use supply and demand to show how a quota differs from a tariff when there is a monopolistic domestic producer?

4. Interpret the economic effects of an overvalued exchange rate in terms of the supply and demand for foreign exchange?

5. Demonstrate the long-run effects of an import substitution strategy, in terms of movements along and shifts in the production possibilities frontier?

Self-Test

Completion

1. An _____ industry is one that requires protection or subsidy to get started, but is expected eventually to become competitive.

2. The margin between the tariff-determined price of a domestic product and that of the inputs that go into the product is called the

   _____.

3. If the effective rate of protection is 127% for manufacturing and 46% for agriculture, there is an incentive for domestic investment in

   _____ rather than _____.

4. The ratio of value-added at domestic prices (in local currency) to value-added at world prices (in foreign currency) is called the

   _____.

5. A nation's exchange rate is overvalued when the price of foreign

   exchange is held artificially too _____.

6. One clear empirical indicator of import substitution is a marked increase in the share of _____ goods in total imports.

7. Where tariffs, quotas, and import licenses are the primary determinants of profits, the most successful managers are those with _____ skills.

8. A tariff on a product will generally cause its domestic price to _____, and domestic consumption of the product to _____ .

True-False If false, you should be able to explain why.

_____ 1. Development of capital goods industries has generally been the initial target of import substitution efforts.

_____ 2. A prohibitive tariff is one high enough to shut off all imports of the good in question.

_____ 3. It is possible for a country's bicycle industry to have a 150% rate of effective protection even if the nominal tariff rate is only 25%.

_____ 4. An industry with a low domestic resource cost (DRC) is more efficient than an industry with a high DRC.

_____ 5. It is clear from data for the period 1960–1983 that fast-growing countries have reduced the ratio of imports to GDP.

_____ 6. In most LDCs pursuing import-substitution industralization, the ratio of imports to GDP declined from 1960 to 1980.

_____ 7. An overvalued exchange rate will increase the domestic currency cost of imported goods.

_____ 8. More often than not import substitution protection has bred inefficient, high-cost producers rather than successful, competitive industries.

Multiple Choice

1. Other things being equal, the effective rate of protection on leather shoes will be higher:
   a. the higher the nominal tariff on shoes.
   b. the lower the nominal tariff on leather.
   c. the smaller the value-added at world market prices.
   d. all of the above.

2. An *ad valorem* tariff is:
   a. a tariff based on the value-added of an imported good.
   b. a tariff based on an imported input to a domestic industry.
   c. a tariff based on the value of an imported good.
   d. a tariff that increases the domestic market price of a good.

3. With import substitution, the structure of effective protection characteristically biases domestic investment in favor of:
   a. production of capital goods.
   b. production of manufactured consumer goods.
   c. production of agricultural export goods.
   d. production of food crops.

4. In Figure 16–1, a tariff rate of *t* is equivalent in most respects to a quota that restricts imports to amount:
   a. *AB.*
   b. *BC.*
   c. *BE.*
   d. *DF.*

5. The textbook's boxed-example case study of Kenya illustrates a country in which import substitution:
   a. quickly led to stagnation.
   b. had become an impediment to more rapid growth by the early 1980s.
   c. was never used to promote industrialization.
   d. was atypical, emphasizing agriculture and capital goods industries.

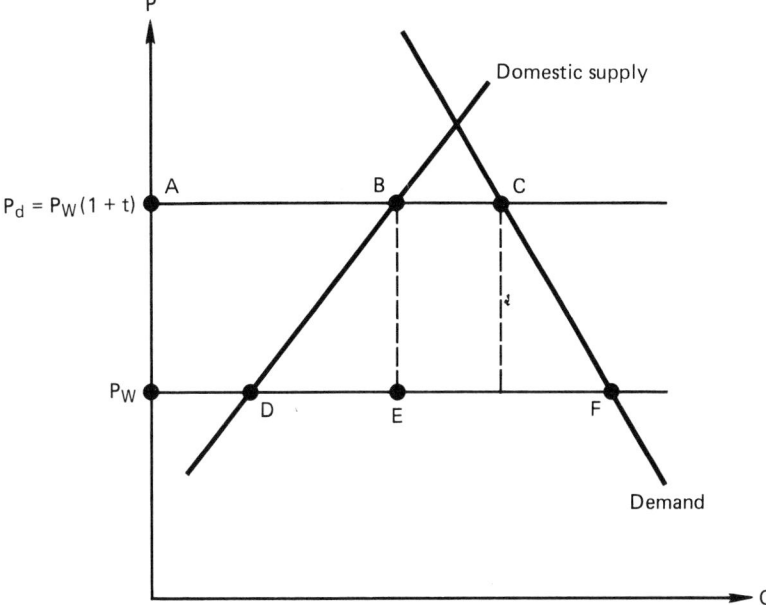

Figure 16–1

6. The term "quota premium" refers to:
   a. the price paid by importers for import licenses.
   b. a government decision to relax a quantitative restriction on a product.
   c. windfall profits gained by those who receive import-license allocations under a quota system.
   d. the effective rate of protection associated with an import quota.

7. In many LDCs the effective rate of protection is especially high for which sector?
   a. manufacture of consumer goods
   b. manufacture of machinery
   c. mining
   d. agriculture

8. Which of the following is *not* part of the "catalogue of woes" associated with the long-term effects of import substitution? [There could be more than one correct answer.]
   a. intensified income inequality
   b. reduced employment growth
   c. encouragement of capital-intensive investments
   d. accelerated population growth
   e. limited backward linkages in manufacturing
   f. creation of high-cost non-competitive industries
   g. exacerbated foreign exchange constraint
   h. slowed growth of domestic food production

Applications

Worked Example: Effects of a Protective Tariff

The Republic of Écouter imports radios. Figure 16–2 shows that the world-market supply of radios to Écouter is perfectly elastic at a price of $P(W) = \$20 = F6,000$ (F stands for francs, the local currency). The domestic demand curve (D) shows that at this price 1,000 radios per year are purchased. The potential domestic supply curve (S) shows that high-cost domestic producers cannot compete against imports as long as the price remains below F7,000.

To promote domestic production of radios, the government decides to levy a 50% *ad valorem* tariff. With this tariff, imported radios now cost $P(D) = P(W)(1 + t) = 6,000(1.5) = F9,000$. The supply curve S shows that domestic producers can now compete against imports up to $Q = 500$ units of output. This is the **protective effect** on domestic output. The marginal cost of further domestic output would exceed F9,000; therefore, additional units of output would not be profitable. In addition to stimulating domestic production, the higher price causes the quantity demanded to drop to 800 radios. Imports of 300 radios fill the gap between domestic consumption and production.

With the tariff in place, consumers spend F7,200,000 on radios (9,000 × 800). Of this total, F1,800,000 (area *f* in the figure) goes to pay the world price of imported radios. This compares to F6,000,000 originally spent on imported radios (areas *e* + *f* + *g*). F900,000 (area *c*) is paid to

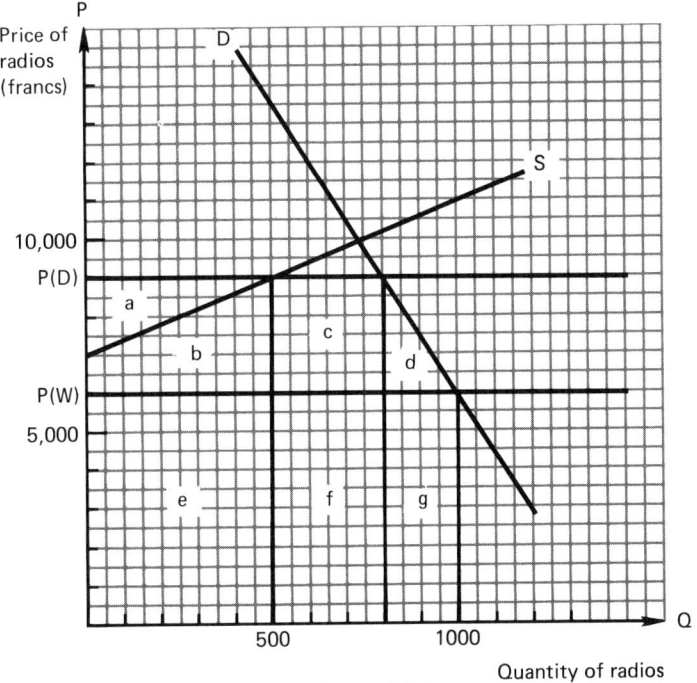

P

Price of radios (francs)

D

S

10,000

P(D)

a

b

c

d

P(W)

5,000

e

f

g

500

1000

Q

Quantity of radios

Figure 16–2

the government in tariff duties on the imported radios. And domestic producers' revenues are F4,500,000 (areas $a + b + e$).

Since the height of the demand curve at each point reflects the consumers' willingness to pay for the marginal unit of the product, the area under the demand curve up to a given point can be interpreted as a measure of the total value to consumers. Subtracting from this total value the amount paid for the radios gives the **consumer surplus**. Prior to the tariff, the consumer surplus equaled the entire area bounded by the demand curve and line $P(W)$. With the tariff, consumers pay more and get less, suffering a loss of consumer surplus equal to area $a + b + c + d$. The protective tariff stimulates domestic production at a cost in terms of consumer welfare and efficiency.

Part of this loss to the consumers is offset by a gain to the government in the form of tariff revenues (area c). Area a is a transfer to domestic producers called **producers' surplus**: payments in excess of marginal costs. The rest (areas $b + d$) is a net **deadweight loss**. Area b is part of the revenue earned by domestic producers but not part of their profit: it covers the excess **resource cost** of diverting resources to radio production from other productive uses.

The welfare and efficiency costs of protection are worth bearing if the radio industry becomes more efficient and overcomes its cost disadvantage. In the figure, this would be represented by a downward shift in S large enough for domestic producers to compete against imports without protection. The irony is that domestic producers often find it easier to lobby for more protection than to improve efficiency.

Exercises

1. It is your turn to analyze the effects of a protective tariff.

   a. Figure 16–3 shows the domestic supply (S) and demand (D)
      curves for tires in Kayak.

      (i) Domestic production will be undertaken only when the price is

         at least Ksh_____. (Ksh stands for the Kayak shilling, the
         local currency).

      (ii) Suppose, however, that imported tires sell for Ksh400. Draw
         the line representing the supply from the world market, and
         label it $P(W)$.

      (iii) Under these conditions the quantity demanded is:

         _____ thousand tires.

         The market price for tires in Kayak is:

         Ksh_____.

         And expenditures on tires total:

         Ksh_____ million.

      (iv) Imports account for _____ % of the market.
      (v) Given that Ksh10 = $1, the foreign exchange cost of tire

         imports is $_____.

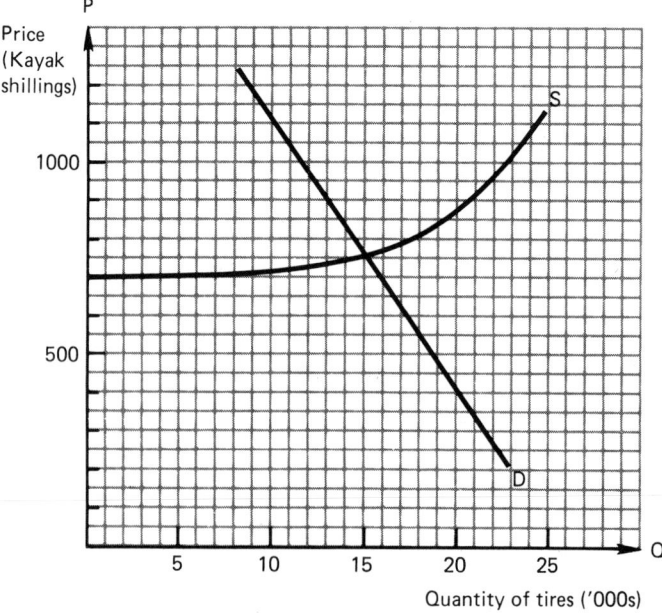

Figure 16–3

b. In order to foster domestic tire production, the government introduces a 100% tariff on imports.
  (i) With this tariff, the domestic price of imported tires becomes Ksh_____ .
  (ii) Draw a line in Figure 16-3 showing this new price of imports and label it P(W)′.
  (iii) Label as *point E* the point showing the new market equilibrium price and quantity. [Hint: Careful! This example differs somewhat from the Worked Example.]
  (iv) At this new equilibrium the quantity demanded is _____ thousand tires. Label this Q(E).
  (v) The new equilibrium price is Ksh_____ . Label this P(E).
  (vi) Total expenditures on tires equal Ksh_____ million.
  (vii) Imports account for _____ % of the market.
  (viii) Government tariff revenues total Ksh_____ .
  (ix) The foreign exchange cost of tire imports is $_____ .
  (x) The protective effect is to stimulate _____ thousand tires of domestic production.
c. Label specific areas in Figure 16-3 with small letters *a, b,* and *c* to identify:
  (i) the loss of consumer surplus due to the tariff;

  (ii) the producers' surplus;

  (iii) the excess resource cost of domestic production; and

  (iv) the deadweight loss.

d. Any tariff in excess of _____ % would be a prohibitive tariff.

e. Given the 100% tariff, briefly describe how the market would adjust in terms of production, imports, and equilibrium price:
  (i) if domestic production were to become less efficient, with costs rising by 10%;

  (ii) if production costs were to rise by 25%;

(iii) if demand were to increase by 50%.

f. Think about the longer run consequences of the protective tariff
    in Kayak's tire industry. With reference to Figure 16–3, how
    would you determine whether this case of import substitution is
    ultimately successful or unsuccessful?

2. This exercise examines the effects of quantitative restrictions on
    imports, using the example of the tire market in Kayak as presented
    in exercise 1. Figure 16–4, which is identical to Figure 16–3, shows
    the initial conditions. Again assume that the world price is $P(W) =$
    Ksh400.

    a. Instead of levying a tariff, suppose the government of Kayak sets
        a zero quota on tire imports.
        (i) In Figure 16– label as *point E* the resulting equilibrium price
            and quantity, assuming that the domestic tire market is a
            competitive market (i.e., no monopoly power).

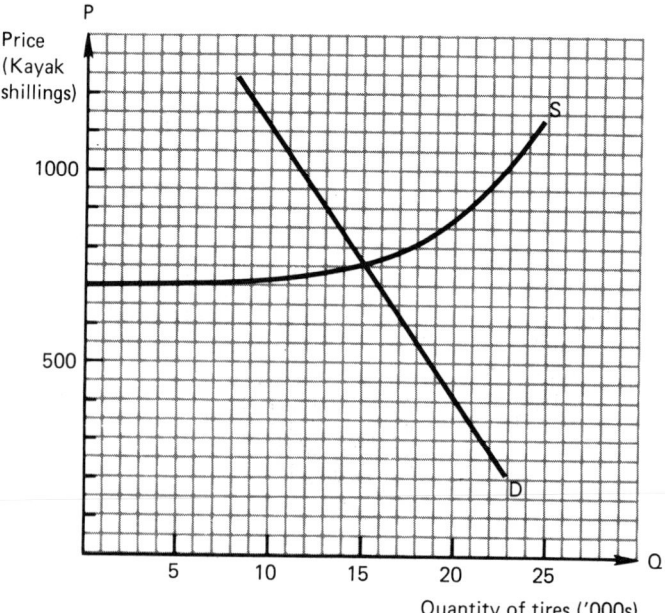

Figure 16–4

(ii) Compare the zero quota to the 100% tariff (analyzed in exercise 1) in terms of the effects on domestic consumption and production.

b. Now consider the effects of the zero quota when there is a single domestic producer acting as a monopolist. Curve S now represents marginal costs (MC).
  (i) Draw in the marginal revenue curve that corresponds to the domestic demand schedule. Label this MR. [Precision is not essential here.]
  (ii) In the figure, clearly identify the monopolist's profit-maximizing output and label it Q(M). [Hint: it is the output such that MC = MR.]
  (iii) Identify the monopoly price and label it P(M).
  (iv) Shade in the loss of consumer surplus that results from imposition of the zero quota when there is a domestic monopoly.

c. When there is a single domestic producer, how will a zero quota differ from a 100% tariff in terms of the effects on domestic price and quantity? Briefly explain why.

d. Return to the assumption that there is no monopoly in the domestic tire industry. Given the zero quota on tire imports, briefly describe how the market would adjust in terms of production, imports, and equilibrium price:
  (i) if domestic production were to become less efficient, with costs rising by 10%;

  (ii) if production costs rose by 25%;

(iii) if demand increased by 50%.

(iv) Compare the three answers above to those in part e of exercise 1.

3. This exercise works through calculations of effective rate of protection (ERP) and domestic cost (DRC).

   a. Cars can be imported into the Republic of Motokah at the world price of $P(W) = \$10,000$ each, or Rs10,000 (Rs stands for rupees), at the exchange rate of Rs1 = $1.

      (i) Car *components* can be imported for domestic assembly at the world price of $C(W) = \$9,000$. In local currency units the

      components cost Rs_____.

      (ii) What is the value-added at world prices of the car assembly operations in Motokah?

$$V(W) = P(W) - C(W) = \$_____$$

$$= Rs_____ .$$

   b. Suppose the government of Motokah levies a tariff of $t_o = 25\%$ on car imports, but permits car components to be imported duty free, so $t_i = 0\%$.

      (i) With this tariff structure, the domestic price of imported cars is:

$$P(d) = Rs_____ .$$

      (ii) The domestic price of components is:

$$C(d) = Rs_____ .$$

      (iii) Domestic assemblers can now compete against import competition as long as their value-added at domestic prices is no higher than:

$$V(d) = P(d) - C(d) = Rs_____ .$$

      Call this the *potential VA(d)* permitted under the tariff structure.

-252-

c. (i) Comparing $V(d)$ to $V(W)$, domestic car assembly can be as

much as _____ % more costly than assembly operations in the world market and still compete with imports.

(ii) So the effective rate of protection is:

$$ERP = \text{_____} \%,$$

although the nominal rate of protection is only:

$$t_o = \text{_____} \%.$$

d. Suppose all conditions remain the same except that a uniform tariff is levied on all imports, such that $t_o = t_i = 25\%$.

(i) In this case, the effective rate of protection on domestic car assembly is:

$$ERP = \text{_____} \%.$$

(ii) In this case, the domestic industry will be able to compete against imports as long as domestic assembly costs exceed the world value-added for assembly operations by no more than

_____ %.

e. Once again let $t_o = 25\%$ and $t_i = 0\%$. But now suppose that components cost $C(W) = \$11,000 = Rs11,000$ on the world market—in other words buying a car in pieces is more expensive than buying a complete assembled car! (It happens, really!)

(i) Use the formula to calculate the effective rate of protection on domestic car assembly operations in this case:

$$ERP = \text{_____} \%.$$

(ii) Under these cost and tariff conditions will domestic assembly be able to compete against imported cars? Explain.

f. With the same tariff structure, return to $C(W) = \$9,000$. But suppose now that the equilibrium price of cars in Motakah rises only to $P(d) = Rs11,000$ because at this price domestic supply satisfies domestic demand. No assembled cars are imported.

(i) You have already calculated that for $t_o = 25\%$ and $t_i = 0\%$, the *potential* value-added at domestic prices is:

Rs_____ , and

$$ERP = \text{_____} \%.$$

(ii) But since the market price in fact rises only to Rs11,000 here, the *actual* value-added at domestic prices is:

$$V(d) = Rs\underline{\hspace{2cm}}.$$

(iii) The value-added at world prices, in dollar units, is:

$$V(W) = \$\underline{\hspace{2cm}}.$$

(iv) So the domestic resource cost per dollar saved through domestic assembly of cars is:

$$DRC = \underline{\hspace{2cm}} Rs/\$.$$

(v) Considering that the exchange rate is Rs1 = $1, explain why the DRC can be interpreted as showing that investment in domestic assembly operations is inefficient.

g. *Optional* (A harder one.) Continue with $P(d) = Rs11,000$ and $C(d) = C(W) = Rs9,000$. Suppose the domestic value-added consisted entirely of wage payments. Because of labor-market distortions the opportunity cost of labor equals 40% of the wage rate.

(i) In terms of **shadow prices** (see Chapter 6), the domestic value-added is therefore:

$$V(d) = Rs\underline{\hspace{2cm}}, \text{ and}$$

$$DRC = \underline{\hspace{2cm}} Rs/\$.$$

(ii) Is domestic assembly efficient under these conditions?

4. This exercise examines the effects of an overvalued exchange rate. The Republic of Cabana earns foreign exchange (FX) through coffee exports. It imports machines and jeans. In Figure 16–5 curves S and D show the supply and demand for FX for any given exchange rate (ER), measured in pesos per dollar.

a. (i) The market equilibrium exchange rate is:

$$ER = \underline{\hspace{2cm}} pesos/\$.$$

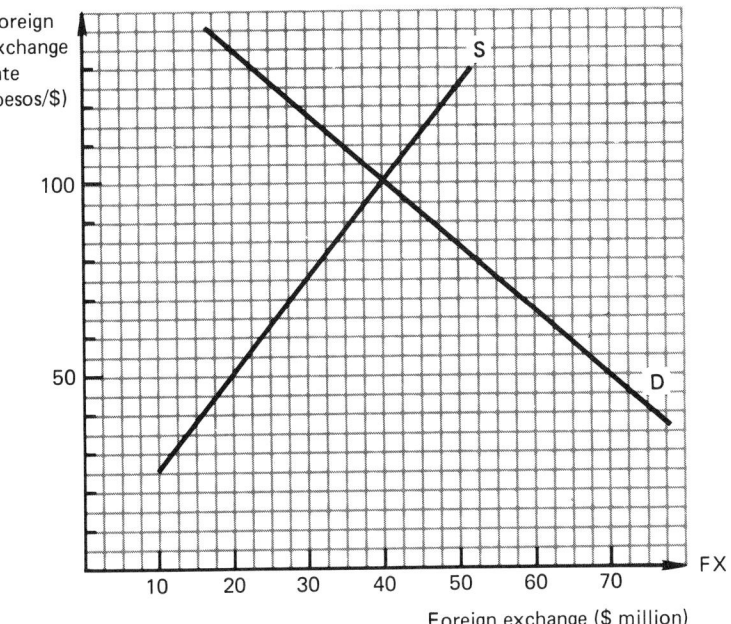

Figure 16-5

(ii) At this exchange rate (and assuming no tariffs or quotas to muddy the exercise), coffee selling for $1 per pound in the world market is worth _____ pesos per pound to the Cabanian exporter.

(iii) For a machine priced at $5,000 on the world market, the equivalent price in Cabanian currency is _____ pesos.

(iv) For a pair of jeans selling at $20 on the world market, the equivalent price in Cabana is _____ pesos.

b. Suppose the supply and demand curves for FX remain as shown in Figure 16-5, but the government requires all foreign exchange earned by Cabanian exporters to be turned over to the central bank at an exchange rate of ER′ = 50 pesos/$. The government then sells the available FX to licensed importers at the rate ER′. At this controlled exchange rate:

(i) Coffee selling for $1 per pound in the world markets will earn _____ pesos for Cabanian exporters.

(ii) A machine selling for $5,000 on the world market will cost a buyer in Cabana _____ pesos.

(iii) A pair of jeans selling for $20 on the world market will cost a buyer in Cabana _____ pesos.

c. (i) Compared to the equilibrium exchange rate, Cabana's peso in part b is _____-valued.

(ii) For Cabanians, exporting has become _____ profitable, while imports have become _____ expensive.

(iii) In Figure 16–5, the quantity of FX demanded at ER' = 50 pesos/$ is $_____million; the quantity supplied is $_____ million.

(iv) There is excess _____ (supply/demand) of

$_____ million.

d. To cope with the disequilibrium situation, the government licenses access to foreign exchange. In pursuit of import substitution, no licenses are granted for importing jeans, but licenses are freely available for importing machines. The effect of these exchange controls amounts to a quota of:

_____ on jeans imports

combined with an implicit subsidy of:

_____ % on imported machines

and an implicit tax of:

_____ % on coffee exporters.

(Hint: compare the peso prices for machines and for coffee with and without the controlled exchange rate.)

e. Suppose instead that licenses to use the scarce foreign exchange are sold in an open auction.

(i) From Figure 16–5, what price would Cabanians be willing to pay for the quantity of FX actually available under the controlled exchange rate?

_____ pesos/$.

(ii) What price, then, would Cabanians be willing to pay for a license permitting them to buy FX for 50 pesos per dollar?

_____ pesos.

(iii) Suppose Cabana has a single domestic producer of jeans. How would this producer's business be affected if foreign exchange licenses were sold at an open auction?

5. This final exercise examines import substitution dynamics using the general equilibrium model as presented in the textbook. Figure 16−6 shows a production possibilities frontier (PPF) for Anglia in 1960. The world price for both coconuts (C) and steel (S) is $1,000 per ton. With free trade Anglia will produce at point A and trade along line TT to consume at point A'.

a. At point A the slope of the PPF is _____; one extra ton of

   S could be produced if C production were reduced by _____.

b. To promote domestic steel production, the government now levies a 100% tariff on S imports, doubling the domestic price of S. The domestic price of C remains unchanged.

   (i) The domestic price ratio will now be:

$$P(C)/P(S) = \underline{\hspace{2cm}}.$$

   (ii) With the tariff on S imports, it becomes profitable for domestic producers to shift resources from coconuts to steel as long as each ton of reduced C output permits S output to

   increase by at least _____.

   (iii) In Figure 16−6 label as *point B* the outcome of this reallocation of resources in response to the new domestic price ratio.

   (v) The slope of the PPF at point B is _____.

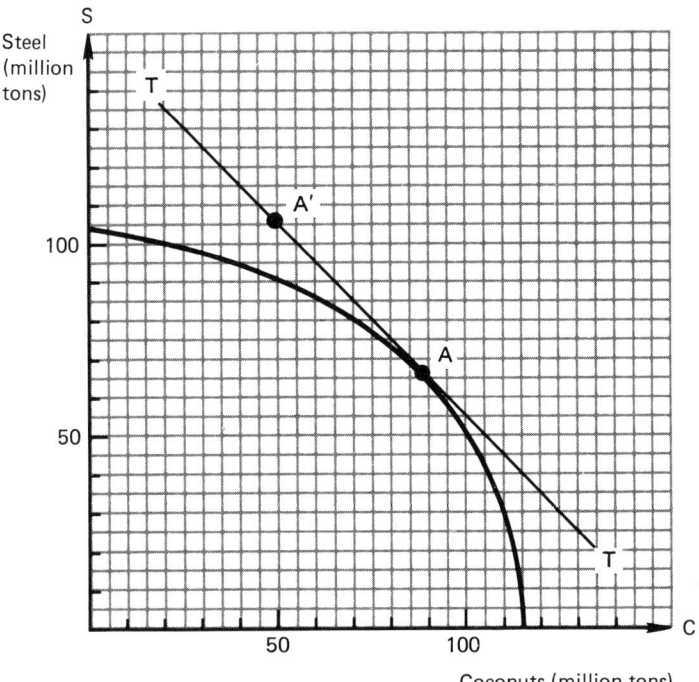

Figure 16–6

c. (i) Carefully draw a line labeled T′ showing the trade possibilities
open to Anglia when it is producing at point B. [Hint: the
world prices have not changed.]

(ii) Label as B′ some point on the new trade line T′ that shows a
situation in which Anglia's exports, imports, and consumption
of both goods have all declined compared to the free-trade
outcome, point A′.

d. Figure 16–7 reproduces Anglia's PPF for 1960.

(i) Suppose that over the subsequent 20 years, Anglia's import
substitution policy is *successful*. Draw a new production
possibilities frontier showing such an outcome for 1980. Label
it *PPF′*.

(ii) For simplicity, assume that relative prices in both the domestic
and world markets are the same in 1980 as in 1960. Identify
the domestic production point in 1980, and label it *B(80)*.

(iii) Identify the consumption point in 1980 and label it *B′(80)*.

e. Explain how to show in Figure 16–7 that Anglia could obtain
more of both goods in 1980 if it eliminated the tariff on steel and
moved to free trade—even though the import substitution policy
has been successful.

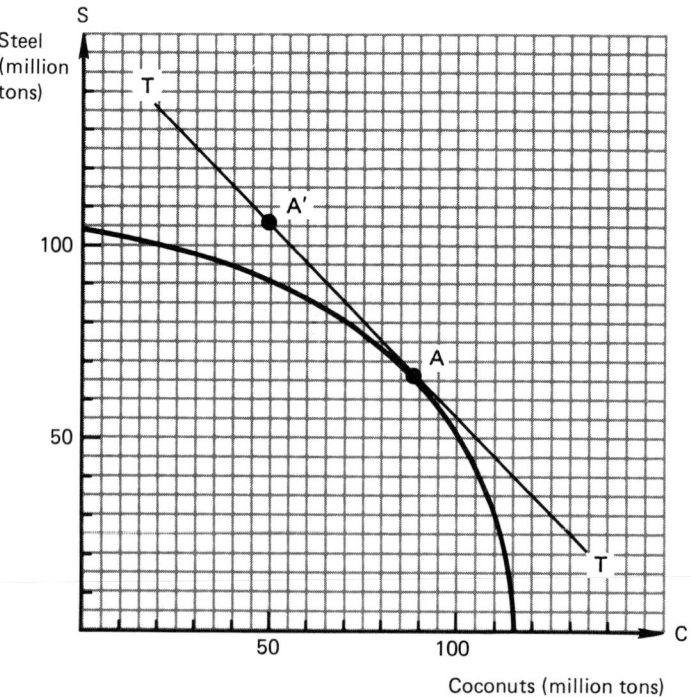

Figure 16–7

f. (i) How would a graphical analysis of *unsuccessful* import substitution differ from what you have drawn in answer to part d?

(ii) What factors explain why import substitution in many LDCs turns out to be unsuccessful? Explain.

Answers to Self-Test

Completion

1. infant
2. value-added at domestic prices
3. manufacturing, agriculture
4. DRC
5. low
6. intermediate
7. political
8. rise, fall

True-False

1. F		5. F	
2. T		6. F	
3. T		7. F	
4. T		8. T	

Multiple Choice

1. d		5. b	
2. c		6. c	
3. b		7. a	
4. b		8. d	

CHAPTER 17   Outward-Looking Development

Overview

Outward-looking export substitution provides an alternative to trade strategies based on traditional primary-product exports or import substitution. The basis of an export substitution strategy is to promote nontraditional exports in which the country has a potential comparative advantage. To promote efficient and competitive industries it is essential to avoid a highly overvalued exchange rate, trade policies that discourage exports, and seriously distorted factor prices.

The experience of countries that have followed this path shows that export promotion policies can produce rapid transformation of exports and rapid growth, with favorable effects on the domestic economy as a whole. The potential benefits are more limited in large countries where trade is less important. In any case, the transition to a more outward-looking trade strategy creates serious political difficulties. Also, protectionism in the industrial countries raises the risk that access to these large markets for LDC products may be restricted. Exports to other third world countries have become increasingly important, and regional trade arrangements offer potential for expanding trade among LDCs.

Main Learning Objectives

After studying this chapter you ought to understand and be able to explain:

1. The basic character of an **outward-looking**, or **export substitution** trade strategy, along with its distinguishing policy features.

2. The meaning and importance of the **effective exchange rate** (EER).

3. The development effects of export substitution, and the conditions under which such policies are most likely to be successful.

4. The emergence of **new protectionism** in the industrial countries, and the consequences for both developed countries and LDCs.

5. The growth of trade among LDCs, and the static and dynamic effects of regional **free-trade areas, customs unions**, or **common markets** to expand intra-LDC trade.

Additional Key Terms, Concepts, and Institutions

Can you identify and explain each of the following?

IEER
transition to export substitution
structural adjustment loans
GATT
most-favored nation principle (MFN)
non-tariff barriers (NTBs)
newly industrializing countries (NICs)
voluntary export restraints
declining industries (in the industrial countries)
complementation agreement

Economic Tools and Techniques

From what you have learned in this chapter, can you:

1. Apply the formulas for calculating the effective exchange rate for exports (EER_x), the effective exchange rate for imports (EER_m), and the index of the price-deflated EER (or IEER)?

2. Explain the costs of non-tariff trade barriers, including the **dead-weight loss** and **revenue rectangle** cost of voluntary export restraints, and the **cost per job saved** in the protected industries?

3. Explain the **trade creation** and **trade diversion** effects of regional preferential trade arrangements?

Self-Test

Completion

1. The measure of the actual amount of local currency paid for a dollar's worth of imports, or received for a dollar's worth of exports, is called the _____.

2. A pro-export trade regime is one characterized by an effective exchange rate for imports that is _____ than the effective exchange rate for exports.

3. If domestic inflation is more rapid than foreign inflation, then _____ may be necessary to maintain export profitability.

4. With wages held artificially high and interest rates held artificially low, resources will be drawn toward more _____-intensive lines of production.

5. Quotas, packaging requirements, health and safety regulations, and customs delays are examples of _____ .

6. In recent years the World Bank has made _____

_____ loans to support liberalization policies as LDC governments move away from heavily protective, inward-looking development strategies.

7. A trade arrangement that eliminates tariffs among member countries but permits each member to maintain its own set of tariffs on im-

ports from other countries is called a _____.

8. A customs union produces a trade _____ effect when domestic consumers are induced to import goods from a partner country rather than from an outside country, even though the partner country produces at higher cost.

9. A _____ agreement allocates various large-scale infant industries among members of a regional trade pact.

10. Most generally, export substitution involves the promotion of any type

of export in which a country has a potential _____

_____.

True-False If false, you should be able to explain why.

_____ 1. An export substitution strategy is one that serves to shift resources into production for the home market rather than production for export.

_____ 2. The more overvalued the exchange rate, the less profitable it is for domestic producers to export.

_____ 3. With very rapid domestic inflation, a fixed-exchange rate rapidly becomes an overvalued exchange rate.

_____ 4. Export substitution policies are especially likely to stimulate widespread structural change and rapid development in large countries such as Brazil or India.

_____ 5. Many manufacturers that thrived under protection from import substitution policies are hurt by a transition to export substitution.

_____ 6. The IEER is an index showing the ratio of the EER for exports relative to the EER for imports.

_____ 7. A customs union differs from a free-trade area in that member countries adopt a common set of tariffs on imports from nonmember countries.

_____ 8. In terms of static effects, a country benefits from a customs union if trade diversion outweighs trade creation.

_____ 9. Increased competition among producers from different member countries can be an important source of dynamic gains from a customs union.

_____ 10. With the growing presence of non-tariff barriers, the quantity of LDC manufactured goods exported to industrial countries hardly increased from 1965 to 1982.

Multiple Choice

1. Which of the following is *not* one of the "Gang of Four" that pursued successful outward-looking strategies of labor-intensive development?
   a. Philippines
   b. South Korea
   c. Singapore
   d. Taiwan

2. Which of the following market interventions is most appropriate for promoting export substitution?
   a. temporary subsidies to exporters
   b. high protective tariffs for favored industries
   c. quantitative restrictions on competing imports
   d. an overvalued exchange rate

3. The cost per job saved in the U.S. textile and clothing industries in 1977 due to tariffs alone has been estimated to be:
   a. $800.
   b. $80,000.
   c. $8 million.
   d. negligible.

4. Which of the following remarks about Korea's export-led growth is incorrect?
   a. Rapid growth was widely spread among manufacturing sectors.
   b. Policies to encourage exports worsened the income distribution.
   c. Producing for export allowed firms to achieve scale economies without creating domestic monopolies.
   d. Export growth depended almost entirely on the manufacturing sector.

5. Which term refers to a system under which a tariff reduction to one country is extended to all trading partners?
   a. non-tariff barrier
   b. customs union
   c. common market
   d. most-favored nation principle

6. How does a common market differ from a customs union?
    a. Restrictions on the movement of labor and capital among member states are substantially reduced.
    b. Tariffs may be levied on imports from other member countries.
    c. A customs union does not include a common set of tariffs on imports from nonmember countries.
    d. There is no difference; they are two names for the same thing.

7. The term "newly industrializing country" refers to countries:
    a. that are predominantly agricultural and just starting to introduce manufacturing.
    b. such as Japan that are no longer ranked as LDCs.
    c. that have built up large industrial sectors behind import-substitution trade barriers.
    d. that have followed the export-substitution path to rapid industrialization.

8. Which of the following groups is a net gainer from a voluntary export restraint agreement on exports of doodads to the United States?
    a. doodad producers in the United States
    b. doodad consumers in the United States
    c. American nondoodad exporters
    d. all of the above

9. What is GATT?
    a. a customs union in Europe.
    b. a type of non-tariff barrier to trade.
    c. an international agreement to negotiate and monitor multilateral tariff negotiations.
    d. an organization set up to promote intra-LDC trade.

10. New protectionism in the industrial countries aims primarily to protect:
    a. infant industries that might be hurt by import competition.
    b. declining industries for which comparative advantage has shifted to the LDCs.
    c. industries that still have a comparative advantage, but are being hurt by cheap labor costs in LDCs.
    d. industries where the cost per job saved is very low.

Applications

Worked Example: Index of the Price-Deflated
Effective Exchange Rate (IEER)

The data required for calculating the *IEER* correspond to the variables that appear in Equation 17–3 from the textbook:

$$IEER = R_o T \, P_w / P_d.$$

To calculate the *IEER* over time, one needs data on the official exchange rate (for calculating R_o), domestic prices (for P_d), and world prices (for P_w), as well as an index of the level of net tariffs (T). Table 17–1 shows

Table 17-1
Data for Calculating the IEER for Indonesia, 1975–1979

Year (1)	Exchange rate (rupiah/$) (2)	Domestic price index[a] (1975 = 100) (3)	World price index[b] (1975 = 100) (4)	Exchange rate index (1975 = 100) (5)	IEER[c] $\frac{(5) \times (4)}{(3)}$ (6)	Constant IEER exchange rate (rupiah/$) (7)
1975	415	100.0	100.0	100.0	100.0	415.0
1976	415	114.4	105.7	100.0	92.4	449.2
1977	415	129.3	111.9	100.0	86.5	479.5
1978	415	143.5	120.2	100.0	83.7	495.4
1979	623	190.2	130.4	150.1	102.9	605.3

Source: World Bank, *World Tables 1983.*

[a]Implicit GDP deflator

[b]U.S. Wholesale Price Index

[c]The term *T* is assumed constant here.

the relevant data for Indonesia over the period 1975–1979—except for T, which for simplicity we will assume to equal 1.0 initially.

From 1975 through 1978, the official exchange rate was fixed at 415 rupiah per dollar. During this period, domestic prices rose more quickly than world-market prices (approximated here by the Wholesale Price Index in the United States). As a result, the *IEER* fell steadily, as can be seen in column 6. In other words, the real exchange rate became increasingly overvalued.

Because domestic costs were rising faster than world-market prices, when exporters exchanged their dollar revenues for rupiahs at the fixed nominal exchange rate, revenues in rupiahs did not keep pace with costs. Nontraditional, nonpetroleum exports were especially affected by the consequent profit squeeze. At the same time, the fixed-exchange rate caused import prices to drop relative to the inflation-ridden prices of domestic goods.

Near the end of 1978, the currency was devalued to 625 rupiah per dollar. Look at the *IEER* for 1979. You can see that the devaluation offset the excess domestic inflation and returned the effective exchange rate to 102.9, approximately its 1975 level. The IEER would have been more stable if the government had adopted a Brazilian-type policy of smaller, more frequent devaluations. Column 7 shows the exchange-rate level for each year that would have held the *IEER* at its base-period value. Thus, column 7 shows the exchange rate for which R satisfies the equation:

$$IEER = R \times P_w/P_d = 100 \quad \text{(ignoring } T\text{).}$$

The steady overvaluation of the rupiah also could have been offset through adjustments in the level of protection (T), with the exchange rate held fixed. Consider the situation for exporters in 1976. The *IEER* for 1976 $(= 92.4)$ shows that the rupiah earnings per unit of exports, adjusted for domestic inflation, dropped to only 92.4% of the value in the base year, 1975. Clearly this hurt export profits. But the profitability of exports could have been maintained at the 1975 level if T_x had increased by 8.2%. (With $R = 1.0$ and $P_w/P_d = 0.924$, the value $T = 1.082$ results in *IEER* $= 1.00$.) From the definition,

$$T_x = (1 - t_x + s_x)$$

one can see that the appropriate T_x would entail lower export taxes or higher subsidies by 8.2%. Similarly, the *IEER* formula reveals that import prices could have been stabilized by raising tariffs or quota premiums by 8.2% in 1976.

Though the *effective* exchange rate could have been maintained through changes in tariffs and subsidies, a simple devaluation (to 449.2 rupiah per dollar) produces identical results with vastly less administrative complexity.

Exercises

1. This exercise involves calculating the effective exchange rate (*EER*) for Zimba, a country that exports copper (*C*) and beef (*B*), and imports medicine (*M*). The world price per unit of each good just

happens to be $1,000, or Kw600 at the official exchange rate of 0.6 kwacha per dollar.

a. Zimba's trade policies include a tax on copper exports (t_c), a subsidy on beef exports (s_b), and a tariff on medicine imports (t_m) as follows:

$$t_c = 25\%;$$

$$s_b = 10\%;$$

$$t_m = 50\%.$$

(i) For every unit exported, copper producers earn $1,000. After changing the dollars into kwacha and paying the export tax,

they end up with Kw_____ .

(ii) So the effective exchange rate faced by the copper industry (i.e., the number of kwacha actually received per dollar of exports) is:

$$EER_c = \text{_____} \text{ kwacha}/\$.$$

(iii) For every unit exported, beef producers earn $1,000. After changing the dollars into kwacha and receiving their subsidy,

they end up with Kw_____ .

(iv) So the effective exchange rate faced by the beef industry is:

$$EER_b = \text{_____} \text{ kwacha}/\$.$$

(v) Every unit of medicine imported costs $1,000 on the world market. Including the import duty, the cost in kwacha to the

importer is Kw_____ .

(vi) So the effective exchange rate faced by the medicine importers is:

$$EER_m = \text{_____} \text{ kwacha}/\$.$$

(vii) If domestic-market prices are equal to world-market prices adjusted for tariffs, taxes, or subsidies, the domestic prices for the three goods will be:

$$P_c = \text{Kw_____},$$

$$P_b = \text{Kw_____}, \text{ and}$$

$$P_m = \text{Kw_____}.$$

b. The tariff protection makes possible import substitution in medicine, for which the unit cost (UC) of domestic production is UC_m = Kw800. The unit cost of production in the copper industry is UC_c = Kw400; in the beef industry it is UC_b = Kw600.

(i) Given domestic prices and costs, the most profitable industry

is _____ .

(ii) The least profitable industry is _____ .

(iii) Briefly explain how the *EER*s for the three sectors reflect resource allocation biases of Zimba's trade policy.

c. Suppose a new trade strategy is adopted. In place of the original tariff, tax, and subsidy, each export industry now benefits from a 10% subsidy while the import substitution industry benefits from a 10% protective tariff.
   (i) The effective exchange rates now become:

$$EER_c = \underline{\hspace{2cm}} \text{ kwacha}/\$,$$

$$EER_b = \underline{\hspace{2cm}} \text{ kwacha}/\$, \text{ and}$$

$$EER_m = \underline{\hspace{2cm}} \text{ kwacha}/\$.$$

   (ii) Assuming that unit costs of production have not changed, the most profitable industry is now _____ .

   (iii) The _____ industry is now not profitable at all!
   (iv) Briefly describe the reallocation of resources that results from the new trade strategy, and explain whether the economy becomes more efficient or less efficient than it was initially.

d. Could a simple change in the exchange rate, with all tariffs, taxes, and subsidies set to zero, produce a resource reallocation the same as that in part c? Explain.

2. This exercise gives you a turn to do some *IEER* calculations. Be sure that you have read the Worked Exercise carefully. The Republic of Pampa exports wheat (W) and produces clothing (C) as an import-substitution industry. Table 17–2 shows data on world prices, the tax and tariff rates, the domestic production costs, and the exchange rate (pesos per dollar, or P/$) for 1986.

Table 17-2

Pampa's Wheat and Clothing Industries

(A)	Wheat 1986	1987	1987a
1. World price ($ per bushel)	$ 4	$4.40	$4.40
2. Exchange rate (P/$)[a]	20 P/$		
3. Exporter receives (pesos per bushel)	P80		
4. Export tax rate (%)	10%		
5. Net revenue per bushel, after tax (pesos)	P72		
6. Domestic production cost per bushel (pesos)	P64	P80	P80
7. Exporter's profits per bushel (pesos)	P12		

(B)	Clothing 1986	1987	1987a
8. World price ($ per unit)	$50	$55	$55
9. Exchange rate (P/$)	20 P/$		
10. Importer cost (pesos per unit)	P1,000		
11. Tariff rate (%)	25%		
12. Domestic price (pesos per unit)[b]	P1,250		
13. Domestic production cost per unit (pesos)	P1,100	P1,375	P1,375
14. Domestic producer's profits per unit (pesos)	P150		

[a]P = pesos
[b]Domestic price = (import price)(1 + tariff), where the tariff is expressed as a decimal.

a. (i) In 1987, world prices for exports and imports increase by 10%, while the price level in Pampa (hence, domestic production cost) increases by 25%. The government maintains the exchange rate and tax and tariff rates at their 1986 levels. Based on this information, fill in the whole 1987 column in Table 17–2. [To assist you, some of the numbers are provided.]

(ii) Table 17–3 translates the wheat industry data from Table 17–2 into index numbers (with 1986 = 100) needed in the formula for calculating the *IEER* for wheat exports:

$$IEER_x = R_o T\, P_w/P_d.$$

Fill in the 1987 column in Table 17–3. [Hint: T stays at 1.00 since there has been no change in the export tax rate].

(iii) Briefly explain how the value of *IEER*$_x$ for 1987 is related to the change in profitability of wheat exports.

b. Table 17–3 showed the data required to calculate the *IEER* for wheat exports. Follow a similar procedure to calculate the 1987 index of the price-deflated exchange rate for *imports*.

$$IEER_m = \underline{\hspace{2cm}}.$$

c. (i) Let all conditions for 1987 remain unaltered except the exchange rate. Suppose that the government devalues the peso by 15% to 23 pesos per dollar in order to offset (approximately) the excess of domestic inflation over world inflation. Fill in the columns labeled "1987a" in Table 17–2 and in Table 17–3 to reflect this change.

Table 17–3

Index Numbers for Wheat Exports

	1986	1987	1987a	1987b
1. R_o	100	_____	_____	___100___
2. T_x	1.0	_____	_____	= _____?
3. P_w	100	_____	_____	___110___
4. P_d	100	_____	_____	___125___
5. $IEER_x$	100	_____	_____	___100___

(ii) Calculate the 1987 index of the price-deflated effective exchange rate for clothing *imports* after the devaluation:

$$IEER_m = \underline{\hspace{2cm}}.$$

d. Suppose now that the government chooses not to devalue the peso, but to support domestic producers by changing tax and tariff rates. Stated more formally, the government wants to maintain $IEER_x = 100$ and $IEER_m = 100$ in 1987 by altering T_x and T_m, with no change in R_o.
   (i) In Table 17−3 fill in the required value for T_x in the column labeled "1987b." [Hint: In this column, $R_o = 100$; given the P_w and P_d values for 1987 that you calculated earlier, you must now find T_x such that $IEER_x = 100$.]
   (ii) Given the value for T_x you have just calculated, and the formula:

$$T_x = (1 - t_x)/(1 - t_x^o),$$

   find the necessary 1987 value of the export tax, t_x.

$$t_x = \underline{\hspace{2cm}}$$

   [Hint: the answer will be a negative number, indicating that an export subsidy is necessary.]

e. (i) Following a procedure parallel to that used in part d, calculate the value of T_m needed to maintain $IEER_m = 100$ in the absence of a peso devaluation.

$$T_m = \underline{\hspace{2cm}}$$

(ii)   Then, using the formula:

$$T_m = (1 + t_m)/(1 + t_m^o),$$

   find the required 1987 value of t_m, the tariff on clothing imports.

$$t_m = \underline{\hspace{2cm}}$$

f. Briefly discuss the difference between using devaluation vs. using changes in tax, subsidy, and tariff rates to support domestic producers, in a country where domestic inflation regularly exceeds world inflation.

3. This exercise explores some of the economic effects of non-tariff trade distortions frequently associated with the new protectionism in the industrial countries. Before starting, you may wish to review textbook Figure 16–1.

    a. Figure 17–1 illustrates the market for paper clips in the United States. Line S_d is the supply curve for paper clips produced domestically. Line S_f shows the supply to the U.S. market of foreign paper clips; it is horizontal for simplicity. Line D shows the domestic demand for paper clips.
       (i) With free trade, the equilibrium price of paper clips in the United States is:

$$P_e = \$\underline{\hspace{2cm}} \text{ per carton.}$$

       (ii) The equilibrium quantity is:

$$Q_e = \underline{\hspace{2cm}} \text{ million cartons per year,}$$

of which _____ million cartons, or _____%, is imported.

    b. Suppose all the imports come from Hong Kong (HK), where paper clip production is a competitive industry. This means that HK producers earn zero economic profits.
       (i) After arm twisting by U.S. trade officials, the HK Paper Clip Association agrees to a "voluntary export restraint," in the form of a self-enforced 50% reduction in paper clip exports to

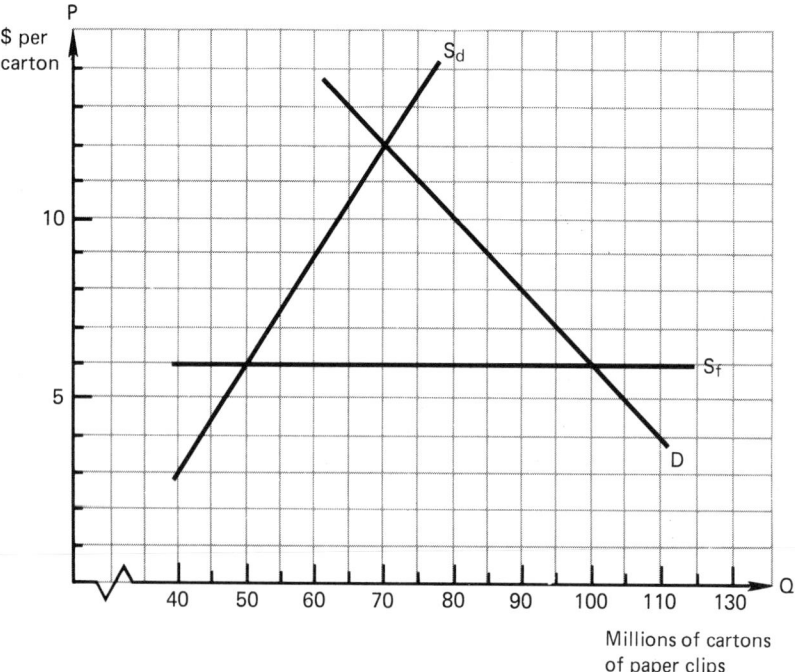

Figure 17–1

-272-

the United States. In other words, they agree to limit exports to:

_____ million cartons per year.

(ii) Accurately draw the effective supply curve of paper clips in the U.S. market following the voluntary export restraint agreement, and label it S'. [Hint: Supply now consists of domestic supply plus the fixed amount of imports from HK.]

(iii) The new equilibrium price of paper clips in the United States is:

$$P' = \$\underline{\hspace{2cm}} \text{ per carton.}$$

(iv) The new equilibrium quantity in the market is:

$$Q' = \underline{\hspace{2cm}} \text{ million cartons per year,}$$

of which _____ million cartons, or _____%, is imported.

c. Let's examine the effects of the voluntary export restraint agreement.

(i) U.S. consumers now face a price for paper clips that is higher by \$_____ per carton.

(ii) For the quantity they are consuming (Q'), U.S. consumers are shelling out an extra \$_____ million due to the higher price.

(iii) Compared to the situation prior to the agreement, U.S. producers are now selling an extra _____ million cartons.

(iv) Compared to the situation before the agreement, the revenues (price times quantity) of U.S. producers have risen by \$_____ million, or _____%.

(v) Suppose the extra production translates into 3,000 extra jobs in the paper clip industry. Based on your answer to part ii, the cost to consumers per job created is \$_____ per year.

(vi) The value of the deadweight loss to the U.S. economy is \$_____ million. [Hint: refer to triangles b plus d in textbook Figure 16–1, and recall that the area of a triangle = 1/2 base × height.]

d. (i) What about the HK producers? They now export _____ million cartons each year to the United States, fetching a price per carton of \$_____. [Note: With the agreement, the HK Paper Clip Association is obligated to act as a cartel. It restricts supply to the United States and then charges the prevailing U.S. market price.]

(ii) Compared to the situation prior to the agreement, their

revenues from paper clip exports have _____ by

$_____ million.

e. Recall, though, that the HK producers *originally* earned zero economic profits on their paper clip exports to the United States. The original export price ($6 per carton) just covered costs, including a normal return on capital, implying that the resources used to produce the extra paper clips could be transferred to other production lines (jeans, radios) and earn roughly comparable returns.

  (i) Consider the resources that remain in paper clip production. The U.S. price now exceeds costs, including a normal return

   on capital, by $_____ per carton.

  (ii) So under the voluntary export restraint agreement, the HK Paper Clip Association members are earning excess profits

   totaling $_____ million. They are selling less, but enjoying it more!

f. Turn now to a related type of protection. Figure 17–2 shows the market for sugar in the United States. The labels are analogous to those used in Figure 17–1. The price of foreign sugar, $0.15 per pound, is determined in the world market.

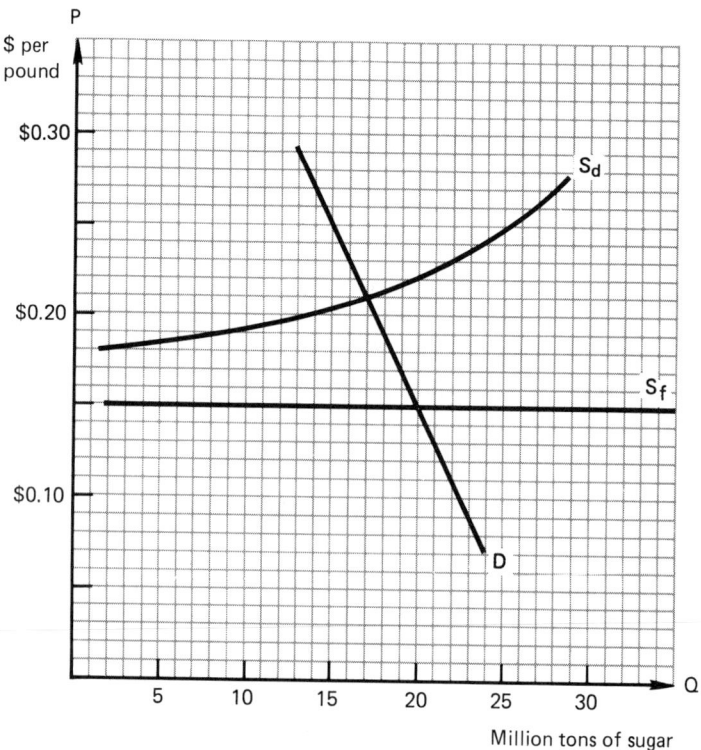

Figure 17–2

(i) Under the conditions shown, the free-market equilibrium price in the United States would be $_____ per pound and imports would account for _____ % of the market supply.
(ii) Suppose the U.S. government adopts a quota restricting sugar imports to 10 million tons per year, while simultaneously guaranteeing *domestic* sugar producers a price of $0.25 per pound. Importers can still purchase foreign sugar at $0.15 per pound, subject to the quota. Carefully draw in Figure 17−2 the new effective supply curve in the U.S. market resulting from imposition of the quota. [See the hint for part ii.] Label this curve S'.
(iii) Carefully draw the new effective demand curve that results from the price guarantee. [Hint: the guarantee price acts as a price floor.] Label this curve D'.
(iv) What are the effects of this policy combination on:

—the domestic-market equilibrium price?

—domestic sugar consumption (excluding government purchases to assure the guarantee price)?

—domestic sugar production?

—earnings of foreign sugar producers on exports to the United States?

—the earnings of U.S traders who import sugar?

g. If the U.S. government decides to deal with the resulting sugar surplus by selling (dumping) most of the excess supply on the world market, what will be the effect on:

—the world market price?

—export earnings of foreign sugar producers?

4. This exercise explores trade creation and trade division in Tanya, following the formation of a customs union with neighboring Kenzania. The exchange rate between the Kenzanian shilling and the Tanyan shilling is Ksh1 = Tsh1; each currency is worth $0.10.

   a. Gaskets, pumps, and tractors can be produced in Tanya, imported from Kenzania, or imported from other countries. Table 17—4 shows the supply costs for each alternative source of the three products.
      (i) Fill in the blanks in the left half of the table, assuming that Tanya levies a 40% tariff on imports of each product prior to entering the customs union.
      (ii) With the uniform 40% tariff, the cheapest source of supply:

      for gaskets is _____ .

      for pumps is _____ .

      for tractors is _____ .

      (iii) Prior to the customs union, Kenzania was also imposing a 40% tariff on all imports. Faced with this tariff, could Tanyan producers export any gaskets, pumps, or tractors? Explain.

   b. After entering the customs union, Tanya still levies a 40% tariff on imports from other countries, but tariffs are set to zero on imports from Kenzania.
      (i) Based on the new tariff structure, fill in the blanks in the right half of Table 17—4.
      (ii) How will Tanya's entry into the customs union alter its pattern of production and trade:

      for gaskets? _____ .

      for pumps? _____ .

      for tractors? _____ .
      [Hint: Be sure to consider potential exports.]

   c. (i) In what sense does Tanya benefit from "trade creation" as a result of the customs union?

Table 17-4
Tanyan Supply Costs

	Prior to Customs Union			After Customs Union		
	Gaskets	Pumps	Tractors	Gaskets	Pumps	Tractors
A. Imports from Kenzania						
1. Price of imports (in Ksh)	Ksh 18	Ksh 6,000	Ksh 100,000	Ksh 18	Ksh 6,000	Ksh 100,000
2. Price of imports (in Tsh)	Tsh 18	Tsh 2,400	Tsh 100,000			
3. Tariff charged (Tsh)	Tsh 7.2				0	
4. Domestic price (= 2 + 3)	Tsh 25.2					
B. Imports from third countries						
1. Price of imports (in $)	$2.00	$500.00	$8,000.00	$2.00	$500.00	$8,000.00
2. Price of imports (in Tsh)	Tsh 20		Tsh 80,000	Tsh 20		Tsh 32,000
3. Tariff charged (Tsh)	Tsh 8	Tsh 2,000				
4. Domestic price (= 2 + 3)	Tsh 28					
C. Production in Tanya						
1. Domestic production price	Tsh 24	Tsh 8,000	Tsh 95,000	Tsh 24	Tsh 8,000	Tsh 95,000

(ii) Is there any loss to Tanya from "trade diversion" as a result of the customs union? Explain.

5. *Optional* In discussing biases created by protection, the textbook mentions that Korea's effective rate of protection (ERP) on production for domestic sales was *negative* 9% in the late 1960s. An exercise in Chapter 16 showed how the ERP can be negative if imports of the components cost more than imports of the finished product. But the Korean situation was different.

a. Suppose Korea's exchange rate is 800 won per dollar.

(i) The world price of textiles is $P(w) = \$10 = $ _____ won per unit. If a tariff of $t(0) = 10\%$ is imposed on textile

imports, the domestic price will be $P(d) = $ _____ won.

(ii) Suppose that cloth is the only intermediate good used in textile production. The world price of cloth is $C(w) = \$9 = $

_____ won. A tariff of $t(i) = 12\%$ is imposed on cloth

imports, so the domestic price will be $C(d) = $ _____ won.

(iii) For textiles, the value-added at world prices is $VA(w) = $

_____ won. Value-added at domestic prices is $VA(d) = $

_____ won.

(iv) The effective rate of protection is therefore:

$$ERP = \underline{\hspace{1cm}} \%.$$

b. This is not a situation in which the value-added at world prices is negative. What, then, is the reason for the negative ERP?

Answers to Self-Test

Completion

1. Effective exchange rate (EER)
2. lower (or, no higher)
3. devaluation
4. capital
5. non-tariff barriers
6. structural adjustment
7. free-trade area
8. diversion
9. complementation
10. comparative advantage

True-False

1. F	6. F
2. T	7. T
3. T	8. F
4. F	9. T
5. T	10. F

Multiple Choice

1. a	6. a
2. a	7. d
3. b	8. a
4. b	9. c
5. d	10. b

CHAPTER 18   Agriculture

Overview

While most topics covered in earlier chapters related in some way to agriculture, Chapter 18 focuses directly on the problems of agricultural development. The chapter begins with a review of the sector's multi-faceted role in development, ranging from poverty alleviation to earning foreign exchange. Land tenure relations and land reform are then discussed. These ownership and organization issues have a major bearing on incentives, efficiency, and equity.

The characteristics of agricultural technology are examined next. Though traditional technology was not entirely stagnant, the rapid pace of change and the scientific basis for innovation—including mechanization and biological advances leading to dramatically improved yields (the Green Revolution)—are modern developments. Agricultural development is not just a matter of technology, however. The infrastructure of roads, irrigation facilities, credit institutions, extension services, and markets must also be established. In addition, pricing policy can have a rapid and profound effect on agricultural production and consumption. Governments encounter conflicts between the interests of farmers and those of urban consumers when setting price policies. Such conflicts are often resolved in a manner that inhibits agricultural development.

Main Learning Objectives

After studying this chapter you ought to understand and be able to explain:

1. Agriculture's role in economic development, and the debate about the desirability of agricultural **self-sufficiency**.

2. The different forms of **land tenure relations** found in developing countries, and the incentive problems that can occur with **tenancy, sharecropping,** and **communal** or **collectivized** agriculture.

3. The institutional and political characteristics of **land reform** measures, and the economic effects of such reforms.

4. The characteristics of traditional and modern agricultural technology, including the **mechanical package** and the **biological package** of modern technology.

5. The importance of road and irrigation systems, credit institutions, **extension services**, and market networks—and the problems faced in developing such **rural infrastructure**.

6. The effect of prices and **subsidies** on farm output, farmers' incomes, the urban cost of living, and the government budget.

Additional Key Terms, Concepts, and Institutions

Can you identify and explain each of the following?

plantation agriculture
latifundia
absentee landlords
free-rider problem
economies of scale
slash and burn
Green Revolution
moneylender
transport costs
overvalued exchange rate

Economic Tools and Techniques

From what you have learned in this chapter, can you:

1. Use isoquants to illustrate characteristics of agricultural technology?

2. Explain how **risk** affects small farmers' decisions about crop specialization and adopting innovations?

3. Apply the profit maximization rule to demonstrate how changes in the relative prices of farm outputs and purchased inputs (such as fertilizer) influence farm production decisions?

4. Analyze the effects of a subsidy or an overvalued exchange rate on the supply and demand for food, and on the government budget.

Self-Test

Completion

1. Economies of _____ are at the heart of farm specialization.

2. _____ is a term used in Latin America to refer to large estates on which the hired labor has a servile relationship to the land owner.

3. The form of tenancy in which the land owner receives a given share of the farmer's harvest is called _____.

4. Land _____ may involve laws limiting the share of the crop that a landlord can demand as rent and laws requiring _____ term contracts for tenant farmers.

5. According to the text, the single greatest barrier to farm specialization in LDCs is the high level of _____ costs.

6. The mechanical package of agricultural technology involves the introduction of machinery primarily as a _____ for labor.

7. _____ services provide the key link between agricultural research institutions and the farmers who must ultimately adopt what the researchers develop.

8. In traditional agriculture the small farmer has only two sources of credit—the family and the local _____ .

9. The one area of government policy that has a rapid and profound effect on agricultural production and consumption is intervention to control _____ .

10. An overvalued exchange rate will tend to _____ food imports and _____ food production.

True-False If false, you should be able to explain why.

_____ 1. A long-run world food crisis is imminent due to the limited supply of productive land.

_____ 2. A low-income nation cannot achieve a high rate of capital formation without a large flow of savings from the agricultural sector.

_____ 3. Depending on conditions, the impact of land reform on productivity can be very positive or it can be very negative.

_____ 4. Compared to the mechanical package of agricultural technology, the biological package results in higher yields per unit of land and lower yields per worker.

_____ 5. Slash-and-burn cultivation methods are most commonly used in agricultural regions that are densely populated.

_____ 6. In countries such as India where labor costs are extremely low, it is never efficient to substitute machines for labor in agriculture.

_____ 7. In general, farmers have not benefited greatly from government take-overs of the marketing functions of private traders.

_____ 8. Experience indicates that rural credit cooperatives are usually successful as long as they operate without government involvement.

_____ 9. Uneducated peasant farmers generally won't increase production when farm product prices rise relative to input prices.

_____ 10. Many LDCs have adopted food price policies that reduce both farm incomes and farm output.

Multiple Choice

1. As defined in the text, collective agriculture is different from communal farming because in collectives:
   a. land is not owned by individual families.
   b. workers share in the output on the basis of the amount of labor they contribute.
   c. land is divided up into family plots for cultivation.
   d. None of the above; the two terms are synonymous.

2. The free-rider problem arises under communal farming in that individuals have little incentive to:
   a. work.
   b. pay for the inputs they use.
   c. maintain and improve the land they cultivate.
   d. all of the above.

3. In which of the following countries was land reform used to consolidate support for a revolution and eliminate the economic base of the landlord class?
   a. China
   b. Mexico
   c. India
   d. all of the above

4. Empirical evidence confirms the general validity of which of the following statements about production by peasant farmers?
   a. They use available resources efficiently.
   b. They are responsive to changing price incentives.
   c. Neither a nor b.
   d. Both a and b.

5. During the three decades from 1955 to 1984, food production failed to keep pace with population in which continents?
   a. Africa only
   b. Asia and Africa
   c. Latin America and Africa
   d. Latin America, Asia, and Africa

6. According to the text, what has been the main difficulty in mobilizing off-season rural labor for public works projects?
   a. Peasant farmers are too tradition bound to care about development.
   b. The lack of direct connection between work and benefits.
   c. Rural workers can earn more money in other jobs.
   d. Governments have neglected rural conditions.

7. The Green Revolution has three key components: the introduction of

   _____ ; the application of chemical fertilizers; and

   adequate and timely supplies of _____ .
   a. tractors; credit.
   b. roads; advice.
   c. plantations; labor.
   d. improved plant varieties; water.

8. An income-maximizing farmer adds fertilizer as long as the incremental fertilizer:
   a. increases output.
   b. increases the value of output.
   c. increases the value of output by more than it increases costs.
   d. is subsidized by the government.

Applications

Worked Example: Farm Production Decisions

Standard microeconomic tools provide insight into farm production decisions and the effects of price changes. Consider a representative farmer in Basmati who owns one hectare (about two and one-half acres) of land for growing rice. The first three columns of Table 18−1 show for various amounts of chemical fertilizer (F), the required labor input (L), and the corresponding quantity of rice output (Q). Figure 18−1 portrays this technical relationship as a rice-fertilizer production function. The graph clearly shows diminishing returns to successive increments of F input.

Technically, the seed variety being used can yield as much as 3,600 kg of rice per hectare. But the actual yield achieved by the farmer is an *economic* decision that depends on prices as well as technical conditions. Suppose that the price of fertilizer is P_F = Rs3 per kg, the price of rice is P_R = Rs1 per kg, and the price of labor is P_L = Rs200 per worker. At these prices, the cost of production (C), the value of output (V), and the farmer's net income (Y) can be calculated for each level of fertilizer usage. The results are shown in columns 4, 5, and 6 of Table 18−1. As can be seen, the maximum income level of Y^* = Rs 800 is achieved when F^* = 200 kg of fertilizer are used, yielding Q^* = 3,000 kg of rice. The farmer will choose to operate at point A in Figure 18−1, even though higher yields are feasible.

Has the extension worker failed to convince the farmer to use the "best" cultivation method? No. Agronomists must recognize that farmers

Table 18-1[a]

Chemical Fertilizer (F) (1)	Labor (L) (2)	Rice Output (Q) (3)	Production Cost (C) (4)	Value of Output (V) (5)	Net Income (Y) (6)	Incremental Cost (ΔC) (7)	Incremental Output Value (ΔV) (8)
0 kg	4	800 kg	Rs 800	Rs 800	Rs 0		
						Rs 350	Rs 700
50	5	1,500	1,150	1,500	350		
						350	600
100	6	2,100	1,500	2,100	600		
						350	500
150	7	2,600	1,850	2,600	750		
						350	400
200	8	3,000	2,200	3,000	800		
						350	300
250	9	3,300	2,550	3,300	750		
						350	200
300	10	3,500	2,900	3,500	600		
						350	100
350	11	3,600	3,250	3,600	350		
						150	0
400	11	3,600	3,400	3,600	200		

[a] Assumes P_R = Rs1, P_L = Rs200, and P_F = Rs3.

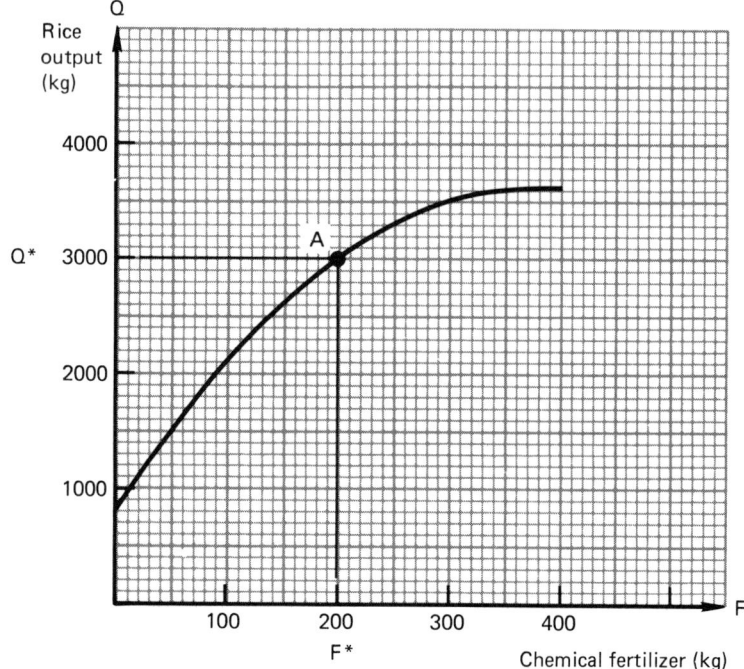

Figure 18-1

will add fertilizer only up to the point that the extra costs are offset by the extra value of rice output. Columns 7 and 8 of Table 18–1 show the incremental cost (ΔC) and the incremental value of output (ΔV) for each successive 50-kg dose of fertilizer. These data clarify the basis for the farmer's decision. Beyond $F* = 200$ kg, incremental costs exceed the resulting incremental value of rice output.

This analysis can be restated in the familiar framework of marginal cost (MC) and marginal revenue (MR), defined with respect to Q. The marginal revenue for successive units of rice output is simply $P_R = 1$ rupee/kg. The marginal cost for successive units of output can be calculated as follows. The 700 kg of extra rice produced when F goes from 0 to 50 are obtained at an incremental cost of Rs350. So for this range of rice output, $MC = 350/700 = $ Rs0.50/kg. Similarly, when F increases from 50 to 100, Q increases by 600 kg (from 1,500 kg to 2,100 kg) and costs rise by Rs350. So $MC = 350/600 = $ Rs0.58/kg. Proceeding in this way, one obtains the MC curve shown in Figure 18–2, along with the MR curve. The level of output that maximizes net income is $Q* = 3,000$ kg, as before.

Two concluding remarks: First, if all rice output were marketed, the MC curve would represent the supply curve for the representative farmer in Basmati. You can see that Q increases as a function of P_R. Aggregation across farmers would generate a standard market supply curve. Second, the effect of prices on the quantity supplied is even more pronounced if one considers that the acreage devoted to rice and the share of rice output that gets marketed will both be positive functions of the market price.

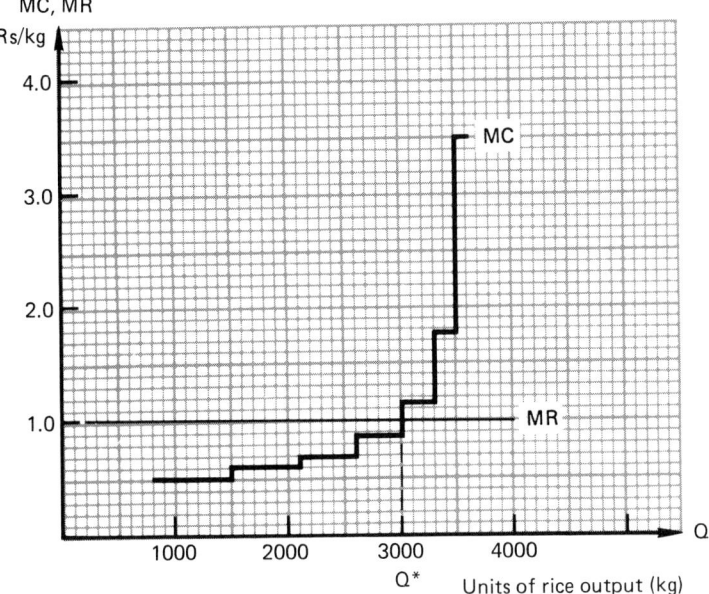

MC, MR
Rs/kg

Figure 18-2

Exercises

1. Now it is your turn to analyze farm production decisions and price effects. This exercise builds upon the Worked Example, so be sure you have read it carefully.

   a. Let's redo the Worked Example using a rice price of $P_R = $ Rs2/kg, while keeping the price of fertilizer at $P_F = $ Rs3/kg, and the price of labor at $P_L = $ Rs200 per worker.

   (i) Table 18-2 has a format similar to that of Table 18-1. The numbers in the first three columns are identical. Fill in all of the blanks in Table 18-2. Some of the numbers are provided to help you with your calculations. Keep in mind that ΔC and ΔV refer respectively to the increase in production cost and in output value for each incremental dose of fertilizer.

   (ii) When P_R changes from Rs1 to Rs2, would any shifts occur in the curves shown in Figures 18-1 and 18-2? Explain.

   (iii) With $P_R = 2$ rupees/kg, the representative farmer in Basmati would choose to produce an output of:

   $$Q' = \text{_____} \text{ kg of rice, using}$$

   $$F' = \text{_____} \text{ kg of fertilizer.}$$

   The farmer's net income in this case would be:

   $$Y' = \text{Rs_____} .$$

Table 18–2[a]

Chemical Fertilizer (F) (1)	Labor (L) (2)	Rice Output (Q) (3)	Production Cost (C) (4)	Value of Output (V) (5)	Net Income (Y) (6)	Incremental Cost (ΔC) (7)	Incremental Output Value (ΔV) (8)
0 kg	4	800 kg	Rs ___	Rs 1,600	Rs ___	Rs ___	Rs ___
50	5	1,500	___	___	1,850	___	___
100	6	2,100	___	___	___	___	___
150	7	2,600	___	___	___	___	800
200	8	3,000	2,200	___	___	___	___
250	9	3,300	___	___	4,050	___	___
300	10	3,500	___	___	___	350	___
350	11	3,600	___	___	___	___	___
400	11	3,600	___	___	___	___	___

[a] Assumes $P_R = Rs2$, $P_L = Rs200$, and $P_F = Rs3$.

b. The effects of increasing the price of rice from Rs1 to Rs2 can now be reviewed.
   (i) As a result of the higher price of rice, the representative

   farmer in Basmati increases output by _____ kg, or _____ %.

   (ii) After adjusting to the higher price, the farmer's net income

   will increase by Rs_____, or _____ %.

   (iii) Suppose that the average farmer only markets rice output in excess of 1,500 kg—the amount needed for family consumption (income in kind). Then the increase in P_R to Rs2 will expand the quantity of rice supplied to the market by the

   average farmer from _____ kg to _____ kg, an

   increase of _____ %.

   (iv) Think about the rural labor market. Will the increase in the price of rice affect the demand curve for farm labor? The labor supply curve? The average wage for farm workers? Explain.

   (v) How will the farmer's outcome be affected by these changes in the rural labor market?

c. Return now to the original rice price of P_R = Rs1, but suppose this time that the price of fertilizer is cut in half, to P_F = Rs1.5.
   (i) Table 18–3 uses a format similar to that of Table 18–1. The numbers in the first three columns are identical. Fill in all of the blanks in Table 18–3.
   (ii) With P_F = Rs1.5, recalculate the marginal cost of producing successive units of rice. Show your answer in Figure 18–2 in the form of a new marginal cost curve, labeled MC'. [Note: Carefully follow the steps explained in the Worked Example.]
   (iii) With P_F = Rs1.5, the representative farmer in Basmati would choose to produce an output of:

$$Q'' = \text{_____} \text{ kg of rice, using}$$

$$F'' = \text{_____} \text{ kg of fertilizer.}$$

   The farmer's net income in this case would be:

$$Y'' = \text{Rs_____}.$$

Table 18.3[a]

F (1)	L (2)	Q (3)	C (4)	V (5)	Y (6)	ΔC (7)	ΔV (8)
0 kg	4	800 kg	Rs 800	Rs 800	Rs ___		
50	5	1,500	___	___	425	Rs ___	Rs ___
100	6	2,100	___	___	___	___	600
150	7	2,600	1,625	___	___	___	___
200	8	3,000	___	___	___	___	___
250	9	3,300	___	___	___	275	___
300	10	3,500	___	___	1,050	___	___
350	11	3,600	___	___	___	___	___
400	11	3,600	___	___	___	___	___

[a]Assumes P_Q = Rs1, P_L = Rs200, and P_F = Rs1.5.

2. This exercise extends the analysis of the Worked Example by introducing a technical innovation and risk. The Basmati Agricultural
   Research Farm (never referred to by its initials) develops a new
   variety of rice that is far more responsive to fertilizer.

   a. Table 18−4 uses a format similar to that of Table 18−1. For each
      level of fertilizer and labor input, the high-yielding rice provides
      the yield shown in column 3. Let prices remain at their original
      levels of P_R = Rs1, P_F = Rs3, and P_L = Rs200.
      (i) Fill in all of the blanks in Table 18−4.
      (ii) In Figure 18−3 carefully draw in the new rice-fertilizer pro-
           duction function. Label the fertilizer input and rice output
           levels that maximize income as F^{**} and Q^{**}, respectively.
      (iii) In Figure 18−4, carefully draw in the MR and MC curves for
            the case under consideration. Identify Q^{**} in this graph.
      (iv) After adapting to the new technology, the net income of the

           representative farmer would be Y^{**} = Rs_____ .

   b. Unhappily, that is not the whole story. In one year out of three,
      the new variety of rice actually does worse than the old variety
      because it is more susceptible to a plant disease. For simplicity,
      assume that the farmer's decision is still F^{**} and Q^{**} as above.
      But when the plant disease strikes, only 55% of the expected crop
      is realized, while costs are unaffected.
      (i) When the plant disease strikes, the farmer's realized output

          will be only _____ kg of rice.
      (ii) When the plant disease strikes, the farmer's net income will

           drop to Rs_____ .
      (iii) Since the plant disease strikes only one year out of three, the
            farmer's net income with the new rice variety will average

            Rs_____ .
      (iv) You should have found that on average the new rice variety
           increases net income. Would it be reasonable then to expect
           peasant farmers to adopt the new variety eagerly? Explain.

3. In this exercise one more variation on the Worked Example is
   investigated: tne effect of different land tenure arrangements. The
   original data shown in columns 1−5 of Table 18−1 provide the background for this exercise.

Table 18.4[a]

F (1)	L (2)	Q (3)	C (4)	V (5)	Y (6)	ΔC (7)	ΔV (8)
0 kg	4	1,000 kg	Rs ___	Rs 1,000	Rs ___	Rs ___	Rs ___
50	5	1,800	___	___	___	___	700
100	6	2,500	___	___	1,000	___	___
150	7	3,100	1,850	___	___	___	___
200	8	3,600	___	___	___	___	___
250	9	4,000	___	___	___	350	___
300	10	4,300	___	___	___	___	___
350	11	4,500	___	___	___	___	___
400	11	4,600	___	___	1,200	___	___

[a]Assumes P_R = Rs1, P_L = Rs200, and P_F = Rs3, but with high yielding rice variety.

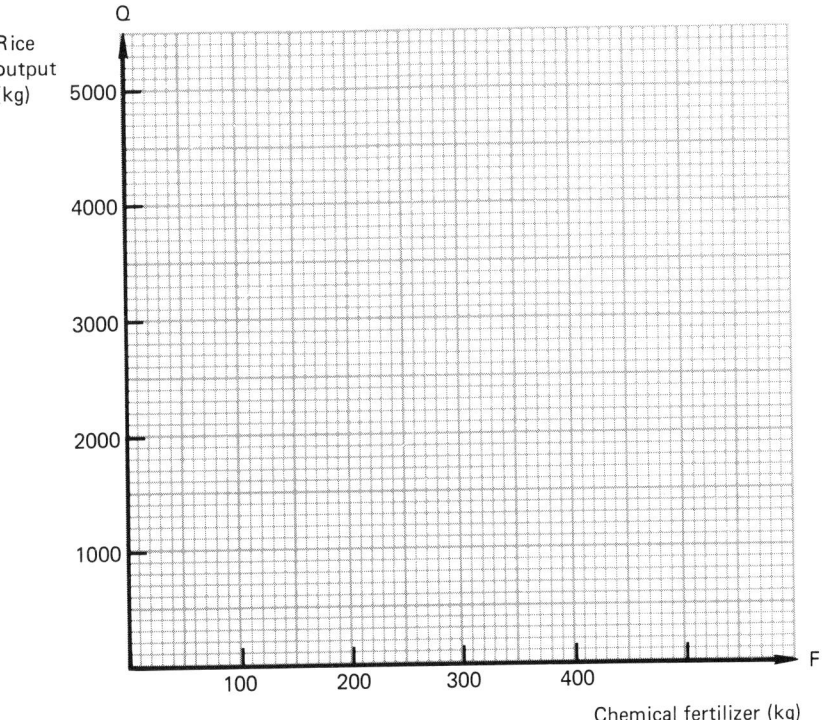

Figure 18–3

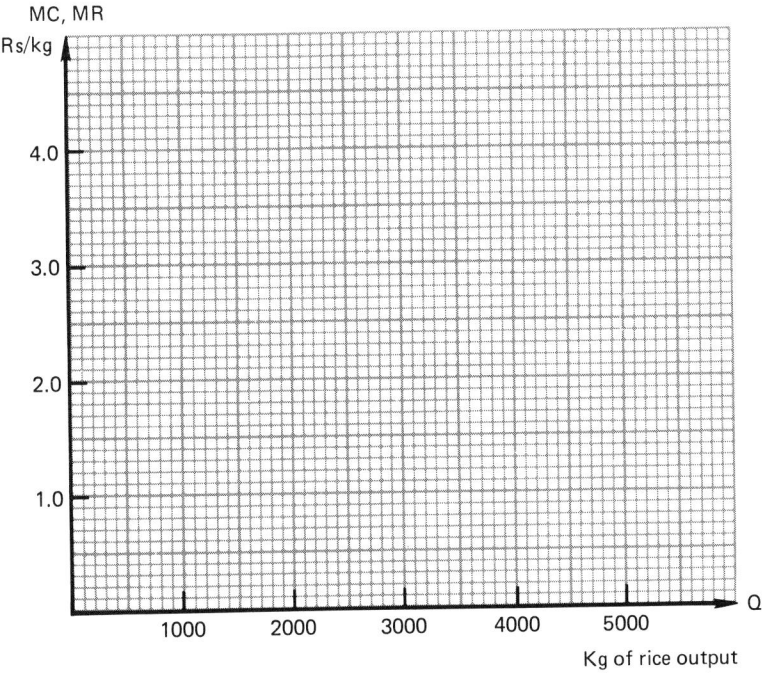

Figure 18–4

a. The net income calculations in Table 18–1 implicitly assume that the rice farmer is an independent proprietor. Suppose instead that farmers are sharecroppers who must pay 25% of their gross crop to the landlords as rent, while bearing the full burden of paying all input costs.

  (i) For each level of output shown in Table 18–5, calculate the net income retained by the sharecrop farmer after paying the landlord. [Hint: $Y = V(0.75) - C$.] Place your answers in the column labeled "sharecrop farmer."

  (ii) What levels of F and Q will be chosen by the sharecropper to maximize net income (after payments to the landlord)?

$$F = \underline{\hspace{2cm}} \text{ kg of fertilizer}$$

$$Q = \underline{\hspace{2cm}} \text{ of rice}$$

  (iii) You should have found that the sharecropper chooses less F and less Q than the independent proprietor. Use the logic summarized by Figure 18–2 to explain why this difference occurs.

  (iv) Whose production decision is economically more efficient—the sharecropper or the independent proprietor? Briefly explain.

Table 18–5

| | Net income retained by | |
Rice output (Q)	Sharecrop farmer	Tenant farmer
800 kg	Rs _____	Rs _____
1,600	−25	_____
2,100	_____	_____
2,600	_____	350
3,000	_____	_____
3,300	_____	_____
3,500	_____	_____
3,600	_____	_____

b. Suppose that instead of paying a given share of the gross crop as rent, the farmer is a tenant who pays the landlord a fixed sum of Rs400.

   (i) Calculate the net income retained by the tenant farmer for each output level shown in Table 18–5 and fill in the blanks in the tenant farmer column of the table. [Hint: $Y = V - (C + 400)$.]

   (ii) What levels of F and Q will be chosen by the tenant farmer to maximize net income (after payments to the landlord)?

$$F = \underline{\hspace{3cm}} \text{ kg of fertilizer}$$

$$Q = \underline{\hspace{3cm}} \text{ kg of rice}$$

   (iii) You should have found that the tenant chooses the same levels of F and Q as the independent proprietor. Explain this result in terms of the logic of the farmer's production decision, as represented by Figure 18–2.

   (iv) Think again about the logic of Figure 18–2. What would be the effect of a sharecropping arrangement in which the landlord received 25% of the gross crop, but also paid 25% of the input costs?

c. Now suppose that the farmer is a worker on a large collective farm, in charge of a one-hectare plot. The farmer pays nothing for fertilizer or for labor, and is rewarded according to the number of workers under his supervision. Briefly discuss the input and output decisions and the efficiency of farming likely to result from this incentive system.

4. This exercise uses supply-and-demand analysis to study the effects of food subsidy policies. Curves D_r and S_r in Figure 18–5 are the retail demand and supply curves for grain in the Republic of Nafaka. Curve S_f shows the farmers' supply curve. As discussed in the textbook, marketing costs account for the vertical gap between S_f and S_r.

In the absence of government intervention, curves D_r and S_r show that the equilibrium price in the retail market would be $P_0 = $ N$1.00 per kg of grain. [N$ stands for the Nafaka dollar, which is worth U.S.$0.50.] The equilibrium quantity would be $Q_0 = 200$ million kg of grain. From curve S_f you can see that the price paid to farmers for supplying quantity Q_0 is $P_1 = $ N$0.60 per kg. So the marketing cost—the cost of moving the food from the farm gate to the retail consumer—is $C_0 = $ N$0.40 per kg of grain.

a. Now suppose that the government of Nafaka issues a price control edict. Grain must be sold in the retail market at a controlled price of $P^* = $ N$0.80 per kg.

(i) From curve D_r you can see that the retail quantity demanded at this controlled price is:

$$Q_1 = \underline{\hspace{2cm}} \text{ million kg of grain.}$$

(ii) The traders still incur the marketing costs (C_0). After deducting these costs from the controlled retail price, rural traders would be paying farmers:

$$P_2 = \text{N\$} \underline{\hspace{2cm}} \text{ per kg of grain.}$$

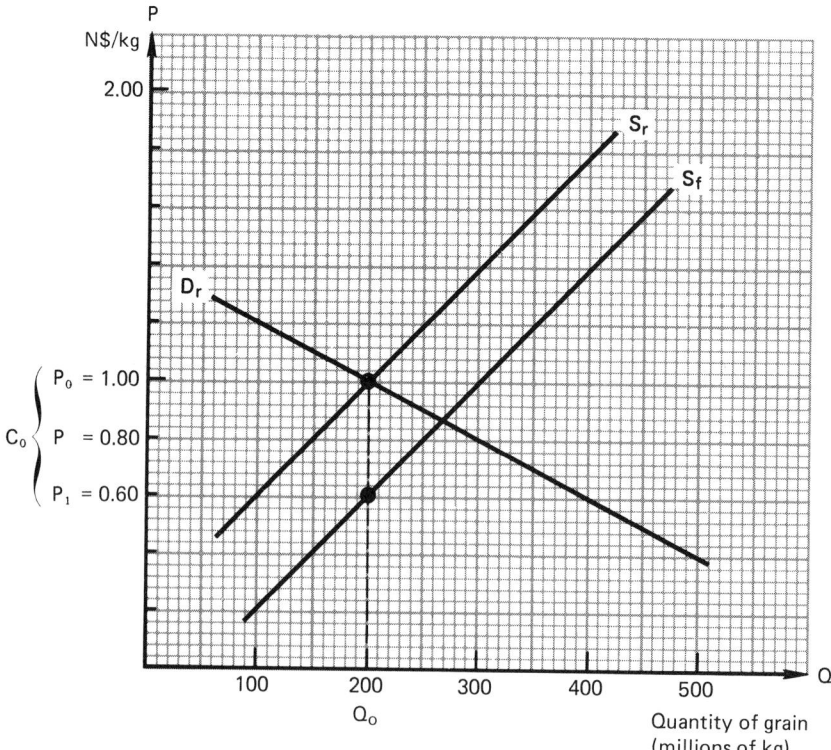

Figure 18–5

(iii) At this price, farmers are willing to supply to the market only:

$$Q_2 = \text{_____ million kg of grain.}$$

(iv) Consequently, there will be a shortage in the market of:

$$Q_1 - Q_2 = \text{_____ million kg of grain.}$$

b. With the price control in effect, market forces leave the government with a number of options for handling the shortage. It can simply tolerate the situation. Or it can import enough grain to cover the shortage.

(i) To eliminate the shortage the government would have to

import $Q_m = \text{_____}$ million kg of grain. If the world price of grain is U.S.$0.50 = N$1.00 per kg, these imports

would entail a foreign exchange cost of U.S._____ million.

(ii) In domestic-currency terms, the government would buy the imports for N$1.00 per kg, and then sell the grain to consumers for $P^* = $ N$0.80. So the government would be providing a subsidy to consumers of $S_0 = $ N_____ per kg of imported grain. Altogether this subsidy would cost the government:

$$Q_m \times S_0 = \text{N\$_____ million.}$$

c. Alternatively, the government can eliminate the shortage by raising farm prices to the point that domestic grain production matches demand ($= Q_1$).

(i) Curve S_f shows that domestic farmers will increase output to Q_1 if they are paid:

$$P_3 = \text{N\$_____ per kg.}$$

Taking into account the required marketing costs, the total procurement price would be:

$$P_4 = P_3 + C_0 = \text{N\$_____ per kg of grain.}$$

(ii) By paying P_4 per kg of grain and then selling the grain for $P^* = $ N$0.80, the government is providing a subsidy of $S_1 = $

N_____ per kg of grain consumed. The total cost of this subsidy to the government is:

$$Q_1 \times S_1 = \text{N\$_____ million.}$$

(iii) Compare the farm price policy with the import policy in terms of budget costs. Then comment on the economic opportunity cost of each policy, and each policy's effect on agricultural development in Nafaka.

d. Finally, consider the longer term effects. Over the ensuing decade, the retail demand curve shifts to the right by 200 million kg, while the farm supply curve shifts to the right by only 50 million kg. Also, bureaucratic politics cause marketing costs to double. Yet political instability prevents any increase in the controlled retail price of $P* = $ N$0.80.

  (i) Use dotted lines in Figure 18–5 to show the position of curves D_r, S_f, and S_r at the end of the decade.
 (ii) At the end of the decade the quantity demanded at price $P*$ will be:

_____ million kg of grain.

At price $P*$ the quantity supplied to the retail market will be:

_____ million kg of grain.

So the government will have to cover a market shortage of:

_____ million kg of grain.

(iii) Given the available information, explain how the cost of the price control will change over time, if the market shortage is covered by:
 − grain imports

− paying higher prices to domestic farmers.

5. This exercise applies isoquant analysis to show how factor productivity in agriculture can depend on factor endowments. East Nasi and West Nasi are identical in terms of land fertility and farmers' capabilities. And they face the same agricultural technology, illustrated in Figure 18–6 by isoquant QQ showing alternative combinations of land (D) and labor (L) that can be used to produce 10 tons of rice. For simplicity, we ignore other inputs such as capital and fertilizer.

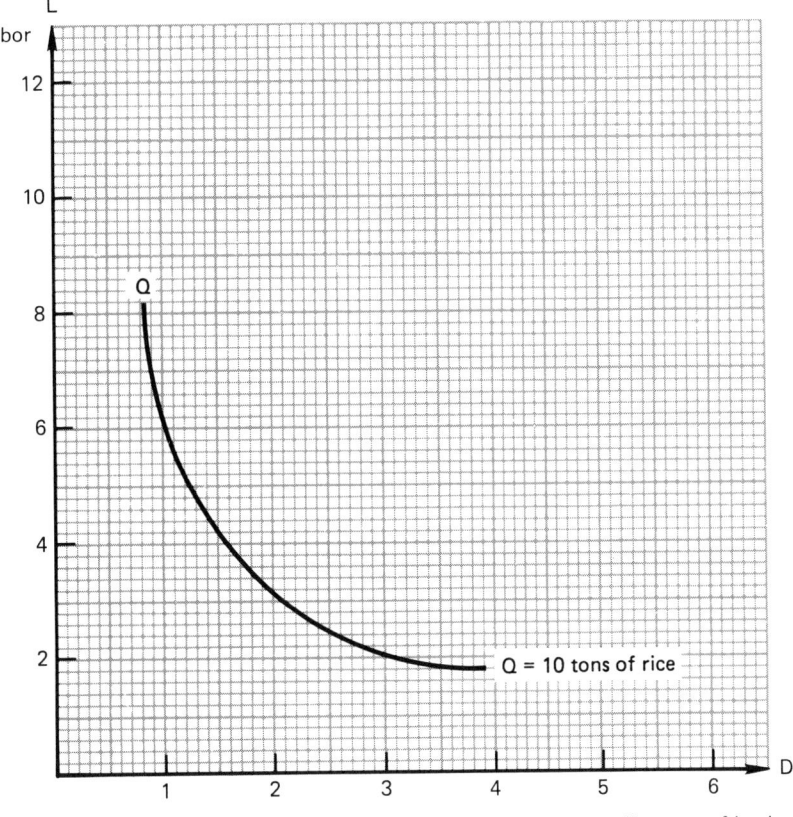

Labor

$Q = 10$ tons of rice

Hectares of land

Figure 18-6

a. The two countries do differ in population density. East Nasi has far more land relative to its population. In East Nasi the annual rental cost of land is $200 per hectare, while labor costs $300 per year. In contrast the annual land rental in West Nasi is 1,800 pesos per hectare, while labor costs P300 per year. You need not know the exchange rate between these currencies just yet.

(i) The optimal factor proportions for a farmer in East Nasi can be determined by finding the point on QQ that lies on the lowest possible budget line. Consider a cost level of $C =$ $1,200. For this cost, a farmer in East Nasi can afford

_____ hectares of land and zero labor, or _____ workers and zero land, or any other combination of L and D costing $1,200.

(ii) In Figure 18-6, draw the $C = $1,200 budget line faced by an East Nasi farmer.

(iii) You should find that this line happens to be tangent to isoquant QQ. Label the point of tangency as *point E**.

(iv) For a farmer in East Nasi the optimal technique for producing 10 tons of rice involves the use of:

$D = $ _____ hectares of land, and

$L = $ _____ workers.

(v) An efficient farmer in East Nasi will produce _____

tons of rice per hectare of land, or _____ tons of rice per worker.

b. Now consider the optimal factor proportions for a farmer in West Nasi, where the wage is P300 and the land rent is P1,800 per hectare.

   (i) In Figure 18–6, construct a few representative budget lines for a farmer in West Nasi. [Hint: try cost levels of P1,800 and P3,600.]

   (ii) Find the point on isoquant QQ that is tangent to a budget line for West Nasi farming. Label the point of tangency as *point W**.

   (iii) For a farmer in West Nasi the optimal technique for producing 10 tons of rice involves the use of:

$$D = \text{_____} \text{ hectares of land, and}$$

$$L = \text{_____} \text{ workers.}$$

[Hint: the answer involves only integers.]

   (iv) An efficient farmer in West Nasi will produce _____

tons of rice per hectare of land, or _____ tons of rice per worker.

c. Farmers in each country are adapting optimally to relative factor costs. Yet factor productivity levels are very different.

   (i) Output per hectare of land is much higher in _____ Nasi.

   (ii) Output per worker is much higher in _____ Nasi.

   (iii) What can one conclude from these differences in factor productivity about the relative efficiency of rice farming in East and West Nasi? Briefly explain.

d. (i) If the exchange rate between the two currencies were $1 = P1, what pattern of rice trade would emerge under free trade?

(ii) If the exchange rate were $1 = P10$, what pattern of rice trade
would emerge under free trade?

Answers to Self-Test

Completion

1. scale
2. Latifundia
3. sharecropping
4. reform; longer
5. transport
6. substitute
7. Extension
8. moneylender
9. prices
10. increase; reduce

True-False

1.	F	6.	F
2.	F	7.	T
3.	T	8.	F
4.	T	9.	F
5.	F	10.	T

Multiple Choice

1.	b	5.	a
2.	c	6.	b
3.	a	7.	d
4.	d	8.	c

CHAPTER 19   Natural Resources

Overview

Chapter 19 begins by acknowledging the very uneven distribution of the world's energy, mineral, and forest resources. Many LDCs are poorly endowed with resource reserves. For those countries that are more richly endowed, natural-resource wealth has proved to be a mixed blessing. Many of these countries have been unable to convert resource endowments into rapid growth or diversified, equitable economic development. If not well managed, earnings from resource exports can lead to inflation and currency overvaluation, hindering development of non-resource exports and import-competing domestic production.

Non-renewable resources are, however, a source of economic rents. LDCs have had considerable success in capturing a large share of these rents through fiscal measures, contracts and state-owned enterprises. Less success has been achieved in shifting taxes onto foreign consumers of resource exports: demand and supply are generally too elastic for such measures to work—particularly in the long run. Nonetheless, with proper policies, LDCs can succeed in transforming natural-resource wealth into physical and human capital, while minimizing adverse effects on other sectors of the economy. The appropriate policies include restrained government spending and borrowing, and judicious exchange-rate adjustments.

Main Learning Objectives

After studying this chapter you ought to understand and be able to explain:

1. The uneven distribution of the world's energy, mineral, and forest **resource reserves**.

2. The mixed record of growth among countries endowed with abundant **natural capital**.

3. The special problems related to tropical forest resources, and possible policy remedies.

4. The concept of **resource rents**, and the distinction between **scarcity rent, differential resource rent**, and **monopoly rent** associated with exploiting natural resources.

5. The policies that LDC governments have used to increase their share of resource rents.

6. The factors that determine the extent to which a tax on natural-resource exports is shifted forward to foreign consumers.

7. The causes, symptoms and potential remedies for **Dutch disease** associated with rapid increases in resource-based exports.

Additional Key Terms, Concepts, and Institutions

Can you identify and explain each of the following?

nonrenewable resources
deforestation
noncommercial energy
mini-devaluation
tragedy of the commons
enclave export sector

Economic Tools and Techniques

From what you have learned in this chapter, can you:

1. Use supply-and-demand analysis to distinguish the three types of rent associated with natural resources?

2. Calculate the ratio of **retained value** (RV) to total proceeds (R), as a measure of the extent to which the host country benefits from natural-resource projects?

3. Apply Equation 19–3 from the textbook to calculate the percentage of a tax on an export commodity that is shifted forward to foreign consumers?

4. Explain the mechanics of **Dutch disease**, and how fiscal restraint or exchange-rate devaluation help to cushion its adverse effects?

Self-Test

Completion

1. Fuel wood, animal dung, and agricultural wastes are examples of

    _____ energy sources in LDCs.

2. When forests are public property and not carefully managed, they tend to be overused and deteriorate rapidly. This is an example of

    the tragedy of the _____.

3. The return accruing to a factor of production in inelastic supply is

    called a _____ rent.

4. The total of wages and salaries, procurement costs, capital income, taxes and royalties accruing to the host country from a natural-resource project is called the _____.

5. According to the text, the prime cause of _____ in many LDCs is the practice of shifting cultivation.

6. Taxes levied against foreign-resource extraction companies will have little adverse effect on investment incentives in the host country, provided they are taxes on _____.

7. _____ occurs when a successful natural resource export sparks domestic inflation while simultaneously causing a large increase in foreign exchange reserves.

8. The text suggests that governments facing Dutch disease can avoid the trauma of a major devaluation by using periodic _____.

True-False If false, you should be able to explain why.

_____ 1. During the period 1973–1983, those developing countries having large endowments of nonfuel mineral resources experienced rapid economic growth compared to LDCs in general.

_____ 2. The world's proven reserves of a natural resource may increase abruptly if formerly unprofitable deposits become commercially recoverable as a result of a price rise.

_____ 3. The major cause of deforestation has been logging operations of multinational corporations.

_____ 4. LDCs account for more than 50% of world production of almost all major nonfuel minerals.

_____ 5. If an LDC government captures 100% of the rent on its natural resources, the rate of return to resource extraction would still be adequate to attract private-sector investors.

_____ 6. A policy of maximizing host-country returns from resource extraction is synonymous with minimizing the return earned by multinational corporations involved in the operations.

_____ 7. The smaller a country's share of the world-market supply for a given commodity, the more fully it can shift a commodity export tax forward to foreign consumers.

_____ 8. Nigeria's agricultural sector was very prosperous prior to the oil boom in the 1970s, and very weak thereafter.

_____ 9. With perfectly inelastic world demand, a commodity export tax imposed by any single producing country is shifted fully to foreign consumers in the form of higher prices.

_____ 10. LDCs have managed to obtain only a very small share of the benefits from natural-resource projects that are operated by multinational corporations.

Multiple Choice

1. Which of the following LDCs has successfully converted natural resource wealth into rapid economic growth?
   a. Zambia
   b. Malaysia
   c. Korea
   d. Bolivia

2. The return to a high-quality resource deposit over and above the return to a marginal commercial deposit is called:
   a. differential resource rent.
   b. monopoly rent
   c. scarcity rent.
   d. monopoly profit.

3. For most resource-extraction projects, the major source of retained value for the host country is in the form of:
   a. wages paid to the local work force.
   b. profits earned by domestic co-owners.
   c. payments made to procure domestically produced intermediate goods and capital goods.
   d. taxes and royalties paid to the government.

4. Which of the following countries was not among the three largest oil producers in 1984?
   a. United States
   b. Saudi Arabia
   c. Nigeria
   d. Soviet Union

5. Which of the following is not one of the basic symptoms of Dutch disease?
   a. rapidly declining per-capita income
   b. rising unemployment
   c. stagnation of major sectors other than resource exports
   d. accelerating inflation

6. The two LDCs that dominate the supply of tropical hardwood timber to the world market are:
   a. Malaysia and Indonesia.
   b. India and China.
   c. Brazil and Colombia.
   d. Nigeria and Zaire.

7. Inflation generally results from a large increase in a country's oil revenues because:
   a. the currency depreciates, making imports more expensive.
   b. so much is exported that scarcities occur domestically.
   c. government spending of the oil revenues generates a large increase in the money supply.
   d. all of the above.

8. The text's boxed example of Indonesia illustrates a case in which the oil boom:
   a. led to a crisis of debt, inflation, and unemployment, despite rapid growth of GNP.
   b. caused GNP growth to decline abruptly.
   c. was followed by a devaluation that succeeded in stimulating exports of manufactured goods.
   d. caused a sharp decline in agricultural output.

Applications

Worked Example: Resource Rents

The Monzanium Monopoly Corporation (MMCo) controls the world's only two known monzanium deposits, both of which are located in Binaro. Deposit I contains high-grade ore; a maximum of 1 million tons of monzanium can be mined annually and processed for sale at a cost of $1,500 per ton. Deposit II contains low-grade ore; up to 1 million tons can be mined annually but at a cost of $3,000 per ton. These costs, which include normal profits, are shown by line *CC* in Figure 19-1. Line *DD* is the world demand curve for monzanium. Line *MR* is the corresponding marginal revenue curve. When MMCo produces the maximum output of $Q = 2$ million tons per year, it can charge $12,000 per ton and earn a return over and above normal profits equal to the entire shaded area. Note that at full production marginal revenue equals $5,000.

All three kinds of rent are represented in this example. First, there is a **scarcity rent** of $2,000 (= $5,000 − $3,000) per ton. This is the maximum tax per ton that would have no effect at all on the allocation of resources in the industry. The tax would be a pure transfer from the company to the government of Binaro. Production incentives would be unaffected— the essence of scarcity rent. Any tax higher than $2,000 would cause marginal cost to exceed *MR* at $Q = 2$ million tons, provoking MMCo to reduce production.

The firm also earns a **differential resource rent** of $1,500 per ton on the rights to deposit I (but not deposit II). Due to the high quality of its ore an *extra* tax or a royalty of up to $1,500 per ton could be levied on deposit I rights without impairing production incentives.

The remaining excess profit, equal to $7,000 per ton (= $12,000 − $5,000) is **monopoly rent** in this example. If the government tries to capture part of this surplus through a tax per ton of monzanium output exceeding $2,000 on deposit II or $3,500 on deposit I, the firm's profit-maximizing production decision would be altered. However, the

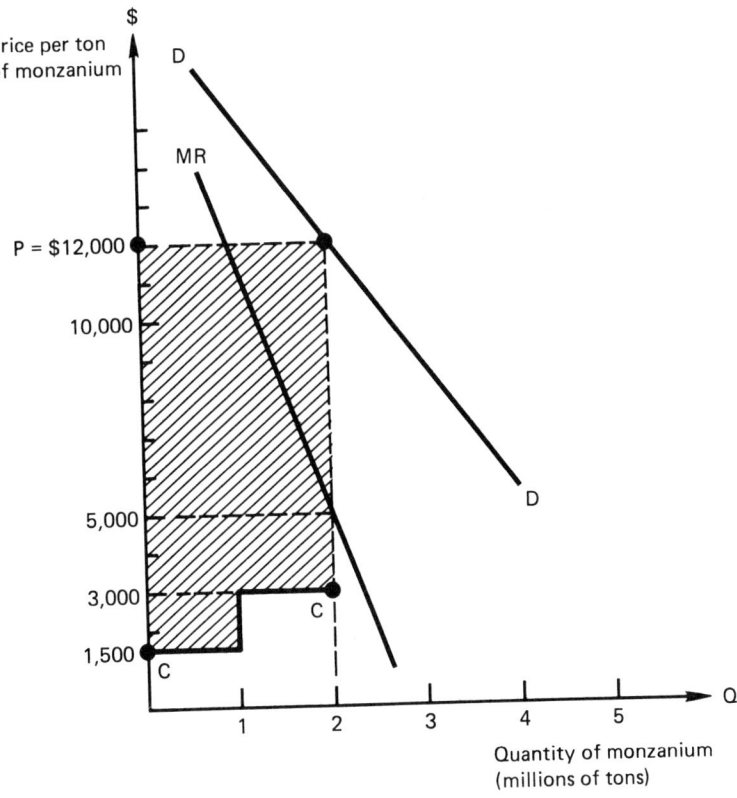

Figure 19-1

government could tap this source of rent in other ways without impairing MMCo's incentives. For example, the government could levy a profits tax—there is no difference between the output that maximizes 50% of profits and the output that maximizes 100% of profits. Or the government could share ownership of MMCo's Binaro venture. Or it could own the venture outright and pay MCCo just enough to cover operating costs, including a normal profit.

If production were competitive rather than monopolized, the *MR* curve would be irrelevant to production decisions and there would be no monopoly rents. In this case the excess of the market price ($12,000) over the supply price ($5,000) would represent scarcity rent.

Exercises

1. Now it is your turn to evaluate rents.

   a. The U.S. government is auctioning off oil exploration rights to plots of land 100 miles from the Alaskan shore. Demand for these rights is shown by line *DD* in Figure 19-2.
   (i) Label as P_1 the scarcity rent per plot earned by the government if $Q = 10,000$ plots were auctioned off.

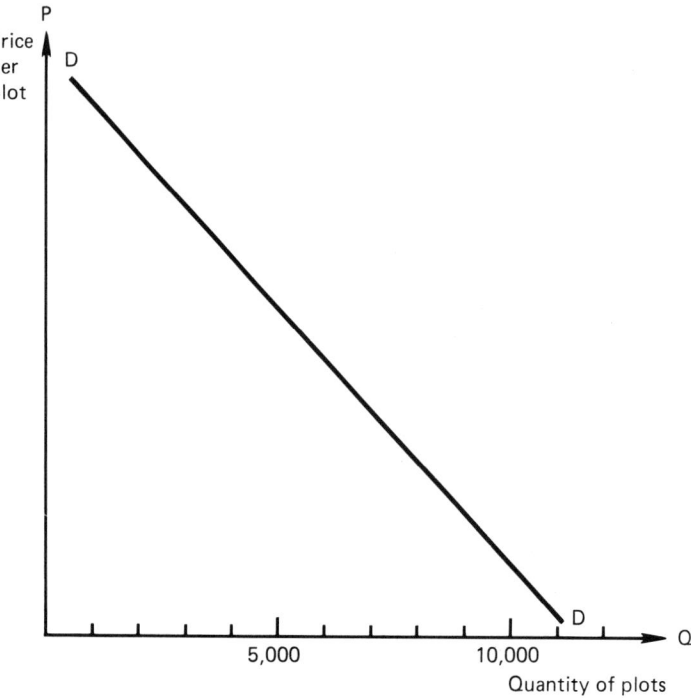

P

Price
per
plot

D

D

5,000   10,000   Q

Quantity of plots

Figure 19–2

(ii) Label as P_2 the scarcity rent per plot earned by the
government if $Q = 2,000$ plots were auctioned off.
(iii) Suppose $Q = 2,000$ again, but now the government gives away
the drilling rights for free on a first-come, first-served basis.
What becomes of the rents?

b. In Figure 19–3, SS shows the world-market supply curve for
bauxite. Production is a positive function of the price up to an
output of OX, representing capacity operation of existing mines.
World demand for bauxite is shown by line DD_1.

(i) The market equilibrium price is $P_1 = \$$_____ .
(ii) The scarcity rent earned by bauxite producers is $R_1 =$

$\$$_____ per ton.
(iii) Zebulon has the world's richest ores, and is therefore the
lowest-cost producer of bauxite. Segment OY of the supply
curve represents supply conditions in Zebulon. Producers in
Zebulon earn a differential resource rent of $R_z =$

$\$$_____ per ton.

c. Now suppose that governments in all bauxite producing countries
imposed a common $500 per ton tax on bauxite production.
From the point of view of the mining companies this tax causes a

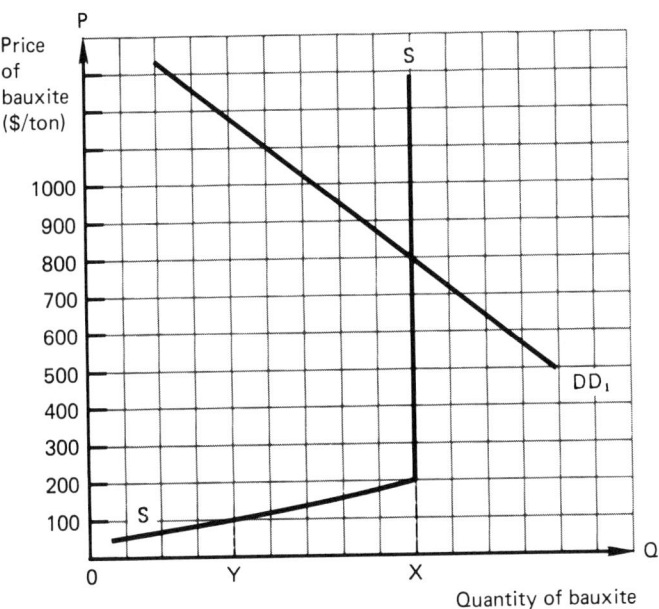

Figure 19-3

$500 drop in the price received for any given level of output. In Figure 19–3 this can be represented as downward shift in the demand curve by the amount of the tax.

(i) Draw in the new demand curve faced by the mining companies and label it DD_2.

(ii) The new equilibrium price (less tax) received by the producers is $P_2 = \$$_____ .

(iii) Bauxite consumers are paying a price (including tax) equal to $P_2' = \$$_____ .

(iv) In this case, the scarcity rent per ton of bauxite equals $R_2 =$ $_____ , of which _____ % is being captured by the host governments.

(v) What is the maximum tax per ton of bauxite that the governments of bauxite producing countries can levy without impairing production incentives? Would the answer be different for Zebulon considered alone?

2. This exercise presents a problem in calculating retained value. You may wish to review Equations 19–1 and 19–2 in the textbook. Table 19–1 shows the 1986 Income and Expenditure account for the Tinland subsidiary of the Imperialistic Tin Corporation (ITC). The following facts are also pertinent:

Table 19-1
Income and Expenditure Statement, ITC-Tinland, 1986
(Figures in millions of dollars)

Sales revenues		$214
Expenses		
wages	$32	
salaries	12	
energy costs	20	
intermediate goods and services	32	
Total operating costs	96	
Operating income		118
Interest on debt	6	
Taxes to Tinland	50	
Royalties to Tinland	35	
NET INCOME		27

100 % of the wage workers are Tinland nationals.

80% of salary payments go to Tinland nationals.

100% of energy inputs are produced in Tinland.

40% of intermediate goods and services are imported; in addition, 30% of the value of local procurements represents import content.

90% of interest payments go to foreign lenders.

45% of the stock in the subsidiary is owned by the Tinland government or by Tinland nationals.

40% of the earnings of expatriate salaried employees is spent on Tinland goods and services.

a. These data provide all of the information you need to calculate each component of retained value (RV):

(i) W_d = labor income for host country workers = $_____ million.

(ii) C_d = income paid to expatriate workers but spent locally = $_____ million.

(iii) $DP(1 - Z)$ = domestic procurement of goods and services (don't forget energy costs), less import content = $_____ million.

(iv) K_d = profits and interest accruing to Tinlandians = $_____ million.

(v) T_d = taxes and royalties paid to the host government = $_____ million.

(vi) RV = RETAINED VALUE = $_____ million.

b. The data also provide all of the information necessary to identify the components of total proceeds (R):

(i) M = import cost of procurements = $_____ million.

(ii) I = interest cost on external loans = $_____ million.

(iii) P = profits accruing to foreigners = $_____ million.

(iv) W_f = salaries paid to expatriates that are not spent locally = $_____ million.

(v) Now check that:

$$R = \text{total sales proceeds} = M + I + P + W_f + RV$$

= $_____ million.

(vi) What is retained value as a fraction of total proceeds?

$$RV/R = \text{_____} \text{ or } \text{_____} \%.$$

c. What factors determine who bears the burden of the taxes and royalties collected by the government of Tinland? Is it ITC? Or foreign tin consumers? Or who?

3. This problem applies Equation 19–3 from the text, which shows the formula for computing T_c, i.e., the fraction of an export tax that is shifted forward to foreign consumers.

The island nation of Pulau is the world's only source of the coveted venus shell, so Pulau's market share = a = 100%. The elasticity of supply to the world market is $E_s = e_{st} = 0.80$. World demand for the shell is highly inelastic, $E_d = 0.20$ (in absolute value). The world-market price per venus shell is $P_v = \$5$. These figures will be referred to as the "initial conditions."

a. (i) Given the initial conditions, if Pulau sets a tax of $2 per shell, the percentage shifted forward to foreign consumers would be:

$$T_c = \text{_____} \%, \text{ or } \$\text{_____} .$$

(ii) Suppose all initial conditions remain unchanged except that the demand of venus shells is highly elastic: $E_d = 2.50$. Then,

$$T_c = \text{_____} \%.$$

(iii) Suppose all initial conditions remain unchanged except that supply is highly inelastic: $E_s = e_{st} = 0.10$. Then,

$$T_c = \text{_____} \%.$$

(iv) Suppose all initial conditions remain unchanged except that Pulau's market share is only a = 50%. Assume that the supply elasticity from all sources is still $e_{sn} = e_{st} = E_s = 0.80$. Then,

$$T_c = \text{_____} \%.$$

(v) Suppose all initial conditions remain unchanged except that Pulau's market share is $a = 50\%$, the elasticity of supply from alternative producers is $e_s = 1.6$, and the overall elasticity of supply is $E_s = 1.2$. Then,

$$T_c = \underline{\hspace{2cm}} \%.$$

b. More generally, the extent of shifting taxes forward to foreign consumers is greater:

(i) the _____ the taxing country's supply elasticity;

(ii) the _____ the world-market-demand elasticity;

(iii) the _____ the taxing country's market share; and

(iv) the _____ the supply elasticity for other producing countries.

c. Now analyze the tax shifting in terms of supply and demand. Suppose that panel a of Figure 19–4 shows the supply and demand curves (S and D) corresponding to initial conditions.

(i) After imposition of the $2 tax, consumers will be paying a price that is $_____ higher than the amount received by sellers.

(ii) From the consumers' perspective, the tax effectively shifts the supply curve upward to the dotted line S'. This line shows that any given quantity will be supplied at a price to the consumer that is $_____ higher than before, to cover the tax.

(iii) With the tax, the new equilibrium price is $P'_v = \$$_____.

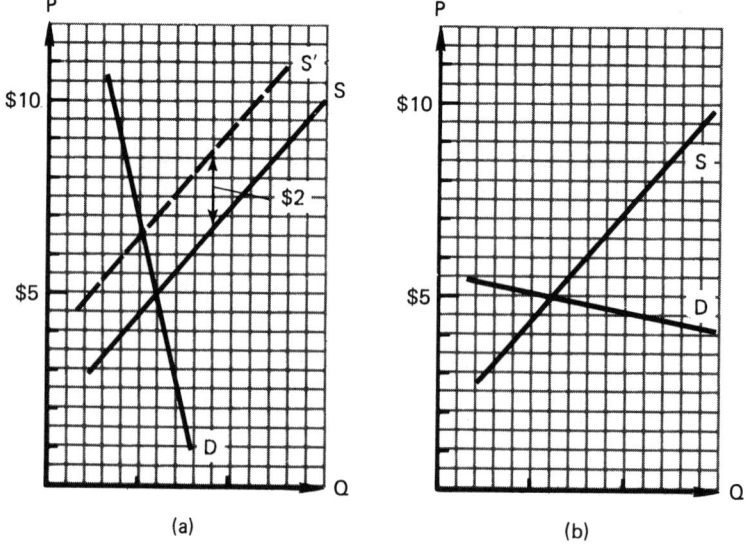

(a)   (b)

Figure 19–4

(iv) Consumers therefore bear $_____ of the $2 tax. Who pays the remainder?

d. Panel b shows the original supply curve with a far more elastic demand curve.
   (i) Show how the supply curve will shift as a result of the imposition of a $2 tax. Label the new supply curve S'.
   (ii) How does panel b compare with panel a in terms of the after-tax equilibrium price and the extent to which consumers bear the tax burden? [Note: The shifting of export taxes is one case of tax *incidence*, as discussed in Chapter 12.]

4. This exercise explores the mechanics of Dutch disease. Until recently, the economy of Providence was based upon producing marbles for export and rice for domestic consumption. Some rice was imported, as well. Total GNP for 1985 was $Y = 100$ billion shillings (Sh). Export earnings totaled $X = \$10$ billion (= Sh10 billion, at the equilibrium exchange rate of Sh1 = \$1). The ratio of money supply to GNP was $M/Y = 10\%$. The government budget was balanced. There was little inflation, little unemployment, and a very modest foreign debt.

   Then in early 1986, bonanza. An enormous diamond lode was discovered. Abruptly, diamond export earnings grew from zero to $40 billion per year, of which $30 billion accrued to the government in the form of royalties paid by foreign mining companies. Sounds good!

   a. The post-bonanza supply of foreign exchange caused the shilling to appreciate dramatically to Sh0.2 = $1.
      (i) The world price of marbles is $5 per box. In local currency,

      marble exporters received Sh_____ per box when the exchange rate was Sh1 = $1. At the new exchange rate following the diamond bonanza, marble exporters receive

      Sh_____ per box.
      (ii) Figure 19-5 shows the supply curve (S) for marbles produced in Providence. Draw in a horizontal line showing the pre-bonanza export price (in shillings). Label it P_0. Identify the corresponding quantity of marble exports as Q_0.

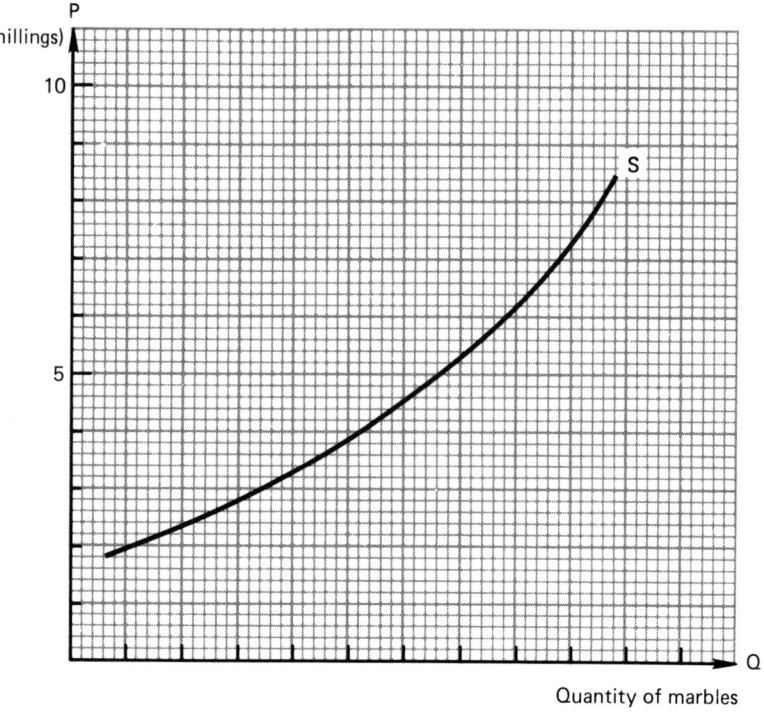

P

Price (shillings)

10

5

S

Quantity of marbles

Q

Figure 19–5

(iii) Draw a horizontal line showing the post-bonanza export price (in shillings). Label it P_1. What happens to the quantity of marble exports as a result of the exchange-rate appreciation caused by the diamond bonanza?

(iv) The world price of rice is $200 per ton. At the original exchange rate the local currency cost of rice imports was

Sh_____ per ton. At the post-bonanza exchange rate, rice

imports cost Sh_____ per ton.

(v) Figure 19–6 shows the supply curve for domestic rice (*SD*) and the domestic demand curve (*D*). Draw in a horizontal line showing the pre-bonanza import supply curve. Label it P_0. Label the initial equilibrium point in the Providence rice market as E_0, and the quantity supplied *domestically* as Q_0.

(vi) Draw in a horizontal line showing the post-bonanza import supply curve. Label it P_1. What happens to sales of domestically produced rice as a result of the diamond bonanza?

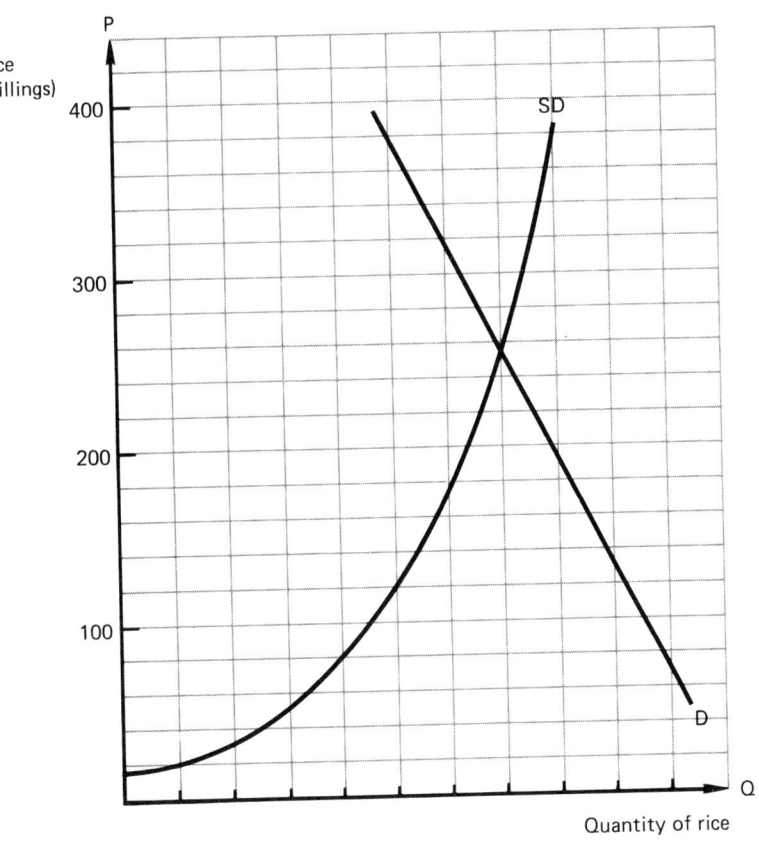

Price
(shillings)

400

SD

300

200

100

D

Q

Quantity of rice

Figure 19–6

(vii) The rice and marble industries are very labor-intensive, whereas the diamond industry employs only a few hundred Providentials. How does the diamond bonanza affect the labor market?

b. The government decides to spend its $30 billion bonanza on domestic services.
  (i) Since the diamond royalties were paid in dollars, the government must first convert the funds to shillings at the central bank. Assume that the government converts the funds at the post-bonanza exchange rate. Then the government's new spending will cause the money supply in circulation to

  rise from Sh_____ billion to Sh_____ billion, an

  increase of _____ %.

(ii) What is likely to be the effect on the domestic inflation rate?

(iii) If the same amount of government spending had been financed by domestic taxes rather than diamond royalties, would the inflation effect have been the same? [Hint: no.] Why?

c. Explain how it might be possible for Providence to end up with a large government budget deficit and a large national debt as a result of the diamond bonanza.

d. If the exchange rate had been held fixed at the initial level of Sh1 = $1, would the domestic rice and marble industries have been saved? [Hint: Think about the effects of inflation with a fixed-exchange rate.] Explain your answer with reference to Figures 19–5 and 19–6.

e. The textbook suggests that the worst symptoms of Dutch disease can be avoided if the government "sterilizes" the sudden flood of royalty revenues by investing the dollars in overseas deposit accounts, or spending on imports.
(i) With reference to Figures 19–5 and 19–6, explain how such sterilization alters the impact of the diamond bonanza on the domestic rice and marble industries.

(ii) How would the people of Providence benefit from the diamond bonanza if the government royalty earnings are not spent domestically?

5. This exercise checks your understanding of the textbook's Figure 19–3, showing the effects of oil exports on agricultural growth. Figure 19–7 here is a reproduction of that figure. Assume that a favorable oil shock occurs in year 5.

a. Why, if the exchange rate remains fixed, would the oil shock push the agricultural sector from line *ABA* down to line *BCB*?

b. What policy response causes agricultural growth to follow line *BDE* rather than line *BCB*? Why would this policy response have such an effect?

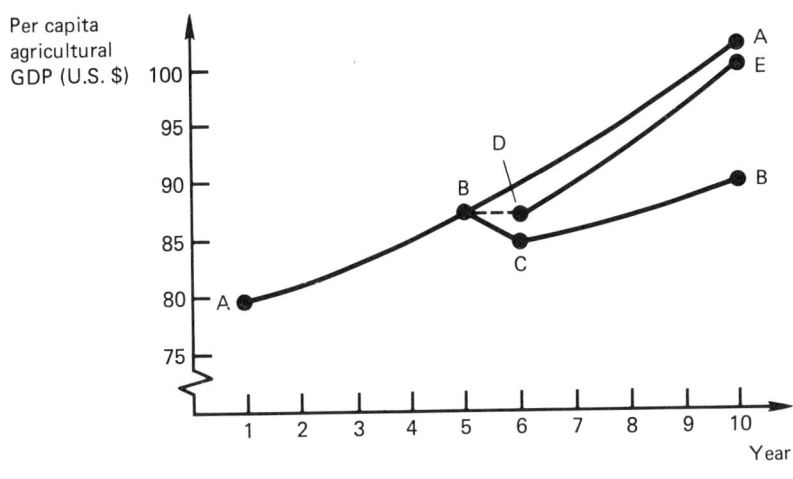

Figure 19–7

c. Draw a line in Figure 19–7 showing the outcome if the policy response were delayed and implemented only in year 8. Label this line *XX*.

Answers to Self-Test

Completion

1. noncommercial (or traditional)
2. commons
3. scarcity
4. retained value
5. deforestation
6. rents
7. Dutch disease
8. mini-devaluations

True-False

1.	F	6.	F
2.	T	7.	F
3.	F	8.	T
4.	F	9.	F
5.	T	10.	F

Multiple Choice

1.	b	5.	a
2.	a	6.	a
3.	d	7.	c
4.	c	8.	c

CHAPTER 20   Industry

Overview

Chapter 20 focuses on two major issues: the role of industry as a leading sector in the development process, and the technical characteristics of investment choices in manufacturing. Value-added in the industrial sector typically grows more rapidly than GDP, so the sector's share of GDP rises with per-capita income. Simple consumer goods industries, such as textiles and food processing, account for the fastest growth at low levels of income; at higher levels of income, producer goods and consumer durables become major growth sectors. After reviewing these empirical patterns, the text explores linkage effects, as well as the association between industrialization and urbanization.

The choice of technique in industry is discussed next. A considerable body of empirical evidence demonstrates that there is in fact a wide range of choice of technique, implying that relative factor prices can have a major impact on factor intensity in production. In connection with technology choice, the role of scale economies is explained and evaluated. In particular, the importance of small-scale industry as a vehicle for employment creation is discussed, along with policy measures to promote small enterprises. The chapter concludes with a review of the special strengths of industry, including the sector's essential contribution to a more productive and better diversified economy.

Main Learning Objectives

After studying this chapter you ought to understand and be able to explain:

1. The broad empirical pattern of changes in the size and structure of the industrial sector associated with rising per-capita income.

2. The meaning and the measurement of **direct backward linkages, total backward linkages,** and **direct forward linkages.**

3. The factors that underlie the strong association between industrialization and **urbanization,** along with the benefits and costs of urban concentration.

4. The range of **technology choice** in manufactoring activities, the scope for capital-labor substitution, and the factors that influence the choice of technology.

5. The nature and implications of **economies of scale** in manufacturing.

6. The pros and cons of promoting **small-scale industry** and the policy measures that can be used for this purpose.

7. The fundamental role that industry plays in the development process—including its relationship to agriculture, employment growth, and national **dependence**.

Additional Key Terms, Concepts, and Institutions

Can you identify and explain each of the following?

backward integration
early developing branches of manufacturing
economies of agglomeration
labor-intensive and capital-intensive technologies
minimum efficient scale (MES)

Economic Tools and Techniques

From what you have learned in this chapter, can you:

1. Compute backward and forward linkages from input-output coefficients data?

2. Explain the **external economies** and **diseconomies** associated with urbanization?

3. Use an isoquant diagram to illustrate the scope for factor substitution in manufacturing, the extent to which factor intensity can vary, and the **appropriate technology** corresponding to a given set of factor prices?

4. Use the **long-run average cost** curve for an industry to explain scale economies?

Self-Test

Completion

1. In most developing countries, value-added in manufacturing grows

   _____ rapidly than GDP as a whole.

2. The process of industrialization requires backward integration from

   _____-goods industries to _____-goods industries.

3. Expansion of the cement industry causes limestone quarrying to

   increase. This is a _____ linkage of the cement industry.

4. Manufacturing firms in urban areas benefit from economies of

   _____ in the form of wide availability of inputs and services due to the proximity of many other firms.

5. The largest direct cost of urbanization is the cost of providing the necessary urban _____.

6. In many LDCs technology choice is distorted in favor of more _____-intensive production methods because of factor-price distortions.

7. The minimum efficient scale is defined as the scale of operation beyond which _____ cost ceases to decline.

8. The contention that small-scale industry can generate more employment is based on the observation that small firms generally use more _____ and less _____ per unit of output.

9. As suggested by the Lewis-Fei-Ranis model, greater productivity in industry is a key to increased _____ income.

True-False If false, you should be able to explain why.

_____ 1. Cross-country data reveal that the manufacturing share of GDP generally rises with per-capita income for both large and small countries.

_____ 2. If the total backward-linkage index equals 2.4 for sector A and 1.2 for sector B, then investment in A is more efficient than investment in B.

_____ 3. Dispersing industrial activity to smaller cities can reduce congestion in the large cities, with no significant offsetting social costs.

_____ 4. Empirical studies show that for many manufacturing activities there is a very wide scope for factor substitution.

_____ 5. The term appropriate technology is used in the text to mean the least-cost technology, given appropriate factor prices.

_____ 6. If the MES in the gadget industry is $Q = 10$ million per year and the domestic market in country X is 4 million, then it is not possible for country X to produce gadgets at a competitive average cost.

_____ 7. Industry-specific studies confirm, without exception, that the labor-output ratio is higher in small enterprises than in large enterprises.

_____ 8. Evidence cited in the text indicates that in most developing countries more than 80% of all manufacturing jobs are found in firms that employ fewer than five people.

_____ 9. Manufacturing provides a far greater scope for efficient diversification than would be possible relying on primary products alone.

Multiple Choice

1. On average in low-income countries, growth of the industrial sector generates new jobs each year for what percentage of the labor force?
   a. 0.06
   b. 0.6
   c. 6.0
   d. 60.0

2. Which of the following industries is an early-developing branch of the manufacturing sector?
   a. food processing
   b. textiles
   c. leather goods
   d. all of the above

3. If value-added in the shoe industry equals 40% of the value of output and imported inputs account for 15% of the value of output, then direct backward linkages equal:
   a. 85% of the value of output.
   b. 60% of the value of output.
   c. 45% of the value of output.
   d. 40% of the value of output.

4. Which of the following is an external diseconomy of urban industrialization?
   a. pollution
   b. congestion
   c. infrastructure costs to support a larger urban population
   d. all of the above are external diseconomies

5. One study found that for $100 million invested in each of nine industries, an LDC can generate 150,000 more jobs and 70% more value-added by using the _____ technology rather than the _____ technology.
   a. appropriate; most capital-intensive
   b. most labor-intensive; most capital-intensive
   c. traditional; modern
   d. efficient; traditional

6. According to the text, technologies that do not minimize cost are more likely to be used by industries that are:
   a. highly protected and monopolistic.
   b. highly protected and competitive.
   c. export oriented.
   d. dominated by privately owned firms

7. An industry is likely to be dominated by a few producers if scale economies are _____ , and the MES is a _____ fraction of the national market.
   a. small, large
   b. small, small
   c. large, small
   d. large, large

8. China's policy slogan of "walking on two legs" meant that the country was trying to develop both:
   a. rural factories and modern urban industry.
   b. agriculture and manufacturing.
   c. export markets and domestic markets.
   d. the economic sphere and the ideological sphere.

9. On what basis does the textbook claim that the capital-goods industry is an essential part of a development strategy?
   a. to assure self-sufficiency
   b. to generate technologies needed to create jobs and save capital
   c. because capital goods industries generate so many jobs
   d. all of the above

Applications

Worked Example: Linkage Effects

The Worked Example in Chapter 6 introduced a three-sector input-output model for Planland. The input-output coefficients matrix from that problem, modified to include imported inputs, is shown in Table 20-1. The first column shows that each $1 of output in agriculture requires $0.08 worth of agricultural inputs, $0.04 worth of manufactured inputs, and no services. The sum of these three figures (= $0.12) gives the *direct* requirement for domestically produced inputs per $1 of agricultural output. The index of direct backward linkages in this case is:

$$L_{b1} = \sum_{i=1}^{3} a_{i1} = 0.08 + 0.04 + 0.00 = 0.12.$$

Table 20-1

Input-Output Coefficients Matrix for Planland

	Agriculture (X_1)	Manufacturing (X_2)	Services (X_3)
1. Agriculture	0.08	0.20	0.375
2. Manufacturing	0.04	0.40	0.25
3. Services	0.00	0.10	0.125
4. Total domestic purchases	0.12	0.70	0.75
5. Imported intermediate goods	0.00	0.15	0.05
6. Payments to labor	0.80	0.06	0.15
7. Payments to capital	0.08	0.09	0.05
Totals	1.00	1.00	1.00

This value equals the figure shown in the matrix row for total domestic purchases (row 4). For the manufacturing industry, the index of direct backward linkages can be identified in the same manner:

$$L_{b2} = \sum_{i=1}^{3} a_{i2} = 0.20 + 0.40 + 0.10 = 0.70.$$

(The corresponding indexes for the service sector will be dealt with in Exercise 1).

To calculate the index of **total backward linkages** one must know the "direct plus indirect" input coefficients per unit of output for each sector—the r_{ij} matrix. The input-output math required to compute these coefficients cannot be explained here. It suffices to understand that r_{23}, for example, shows the total amount of the industry 2 product required to support $1 of additional final product in industry 3, after tracing through all of the interindustry linkages.

For Planland, the appropriate calculations show that a $1 increase in agriculture demand requires a total of $r_{11} = 1.11 worth of agricultural output, $r_{21} = 0.08 of manufactured products, and $r_{31} = 0.01 worth of services. Note that the services requirement is entirely indirect, since agriculture itself uses no service inputs. The sum of these three figures (= $1.20) gives the *total* requirement for domestically produced inputs per unit of agricultural product. The index of total backward linkages in this case is:

$$L_{t1} = \sum_{i=1}^{3} r_{i1} = 1.11 + 0.08 + 0.01 = 1.20.$$

For manufacturing, the corresponding figure is:

$$L_{t2} = \sum_{i=1}^{3} r_{i2} = 0.47 + 1.78 + 0.20 = 2.45.$$

Each $1 of manufactured product creates a requirement for $2.45 worth of domestic output, after taking into account the interindustry flows of intermediate goods.

Take note that the previous sentence says "creates a requirement for." Does this in fact mean that $2.45 worth of direct plus indirect domestic output will result per $1 increase in manufacturing-sector production? Not at all. The following illustrate some possible results. Domestic suppliers of intermediate goods may be unable to increase production capacity to satisfy the increased demand or they may be undersold by imports. Or the input requirements might be met by diverting supplies from other uses. Or the particular input demands of a specific type of manufacturing may be quite different from the aggregate average coefficients displayed in the country's input-output table. Or inputs previously imported (see line 5 of the coefficients matrix) may be replaced by domestic inputs. In short, the linkages index gives only a rough indication of where effective linkages effects might be lurking.

Similar remarks apply to forward linkages, which will be covered in Exercise 1.

Exercises

1. Now it is your turn to calculate linkages from input-output coefficients, using the Planland data shown in Table 20–1 as the raw material.

   a. (i) The Worked Example showed how to calculate the index of direct backward linkages for Planland's agricultural and manufacturing sectors. For the service sector, one would apply the formula:

   $$L_{b3} = \sum_{?} a_{??}.$$

   Rewrite this equation, replacing the question marks with the proper symbols:

   $$L_{b3} = \sum a$$

   (ii) Using the appropriate numerical values from Table 20–1, the value of the backward-linkages index for the service sector is:

   $$L_{b3} = \underline{\hspace{2cm}}.$$

   (iii) Compare L_{b3} with the corresponding index value for agriculture and for manufacturing (reported in the Worked Example). It should be clear that the _____ sector has the largest index of direct backward linkages.

   b. In order to calculate the index of total backward linkages for the service sector, you will need to know the following r_{ij} values:

   $$r_{13} = 0.61;$$

   $$r_{23} = 0.54; \text{ and}$$

   $$r_{33} = 1.20.$$

   (i) Considering that the input of manufactured goods required per unit of service output is $a_{23} = 0.25$, what is the meaning of $r_{23} = 0.54$, as reported above?

   (ii) What is the meaning of the fact that the value of r_{33} is greater than unity? [Note: The Worked Example reported that the values for r_{11} and r_{22} also exceeded unity.]

(iii) Calculate the value of the index of total backward linkages for the service sector in Planland:

$$L_{t3} = \sum_{i=1}^{3} r_{i3} = \underline{\hspace{2cm}} .$$

(iv) Comparing L_{t3} with the index values for agriculture and manufacturing (reported in the Worked Example), you can see that the _____ sector has the largest index of total backward linkages.

(v) You should have found that the sector with the largest direct backward linkages does not have the largest total backward linkages. Briefly explain how this can occur.

c. Turn now to forward linkages. It is necessary to refer to the interindustry flow matrix for Planland rather than the coefficients matrix. Table 20–2 provides the required data.

(i) Looking at agriculture first, Table 20–2 shows that in 1985 the total value of output for this sector equaled:

$$Z_1 = \$\underline{\hspace{2cm}} .$$

(ii) The value of agricultural output used as an input:

—to agriculture $= X_{11} = \$\underline{\hspace{2cm}}$;

—to industry $= X_{12} = \$\underline{\hspace{2cm}}$; and

—to services $= X_{13} = \$\underline{\hspace{2cm}}$.

(iii) Altogether, the value of agricultural output purchased as a productive input equaled:

$$\sum_{j=1}^{3} X_{1j} = \$\underline{\hspace{2cm}} .$$

(iv) Therefore the index of direct forward linkages for agriculture is:

$$L_{f1} = \left(\sum_{j=1}^{3} X_{1j} \right) / Z_1 = \underline{\hspace{2cm}} .$$

(v) Following a similar procedure, you should find that the index of direct forward linkages is $L_{f2} = 0.55$ for manufacturing, and $L_{f3} = \underline{\hspace{2cm}}$ for services.

(vi) The sector having the largest index of direct forward linkages is _____ .

Table 20-2

Interindustry Flow Matrix for Planland, 1985 (values in dollars)

	Using Sectors			Total intermediate use	Final use	Total use
	Agriculture (1)	Manufacturing (2)	Services (3)			
1. Agriculture	20	40	30	90	160	250
2. Manufacturing	10	80	20	110	90	200
3. Services	0	20	10	30	50	80
4. Total domestic purchases	30	140	60	230		
5. Imported intermediate goods	0	30	4			
6. Payments to labor	200	12	12			
7. Payments to capital	20	18	4			
8. Total output	250	200	80			530

d. (i) What does $L_{f2} = 0.55$ mean? More specifically, if production
in manufacturing increases by one unit, then the index of
direct forward linkage indicates 0.55 what? [Think!]

(ii) More generally, what does this index value say about the
suitability of manufacturing as a leading sector for Planland's
economic development?

2. The textbook explains why the industrial sector in low-income
countries creates jobs for only about 0.6% of the labor force each
year. This exercise works through a similar analysis for lower-
middle-income countries. The basic data, taken from the World
Bank's *World Development Report 1985*, are shown in Table 20–3.

a. The first step is to find the growth rate of employment in
industry, $g(E_i)$. This statistic is not reported directly, but it can be
calculated from the available data.
(i) Let LF_0 refer to the size of the labor force in 1965. With the
labor force growing at a rate of 2.32% per year, what
formula would you use to calculate LF', the size of the labor
force 18 years later (in 1983)?

$$LF' = \underline{\hspace{2cm}} \times LF_0 = 1.51 \, LF_0.$$

[Hint: If X grows by 5% per year, after t years its value will
be $X' = X(1.05)^t$.]
(ii) In 1965, 13% of the labor force worked in industry, so
employment in industry was:

$$E_i = \underline{\hspace{2cm}} LF_0.$$

Table 20–3

Data for Lower-Middle-Income Countries

Growth rate of value-added in industry	1965–83	7.1% per annum
	1973–83	4.4% per annum
Growth rate of total labor force	1965–83	2.32% per annum
Industry's share of total labor force	1965	13%
	1981	17%

Source: World Development Report 1985, Annex Tables 2 and 21.

By 1983, 17% of the labor force worked in industry, so employment in industry was:

$$E_i' = \underline{\hspace{1.5cm}} \quad LF' = \underline{\hspace{1.5cm}} \quad LF_0.$$

(iii) Therefore, over the eighteen-year period 1965–1983,

employment in industry grew by a factor of $y = \underline{\hspace{2cm}}$.
This translates into a growth rate of:

$$g(E_i) = \underline{\hspace{1.5cm}} \% \text{ per annum.}$$

[In case your calculator can't handle it, the indicated value of y gives: $(1 + i)^{18} = y \longrightarrow i = 0.0386$.]

b. You can now calculate the elasticity of employment growth in industry.
   (i) Over the period 1965–1983, value-added in industry grew by

   $\underline{\hspace{1.5cm}}$ % per year, while employment in industry grew by

   $\underline{\hspace{1.5cm}}$ % per year.
   (ii) For every 10% increase in industrial value-added, employment

   in that sector increased by $\underline{\hspace{1.5cm}}$ %.
   (iii) The elasticity of industrial employment with respect to industrial value-added was:

   $$\eta = \underline{\hspace{1.5cm}}.$$

   (iv) From the growth rate of value-added and the growth rate of employment in the industrial sector, you can see that labor productivity (VA/L) in this sector grew by approximately

   $\underline{\hspace{1.5cm}}$ % per year.

c. In the early 1980s, 170 workers were employed in industry for every 1,000 workers in the labor force, in the lower-middle-income countries.
   (i) With industrial value-added growing 4.4% per year after 1973, the elasticity value calculated in b.iii implies that

   employment in industry grew by $\underline{\hspace{1.5cm}}$ % per year.

   (ii) In other words, in the early 1980s $\underline{\hspace{2cm}}$ new jobs were being created in industry for every 1,000 workers in the labor force—assuming that the employment elasticity was unchanged.
   (iii) The labor force was growing by 2.3% per year. This means

   that there were $\underline{\hspace{2cm}}$ new workers each year for every 1,000 members of the labor force.
   (iv) The bottom line, then, is that industry was creating jobs for

   $\underline{\hspace{1.5cm}}$ % of the new job seekers in the lower-middle-income countries.

3. This exercise investigates the choice of technology in industry. Three alternative technologies for producing knives are available in Republique Couteau. The amount of capital (K) and labor (L) required to produce 1,000 knives per year using the traditional handicraft technology (T1), the labor-intensive intermediate technology (T2), and the automated modern technology (T3) are shown below:

	Capital Required	Labor Required
Handicraft Technology (T1)	10	80
Intermediate Technology (T2)	20	40
Automated Technology (T3)	50	20

a. (i) From the data shown above, calculate the capital-labor ratio for each technology:

$-K/L$ for T1 = _____;

$-K/L$ for T2 = _____; and

$-K/L$ for T3 = _____.

(ii) The automated technology has a capital-labor ratio _____ times that of the intermediate technology, and _____ times that of the handicraft technology.

(iii) Is the range of capital-labor ratios in this exercise unrealistic, compared to the range of technology choice actually observed for many industries in the LDCs? Support your answer using data cited in the textbook.

b. In Figure 20–1, plot the point representing the amount of K and L required to produce 1,000 knives per year using each technology. Label the three points T1, T2, and T3, respectively. Then connect the three points to form the corresponding isoquant.

c. Firms in Couteau's informal sector face a market wage that reflects the opportunity cost of labor. But because of segmented capital markets, they face a cost of capital far exceeding the opportunity cost. In contrast, firms in the modern sector face a subsidized price of capital along with a minimum wage well above the market wage. Specifically, factor prices (in francs) are as follows:

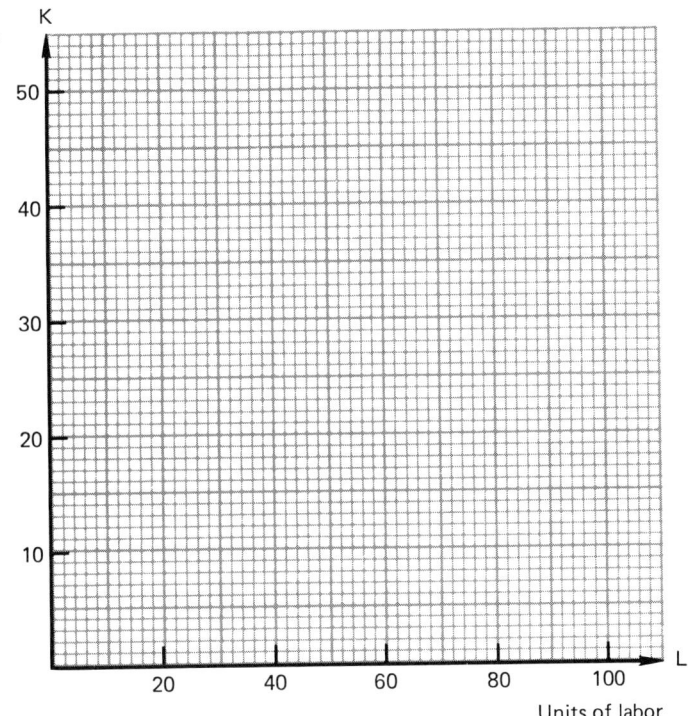

K

Units of
capital

50

40

30

20

10

20   40   60   80   100   L

Units of labor

Figure 20–1

	P_K	P_L
In the modern sector:	F100	F200
In the informal sector:	F500	F100
At shadow prices:	F175	F100.

(i) Given the factor prices faced by firms in each sector, which is
the minimum cost choice of technology

—for firms in the modern sector?   T_____

—for firms in the informal sector?   T_____

[Hint: You already know how much K and L are required by
each technology choice.]

(ii) Which is the appropriate technology, i.e., the one that
minimizes costs in terms of shadow prices?   T_____

(iii) Draw a budget line showing the minimum level of costs for
modern-sector firms. Label it B_m. [Hint: the line must have a
slope equal to $-2 = -P_L/P_K$.]

(iv) Draw a budget line showing the minimum level of costs for
informal sector firms. Label it B_i.

(v) Draw a budget line showing the minimum level of costs in
terms of shadow prices. Label it B_s.

d. Altogether in Couteau there is a market for 1 million knives per year. Keep in mind that the isoquant in Figure 20-1 is drawn for $Q = 1,000$ knives per year.

(i) How many units of capital are required to produce 1 million knives per year with the technology being used

—in the modern sector? $\qquad$ $K =$ _____ thousand

—in the informal sector? $\qquad$ $K =$ _____ thousand

(ii) How many workers are required to produce 1 million knives per year with the technology being used

—by the modern sector? $\qquad$ $L =$ _____ thousand

—by the informal sector? $\qquad$ $L =$ _____ thousand

(iii) Using shadow prices to value capital and labor, what is the factor cost of producing 1 million knives per year using

—the modern-sector technology? $\qquad$ F_____ million

—the informal-sector technology? $\qquad$ F_____ million

—the appropriate technology? $\qquad$ F_____ million

(iv) Compared to the informal sector, production of 1 million knives per year in the modern sector requires _____ times as much capital, creates only _____ % as many jobs, and has an opportunity cost that is _____ % higher.

e. (i) Given the prevailing factor prices in each sector, what is the production cost per 1,000 knives?

—in the modern sector? $\qquad$ F_____

—in the informal sector? $\qquad$ F_____

(ii) Assume that overhead costs in the modern sector total F3,000 per 1,000 knives, while the informal sector has zero overhead costs. Given the factor prices actually being paid, firms in the

_____ sector can produce knives at a lower cost.

Thus firms in the _____ sector will tend to be driven out of business.

4. This exercise examines the relationship between scale economies and the size of the market. Figure 20-2 shows long-run average costs (including a normal return on capital) for the brick industry in Amigo. The figure clearly exhibits economies of scale, since long-run average cost declines with the capacity of the production unit.

a. Brick production entails a number of processes, including mixing clays, molding bricks, firing the bricks in a kiln, and drying them, in addition to handling, storage, and business operations.
(i) Name two factors that might plausibly account for the presence of scale economies in the brick industry.

(ii) What output-capacity level is the minimum efficient scale (MES) of operation in the brick industry in Amigo?

MES = _____ thousand tons per year.

(iii) A production unit with a capacity of 1/2 MES will have an average cost per ton of bricks that is _____ % higher than that at the MES.

(iv) A production unit with a capacity of 1/4 MES will have an average cost per ton of bricks that is _____ % higher than that at the MES.

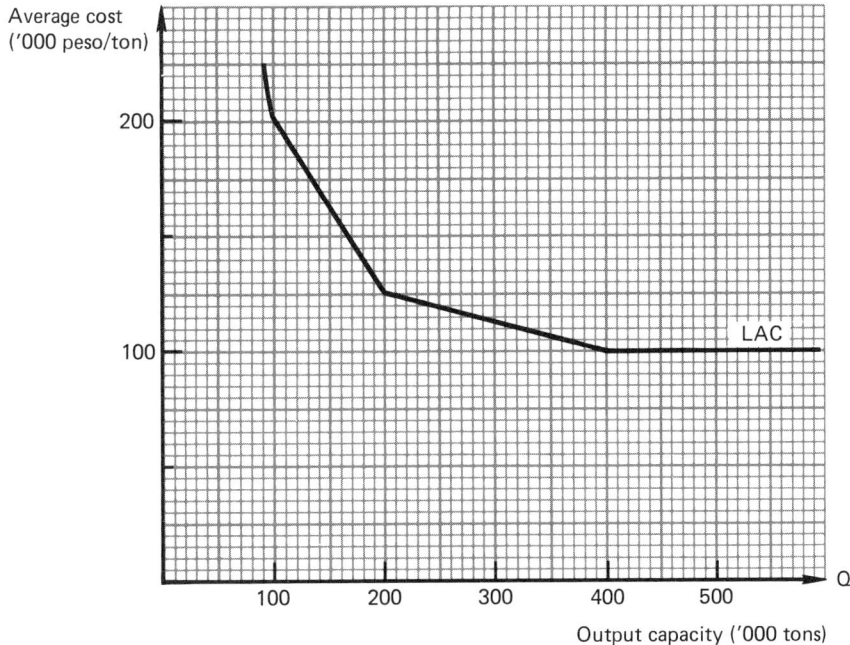

Figure 20-2

b. With a market price of P100,000 per ton (P = pesos), the quantity demanded in Amigo will be 2 million tons of bricks per year.

    (i) The MES in the brick industry equals _____ % of the market in Amigo.

   (ii) What does this number imply about the possibility of developing an efficient, competitive brick industry in Amigo?

  (iii) Suppose brick producers in Amigo could export bricks to El Toro, a neighboring country that lacks quality clays. Including exports, the market for Amigoan bricks would equal 8 million tons per year. How would this alter the prospects of developing an efficient, competitive brick industry in Amigo?

c. Suppose that the size of the market expands by 200,000 bricks per year.

    (i) One clay press is needed per 10,000 bricks per year. So each year expansion of the brick industry creates a requirement for

    _____ new clay presses. In addition, 50 presses are needed for replacement purposes. Altogether then, there is a

    market for _____ clay presses each year in Amigo.

   (ii) Figure 20–3 shows the long-run average cost curve for production of clay presses. The MES in the clay-press industry

    is a capacity of _____ presses per year.

  (iii) How do scale economies affect the prospects for backward-linkage import substitution in the production of clay presses in Amigo?

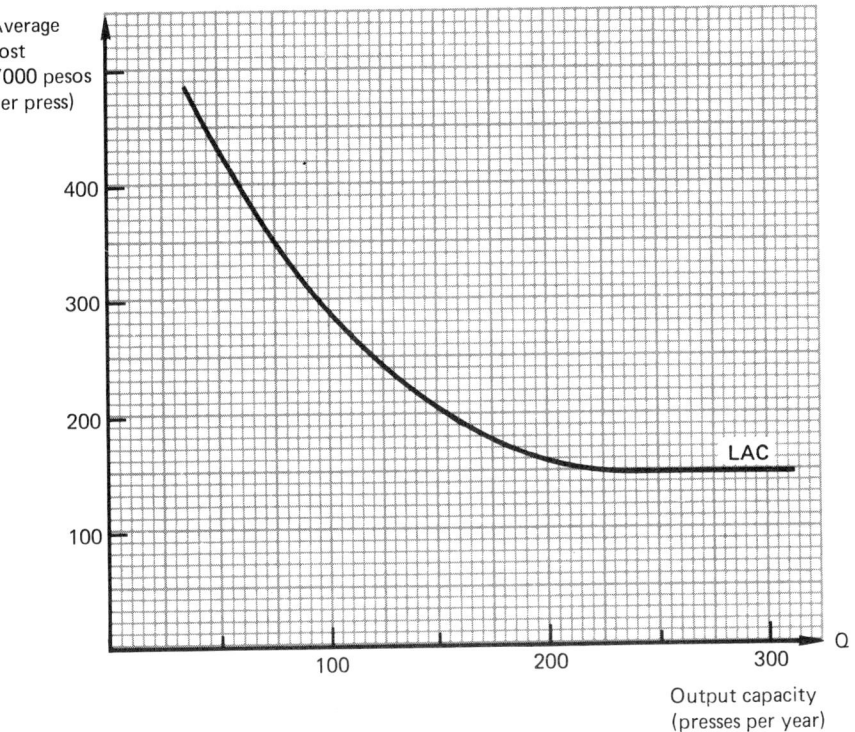

Average
cost
('000 pesos
per press)

Figure 20-3

d. (i) How might the LAC curve, and hence the strength of scale economies in Amigo's brick production, be influenced by government policies? [Hint: factor prices.]

(ii) Including exports to El Toro, you should have found that there is room for a sizable number of competing brick companies in Amigo. Does this mean that there *will be* a sizable number of competing brick companies? How might government development policies encourage monopoly power in the brick industry, even when scale economies are not important?

Answers to Self-Test

Completion

1. more
2. consumer; producer
3. (direct) backward
4. agglomeration
5. infrastructure
6. capital
7. (long-run) average
8. labor; capital
9. per-capita

True-False

1.	T	6.	F
2.	F	7.	F
3.	F	8.	F
4.	T	9.	T
5.	T		

Multiple Choice

1.	b	6.	a
2.	d	7.	d
3.	c	8.	a
4.	d	9.	b
5.	a		

CHAPTER 21   Public Enterprises

Overview

In the past few decades, state-owned enterprises (SOEs) have been a rapidly growing presence in LDCs of all ideological shades. They have been especially prominent in industries requiring large, capital-intensive investments, industries previously dominated by colonial or neo-colonial interests, and industries considered to be of strategic importance to development. Economic motives have been important elements in the rationale for creating SOEs. These motives include the potential contribution to savings and employment, the inability of the private sector to mount large scale investment projects, and the tendency of market power to become concentrated in a few hands.

In only a few countries, however, has the economic performance of SOEs been satisfactory. SOEs often contribute little to savings, and are sometimes a major drain on government finance. State enterprises often absorb a large share of investment funds in capital-intensive operations that fail to make a major contribution to job creation. Furthermore, SOEs are often highly inefficient due to protection from competition, bureaucratic controls, and distorted prices, among other things. But poor performance is not an inherent characteristic of SOEs, as demonstrated by the experience of a few countries like Korea. With good management and sound policies, SOEs can justify their economic rationale, while also contributing to social goals.

Main Learning Objectives

After studying this chapter you ought to understand and be able to explain:

1. The criteria characterizing **state-owned enterprises** (SOEs), or **parastatal enterprises**.

2. The rapid growth and prominent role of state-owned enterprises in LDC economies, irrespective of government ideology.

3. The major economic and noneconomic motives underlying the expansion of SOEs in the third world.

4. The mixed, but generally unsatisfactory performance of SOEs in terms of savings mobilization and job creation.

5. How SOEs have been used as instruments to serve social objectives such as equity and regional balance, and to provide a counterbalance to the economic power of multinational firms.

Additional Key Terms, Concepts, and Institutions

Can you identify and explain each of the following?

savings mobilization
capital lumpiness
commanding heights
joint ventures

Economic Tools and Techniques

From what you have learned in this chapter, can you:

1. Use isoquant analysis to distinguish between **technical efficiency, allocative efficiency**, and **X-inefficiency**?

Self-Test

Completion

1. The acronym SOE stands for _____ .

2. Private domestic firms may be unable or unwilling to mobilize the required volume of investment funds where productive projects are characterized by _____ lumpiness.

3. _____ is a term applied to sectors of the economy that are so strategic and generate such important linkages that they cannot, it is argued, be left in private hands.

4. The term _____ refers to the extent to which a firm fails to minimize costs.

5. The principal reason that SOEs in developing countries have not been more successful in creating new jobs is their _____ intensity.

True-False If false, you should be able to explain why.

_____ 1. The term state-owned enterprise applies only to enterprises that are 100% owned by the government.

_____ 2. The expansion of SOEs in LDCs is strongly correlated with socialist ideology; in the market-oriented countries, SOEs are of little importance.

_____ 3. Since the mid-1970s the World Bank has supported expansion of state enterprises in mining and manufacturing.

_____ 4. In all but a few cases, state-owned enterprises in LDCs have failed to generate a significant volume of savings.

_____ 5. According to the text, SOEs are no more prone than private enterprises to suffer from serious X-inefficiency.

Multiple Choice

1. By the textbook's definition, which of the following is a defining characteristic applying to all SOEs?
   a. prominence of social objectives over profits
   b. production of goods and services for sale
   c. government involvement in the day-to-day operations
   d. operation at a loss, with government subsidies

2. The "savings mobilization" rationale for SOEs is based on which of the following contentions?
   a. Private capitalists save too little.
   b. Raising public-sector savings through taxation is politically difficult and administratively complex.
   c. SOEs will generate operating surpluses that can be used by government for financing capital formation.
   d. All of the above.

3. Which of the following is not a factor contributing to X-inefficiency in public-sector firms?
   a. lack of competition
   b. distorted factor prices
   c. lack of bankruptcy threat when losses are sustained
   d. government directives mandating unnecessary hiring

4. The high degree of capital intensity in SOEs is directly related to each of the following factors except:
   a. rigid government controls on product prices.
   b. concentration of SOE investment in sectors that would in any case be capital-intensive.
   c. distorted factor prices.
   d. lack of competitive pressure to minimize costs.

5. On balance, state-owned enterprises in LDCs have been fairly successful as instruments for:
   a. mobilizing domestic savings.
   b. implementing decolonization.
   c. improving technical and allocative efficiency.
   d. none of the above.

Applications

Worked Example: Allocative Inefficiency and X-Inefficiency

The alternative production techniques available to a state-owned cement factory in Bengili are represented by the isoquant II shown in Figure 21–1. Any point on the isoquant is **technically efficient**: it is not feasible to produce the given output using less of both factors.

If the factors of production were priced to reflect their scarcity value, the cost of capital services per year would be 1 million taka (the name of the currency), and the wage rate would be 25,000 taka per year. Isocost line B_1 has a slope of $-1/40$ reflecting these relative scarcity prices. Point 1 shows the production process that is **allocatively efficient**. Every other point on the isoquant lies on a higher isocost line, when costs are appraised at the scarcity value of capital and labor. In other words, the opportunity cost to the economy of producing cement is minimized at point 1. If actual factor prices properly reflected scarcity values, a profit-maximizing firm would choose to operate at this point.

But suppose that political factors compel the cement factory to hire 50% more labor than required. It would then produce at point 3. Alternatively, inefficient management could lead the firm to use more capital and more labor than necessary, as at point 4, or management could over-build production capacity by 50%, thus operating at point 5. Each of these is a case of X-inefficiency: the firm is failing to minimize costs given the available technology and prevailing factor prices. The firm is failing to operate on its isoquant.

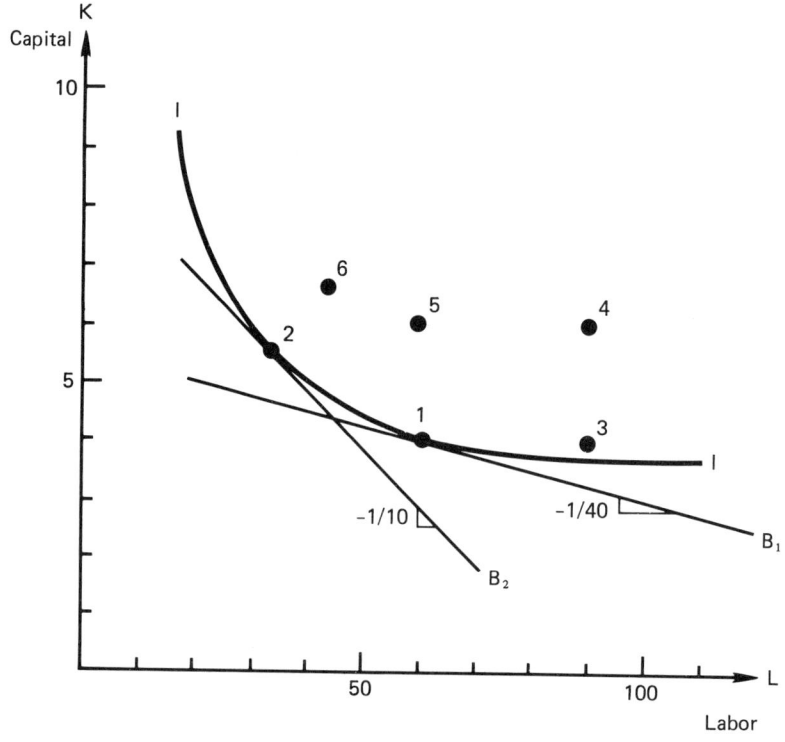

Figure 21–1

Now suppose that the firm borrows at subsidized interest rates, that it receives preferential access to foreign exchange, and that it must adhere to minimum wage laws. Let the actual cost of capital and the actual wage be Tk500,000 and Tk50,000, respectively. Isocost line B_2 has a slope of $-1/10$ reflecting these factor prices. Point 2 is now the cost-minimizing production process. Production at point 2 is technically efficient. This is *not* a case of X-inefficiency. Yet production is allocatively inefficient since the opportunity cost of cement production is higher than necessary. The inefficiency in this case is a result of the distorted factor prices. On top of this, the firm may *also* be X-inefficient. For reasons like those given above, it may fail to minimize costs given the prevailing factor prices, as at point 6. This accentuates the allocative inefficiency.

In short, allocative inefficiency can be a result of X-inefficiency, distorted factor prices, or (quite often) a combination of both.

Exercises

1. This exercise gives you a chance to investigate X-inefficiency, savings, and employment in a state-owned enterprise. With available technology, a state-owned textile monopoly in Mwanzi can produce cloth each month using either of two methods. Process A uses 3 units of capital (K) and 5 workers (L) per 1,000 bales of cloth. Process B uses 1 K and 10 L per 1,000 bales. The cost of capital to the enterprise is $P_K = 2,500$ shillings per month, and the wage rate is $P_L = 800$ shillings per month. These are the prices that reflect the scarcity value of the factors.

a. (i) The production cost per 1,000 bales of cloth is:

   _____ shillings using process A and

   _____ shillings using process B.

   (ii) A profit-maximizing firm will minimize costs using process

   _____, which is the more _____-intensive process.

   (iii) For the firm to avoid operating losses, the price of cloth must

   be at least $P_C = $ Sh_____ per bale.

   (iv) If the quantity demanded at this price is 100,000 bales per

   month, then total employment will be _____ workers.

b. For reasons of social policy, the government imposes a number of controls on the textile enterprise:
   —in order to make cloth more affordable, the price is controlled at 1 shilling below the level P_C identified above.
   —In order to improve labor incomes, the government sets a minimum wage of Sh900 per month.
   —The textile enterprise is obligated to produce enough to satisfy demand, which rises to 110,000 bales per month when the new, lower price is introduced.

(i) Under these conditions the production cost per 1,000 bales of cloth is:

Sh_____ using process A and

Sh_____ using process B.

(ii) The minimum-cost process now is _____.
(iii) Using this process on a monthly volume of 110,000 bales, the enterprise will now have:

total revenues (price times quantity) equal to Sh_____ and

total costs equal to Sh_____.

(iv) So the firm will be making a loss of Sh_____ per

month, while employing a total of _____ workers.
(v) Is the loss attributable to X-inefficiency? Explain.

c. To alleviate this loss, while avoiding a direct subsidy, the government requires banks to provide cheap credit, as well as favorable access to foreign exchange, so that the enterprise can import equipment more cheaply. Also, the firm is exempted from paying income taxes. The combined effect of these policies is to lower P_K to Sh1,500. Other conditions remain as in part b, including P_L = Sh900.

(i) The operating cost per 1,000 bales of cloth is now:

Sh_____ using process A and

Sh_____ using process B.

(ii) The minimum cost process adopted by the enterprise is _____.

Using this process the production cost per bale is Sh_____.
(iii) On its volume of 110,000 bales:

—total revenues are Sh_____;

—total costs are Sh_____;

—the firm makes a _____ (profit/loss) of

Sh_____; and

—total employment equals _____ workers.
(iv) Evaluate the enterprise operations from the point of view of allocative efficiency, technical efficiency, and X-inefficiency.

(v) Evaluate the enterprise in terms of its contribution to savings and to employment.

d. With the above conditions still intact, political appointees are put in charge of the enterprise. The firm becomes overstaffed as redundant employees are hired. Maintenance problems cause machines to be out of operation frequently, so extra equipment is acquired to sustain production. The overall effect is that $4 K$ and $8 L$ are now employed per 1,000 bales of cloth.

(i) The cost per bale is now Sh_____.

(ii) On its volume of 110,000 bales:

—total revenues are Sh_____;

—total costs are Sh_____;

—the firm makes a _____ (profit/loss) of

Sh_____; and

—total employment equals _____ workers.

(iii) Evaluate the enterprise operations from the point of view of allocative efficiency, technical efficiency, and X-inefficiency.

(iv) Evaluate the enterprise in terms of its contribution to savings and to employment.

2. This exercise develops the graphical analysis of the conditions faced by the cloth enterprise in Exercise 1.

    a. (i) In Figure 21–2, draw an isoquant for $Q = 1,000$ bales of cloth, using the technical specifications for processes A and B defined at the beginning of Exercise 1. [Hint: Plot the point representing the amount of K and L required using process A. Then the point for process B. Connect these two points.]

      (ii) Draw in the isocost line, or budget line representing the minimum cost level for producing $Q = 1,000$, given the factor prices in part a of Exercise 1. Label it C_1.

     (iii) Identify the point on isoquant $Q = 1,000$ that minimizes costs, given these factor prices. Label it *point 1*.

    b. (i) Draw in the isocost line representing the minimum cost level for producing $Q = 1,000$, given the factor prices in part c of Exercise 1. Label it C_2.

      (ii) Identify the point on isoquant $Q = 1,000$ that minimizes costs, given these factor prices. Label it *point 2*.

    c. (i) Identify the point that corresponds to the production operations in part d of Exercise 1. Label it *point 3*.

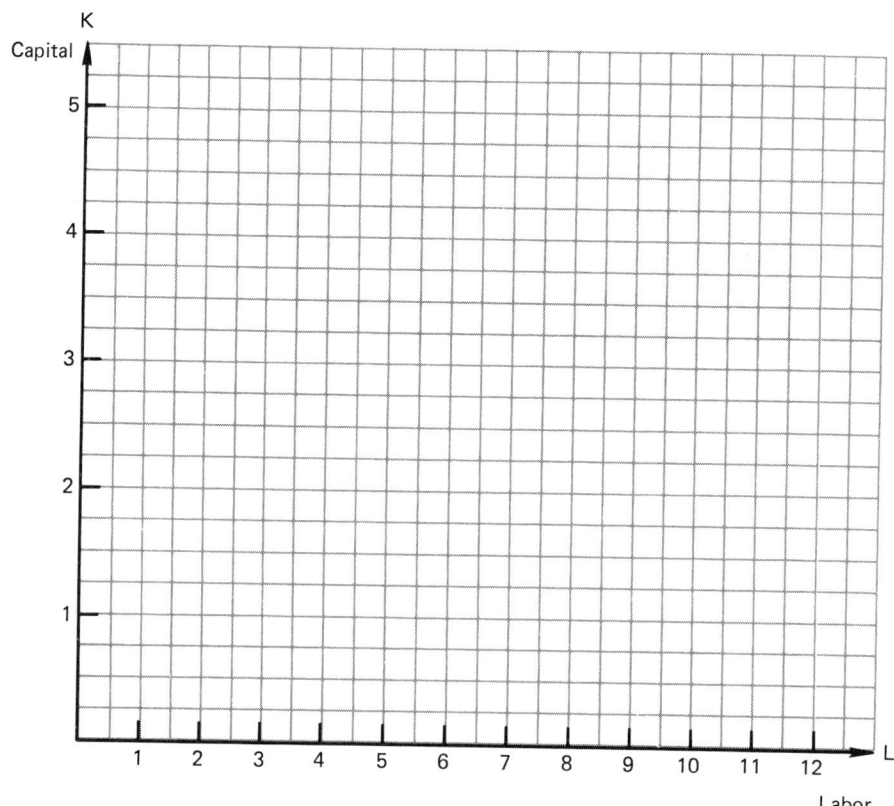

Figure 21–2

(ii) Draw an isocost line through *point 3* that reflects the **scarcity** prices of capital and labor. Label it C_3. [Hint: The scarcity prices are those embodied in line C_1; so C_3 should be parallel to C_1.]

(iii) Indicate clearly on the graph the extent to which the gap between C_1 and C_3 can be attributed:

—to factor price distortions;

—to X-inefficiency.

[Hint: Start by constructing a line through point *2* parallel to C_1.]

3. This final exercise addresses the advantages of a direct subsidy over a hidden subsidy that accentuates factor-price distortions. Consider, one last time, the state-owned textile monopoly in Mwanzi.

a. The social policies introduced in part b of Exercise 1 included a minimum wage, together with a Sh1 reduction in the product price and an increase in the volume of cloth sales.

(i) These social policies resulted in an operating loss of

Sh_____ per month for the company on its volume of 110,000 bales of cloth. This translates into a loss of

Sh_____ per bale.

(ii) This operating loss could be eliminated by a simple, direct

subsidy equal to Sh_____ per bale of cloth.

b. Suppose that the direct subsidy policy were used, rather than the hidden indirect subsidies examined in Exercise 1. In this case the factor prices would remain at $P_L = $ Sh900 and $P_K = $ Sh2,500.

(i) The minimum cost process in this case is _____ .

(ii) The firm will employ a total of _____ workers to produce 110,000 bales per month of cloth.

(iii) By making the policy costs explicit, the direct subsidy obviously makes it easier to appraise costs for the purpose of policy evaluation. But how does the direct subsidy policy compare with the indirect subsidy policy in terms of:

—allocative efficiency, and

—employment effects?

Answers to Self-Test

Completion

1. state-owned enterprise
2. capital
3. Commanding heights
4. X-inefficiency
5. capital

True-False

1. F
2. F
3. T
4. T
5. F

Multiple Choice

1. b
2. d
3. b
4. a
5. b